Genetic Geographies

Genetic Geographies

The Trouble with Ancestry

Catherine Nash

University of Minnesota Press
Minneapolis
London

A different version of chapter 3 was previously published as "Genetics, Race, and Relatedness: Human Mobility and Human Diversity in the Genographic Project," *Annals of the Association of American Geographers* 102, no. 3 (2012): 667–84. A different version of chapter 4 was previously published as "Genome Geographies: Mapping National Ancestry and Diversity in Human Population Genetics," *Transactions of the Institute of British Geographers* 38, no. 2 (2013): 193–206, copyright 2012 Catherine Nash, Transactions of the Institute of British Geographers, and Royal Geographical Society (with the Institute of British Geographers). A different version of chapter 5 was previously published as "Gendered Geographies of Genetic Variation: Sex, Power, and Mobility in Human Population Genetics," *Gender, Place, and Culture: A Journal of Feminist Geography* 19, no. 4 (2012): 409–28.

Published by the University of Minnesota Press
111 Third Avenue South, Suite 290
Minneapolis, MN 55401–2520
http://www.upress.umn.edu

Library of Congress Cataloging-in-Publication Data
Nash, Catherine.
    Genetic geographies : the trouble with ancestry / Catherine Nash.
    Includes bibliographical references and index.
    ISBN 978-0-8166-9063-3 (hc : alk. paper)
    ISBN 978-0-8166-9073-2 (pb : alk. paper)
    1. Human population genetics—Social aspects. 2. Genealogy—Social aspects. 3. Historical geography. I. Title.
    GN289.N37 2015 576.5'8—dc23   2014019924

Printed in the United States of America on acid-free paper

The University of Minnesota is an equal-opportunity educator and employer.

21 20 19 18 17 16 15   10 9 8 7 6 5 4 3 2 1

Contents

Acknowledgments

At the heart of this book is a critique of the idea that those to whom we are closest in terms of ancestry naturally matter most. It is an argument about the dangers of figuring genetic similarity through shared ancestry as the basis for senses of affinity, care, and commonality. In the pages that follow, I explore how that idea runs through what is widely taken to be either a simply fascinating or, more particularly, progressive exploration of ancestry, origins, and relatedness through the scientific study of geographical patterns of human genetic variation and their use in genetic genealogy. In fact, this idea of the primacy of ancestry is challenged all the time. So this is a fitting place to express heartfelt thanks to all those who show that it is how we do kinship, friendship, and work together that matters. I give my deep thanks to all those who practice collegiality, friendship, and family with me so generously within and across the conventions of these categories, sharing and not sharing ancestry or views on whether it is of any interest or any cause of trouble.

I am very grateful especially to Alison Blunt, Beth Greenhough, Caron Lipman, Alastair Owens, David Pinder, and other friends and colleagues who make the School of Geography at Queen Mary University of London such a supportive academic and social context for working life. Many people have inspired and encouraged the project in different ways, including Noel Castree, Ian Cook, Phil Crang, Felix Driver, Dydia DeLyser, Jeanette Edwards, Sarah Franklin, Joan Fujimura, Jane Jacobs, David Livingstone, Jonathan Marks, Sallie Marston, Jon May, Amade M'charek, Holly McLaren, Jane Ogborn, Bronwyn Parry, Chris Philo, Katharina Schramm, David Skinner, Susan Smith, Marianne Sommer, Katharine Tyler, Heather Winlow, and Sue Wright. Many thanks also to all those who commented on the work as I presented it in conferences and seminars in Ireland, the United Kingdom, the United States, and Australia or invited me to be part of specialist workshops and symposia, including Rachel Hughes and the Cultural Geography Study Group of the Institute of Australian Geographers, who gave me the luxury of time to talk at length with all those who participated in the Geographies of Relatedness workshop in 2009. I am especially grateful to Audrey Kobayashi and Peter Wade, who generously reviewed the manuscript and supported the book.

The research for this book was also supported in practical ways. It was funded initially through an Economic and Social Research Council fellowship (2004–2007) and was supported by a British Academy grant in 2006. My work has benefited from the input of editors and reviewers of journal papers, and I am grateful for this and for permission to publish revised and extended versions in this book. I am also grateful to the population geneticists who talked to me about their work over the course of this research (Mark Jobling, Walter Bodmer, Mark Thomas, and Bruce Winney) and helped me understand how our perspectives and approaches overlap and differ.

I thank my editor Jason Weidemann for his vision of this book and wise counsel in the process of its writing and his colleague Danielle Kasprzak at the University of Minnesota Press, as well as Danny Constantino and Jessica Firpi at Scribe Inc., for their thorough and stylish approach to production. I am also very grateful to Eimear Kelly for her proofreading help and Denise Carlson for her skillful indexing.

This is also the place to thank Hester Parr and Clare Fisher for being such wonderful friends; to thank my loving parents, to whom I dedicate this book with all my love; and to say a big thank you to dearest Declan, Breda, Gráinne, David, Kieran, and Damian for doing family at its best. Finally, thank you to Eve, my pride and joy, and to Miles Ogborn, darling fellow geographer from the start.

Geography, Genetics, Kinship

In July 2012, visitors to the Royal Society's Summer Science Exhibition, an annual event held in London "showing the most exciting cutting edge science and technology" to the general public, could take away a free silicone wristband. Printed on it were the words "Genetic Differences Reveal Our Ancestry." These wristbands, of the sort usually associated with charity fundraising, were available at one exhibit that featured the People of the British Isles project exploring the premodern settlement of Britain through studies of contemporary human genetic variation in the United Kingdom. When I visited on one of the last few days, the researchers on hand were busy responding to queries. People crowded around the exhibition panels, which explained the scientific basis of the project and offered interpretations of the project's maps of the geography of genetic variation in western Europe and in the British Isles. Those viewing a detailed regional map of genetic variation in Britain were encouraged to "note the striking correspondence between geography and genetics, and the subtle differences (e.g., between Devon and Cornwall, or two islands within Orkney) that can be picked up by the genetic analysis."[1]

This "Genetic Maps" exhibit represents just one of many studies of this kind being undertaken by human population geneticists who study geographical patterns of contemporary human genetic variation in order to reconstruct the history and geography of ancient human origins and early human migration and the demographic histories of, and ancestral relationships between, specific human groups. The aim of this strand of human population genetics—or, more specifically, anthropological genetics—is to tell us "who is related to whom" and "where we come from" as individuals, groups, and humanity as a whole.[2] These questions are figured as fundamental to collective and personal self-knowledge in this science of origins, ancestry, and relatedness.

But the field's claims to significance do not end there. It has recently extended its analytical focus and claims to interpretative power from reconstructing human migration histories to addressing the genetic impact of, and genetic evidence for, the social dynamics of human societies. Questions of sex, reproduction, and kinship are central to these new directions in anthropological genetics. This is a science of addressing not only who is related to whom but also increasingly the genetic effects of, and genetic evidence for, patterns of reproduction and migration in ways that differentiate between what have been described as "men's and women's histories."[3] Its focus of investigation is not only a matter of who is related to whom and how but also a matter of the nature and social organization of sex, marriage, and sexually differentiated mobility. Studies of human genetic variation are being applied—as geneticist Spencer Wells, one of the most prominent public scientists in the United States, puts it—to address "profound questions" especially about "traditional gender roles" and "patterns of marriage."[4] Adding sex to origins, ancestry, and relatedness makes for a set of concerns and claims that generate considerable public interest, given the personal and political significance of ideas of individual and shared identity via descent, and the appeal and contested power of biological explanations of social life especially regarding sex, sexuality, and reproduction.

This book considers the making of ideas of human connection and distance, sameness and difference, belonging and origins in the entangled science, culture, and commerce of human population genetics as they are shaped by and implicated in the politics of identity, belonging, and difference.[5] This is a field that has grown rapidly since the possibilities for reconstructing human lineages through the analysis of variable forms of inherited genetic material, known as markers, were first explored in the late 1990s, and it has had a particularly high public profile. New accounts of the origins and migration pathways of early humanity or of specific human groups have been the subject of numerous popular science books, websites, newspaper articles, and radio and television documentaries. Since the early 2000s, celebrities and others have been viewed by millions of television viewers in the United States and United Kingdom, the contexts I focus on here, responding to the results of personalized genetic tests for ancestral information that have been developed as a commercial application of the techniques and data of human population genetics and for sale online.[6] Those encountering the message that "genetic differences reveal our ancestry" are very likely to have already encountered the science, commerce, and culture of human population genetics.

Accounts of what can be known through comparisons of human genetic markers are of individual and collective pasts: personal ancestry, the history of a group, or humanity as a whole. As Marianne Sommer argues, in contrast to medical genomics, anthropological genetics is "retrospective and conservative rather than prospective and interventionist."[7] The now pervasive discourse of the gene as historical document, and DNA as archive, and the accounts of the past that are being produced by human population geneticists and culturally figured in popular forms shape what she aptly describes as "biohistories." In what Nadia Abu El-Haj has also characterized as "genetic history,"[8] these pasts are variously figured in terms of what is shared and universal and what is distinctive and differentiated: a shared human story of origins and migration or the different roles and mobilities of women and men—a universal feature of human societies or accounts of the peopling of particular places by particular groups.

These pasts are, of course, a matter of not only historical reconstructions, imaginations, and temporalities of ancestry and origins but also historical geographies. They are about geographies of origins in a spatial sense, of migratory pasts that are journeys across space at different scales, and of ancestries that stretch back in time and across the geographies of those migrations. The object and aims of these reconstructions are simultaneously geographical and historical; the focus of investigation and source of knowledge itself is the geographical pattern of human genetic variation, as that injunction to "note the striking correspondence between geography and genetics" in the "Genetic Maps" exhibition suggests. Anthropological genetics involves the geographical sampling of human genetic variation, the mapping of patterns of variation, and the interpretation of the "history and geography of human genes" (to use the title of a prominent overview of knowledge in the field published in 1994) in terms of geographical origins and geographies of migration.[9] The term "genography" has recently emerged to describe the identification of geographical patterns in plots of genetic variation and these spatial patterns themselves.[10] "Genography" itself can be encompassed within the broader field of "phylogeography," a term coined in 1987 to describe the integrative multistranded exploration of the relationships between gene genealogies—the genealogical lineages of genes that stand for the evolutionary and ancestral relationships within and between members of a species that are the focus of phylogenetics—and geography. Phylogeography is concerned with "the processes governing the geographic distributions of genealogical lineages, especially those within and among closely related species," including humans.[11]

But what is meant by geography in this instance of "the striking correspondence between geography and genetics" and "subtle differences" and in wider recent claims that patterns of human genetic variation "mirror geography"?[12] Does geography simply stand for absolute space, a neutral plane across which patterns or clusters of variation can be discerned? Or does geography also sometimes deliberately or inadvertently evoke political geographies of national borders or senses of difference across space? How are these geographies of human genetic variation—identifiable patterns in general spatial gradations—figured in relation to other geographies of difference and belonging?

This book explores the making and implications of ideas of human relatedness and difference in human population genetics through an attentiveness to the geographies that constitute the practice, imaginaries, interpretations, and implications of accounts of human genetic variation as sources of knowledge about the human past. It attends to the field's own geographies: the social, political, and cultural situatedness of specific projects; their geographical techniques and imaginaries of interconnection, boundedness, and mobility; and their scales of analysis and claims. This is not simply to emphasize what may seem like the self-evident spatialities of "genetic history"—to consider origins in terms of first place as well as foundational period, or accounts of migration as historical geographies, not just histories—but to offer and apply a fruitful analytical framework for addressing the production, meaning, and politics of genetic accounts of origins, ancestry, relatedness, and difference.[13]

Setting out and putting a geographical interpretive framework to work in this book is not meant, however, to mark a territorial claim on the subject matter nor to competitively promote one exclusive disciplinary community over others. Given the spatial turn across the humanities and social sciences over the last decades, it would be inappropriate to claim that a geographical perspective is an exclusively disciplinary one.[14] Yet the geographical approach I apply here is informed by the discipline's reflexive critique of its contribution to the making of ideas of human difference in the late nineteenth and early twentieth centuries through cartographic, climatic, and discursive constructions of race.[15] In one sense then, this book is a contribution to geography's necessary engagement with the making of contemporary geographies of human genetic variation and geographies of difference more widely, in light of its own disciplinary history of measuring, mapping, and theorizing human diversity, and one that draws on the sustained interrogation of geographical concepts and the critical spatial attentiveness that has been pursued within the discipline over the last four decades.

There are clear parallels here with anthropology, in terms of both the history of the discipline and recent social and cultural anthropological work on human population genetics. Anthropologists have argued for the importance of anthropological engagement with genomic accounts of human genetic variation and relatedness, or what Jonathan Marks describes as "molecular anthropology," similarly informed by anthropology's reflexivity regarding its own history of the making of race.[16] This is apposite given the complex relation of genetics to physical anthropology over the course of the twentieth century and the recent anthropological framing of human population genetics. But this is not just a matter of parallel disciplinary histories and developments, since geography and anthropology were entangled disciplines in the early twentieth century in terms of key figures and in terms of their interests in human difference and contributions to the making of race.[17] Drawing geographical and anthropological perspectives together here reestablishes the once close relationships between the two disciplines in the early twentieth century around shared interests in the pattern of human racial and then cultural difference—or anthropogeography—but now through a shared critical attention to the making of difference and relatedness within accounts of genetic variation.[18] But even this might suggest an exclusive disciplinary alliance rather than reflect the spirit of an open multidisciplinary project of addressing current genomic developments to which I bring this anthropologically inflected geographical perspective.

In bringing this geographical attentiveness to bear on the field's aims, sources, practices, imaginaries, interpretive tools, and contexts, I focus on three concepts that are central to the science of studying human genetic variation as a source of knowledge about the past and to the cultures in which it is embedded—origins, ancestry, and relatedness—in ways that foreground their geographical dimensions. Exploring ideas of origins geographically includes highlighting the personal and political potency of answers to the question "where do I, or we, come from?" for belonging, inclusion, and identification. But it also involves exploring the specific meaning and intersections between ideas of origins and indigeneity in different contexts. What do origins and what does indigenous mean in genetic accounts of ancestry? How do those meanings relate to the wider cultural and political weight of these terms, especially in the contexts of the United States and the United Kingdom that I explore here? It is also worth considering, as I will do here, the ways in which the similarly potent, but less obviously spatial, ideas of ancestry and relatedness are understood, in both scientific and ordinary senses, in terms of different geographies of both distance and proximity and geographical imaginaries of sameness and difference at different scales.

Following the expanded claims of anthropological genetics, I consider relatedness not only in terms of "who is related to whom" but also in terms of the broader concept of kinship that encompasses questions of the social organization of sex and reproduction. I do so to address what models of relatedness and difference are mobilized and remade in studies of the geography of human genetic variation. Maternally inherited mitochondrial DNA (known as mtDNA) and the paternally inherited Y chromosome have been central to much work in studying patterns of human genetic variation in evolutionary and anthropological genetics. This genetic material is central also to genetic genealogy. This derives from their particular form of direct inheritance and thus their role as indicators of maternal or paternal descent and, in anthropological genetics, as proxies for wider patterns of variation. But this genetic material is not figured as simply a handy source for studying patterns of genetic variation and ancestral relationships between human groups. Instead, this genetic material itself, genetic maternal and paternal lineages, and the geographies of mtDNA and Y chromosome variation are framed by ideas of maternity and paternity, femininity and masculinity, and sexual difference itself. My attention to the making of difference in human population genetics includes addressing geneticists' production and interpretations of sexually differentiated geographies of genetic variation that rely on and claim to verify particular models of sex, sexual difference, and reproduction. The making of ideas of similarity and difference in human population genetics involves not only ideas of genetic relatedness through degrees of shared ancestry within and between human groups but also, and increasingly, ideas of sexual difference.

My focus on *geographies of relatedness*, which I set out in this introduction and deploy in the chapters that follow, provides a critical framework for engaging with the nature and implications of genetic accounts of origins and ancestry, connection and distance. This entails considering the place of ideas of relatedness within human population genetics, and in relation to the wider social meaning and practice of kinship, addressing the emergence of a focus on sexual difference in the science of human origins and relatedness, and pursuing the geographical dimensions of questions of relatedness, origins, ancestry, and indigeneity that feature so strongly in the science and culture of human population genetics. What sort of geographical imaginations of settlement, mobility, interaction, and isolation underpin accounts and interpretations of human genetic variation? How do they reflect and inform the particular contexts of their making as science and as culture?

From "Race" to "Relatedness"

The text of that wristband—"genetic differences reveal our ancestry"— would have no meaning, no purchase, without a widely shared understanding that ancestry is itself meaningful, informative, and formative. The idea that ancestry matters as a source of personal and collective self-knowledge underpins that reference to "our ancestry." The statement intends to convey one fundamental principle of human population genetics: patterns of genetic variation are sources of knowledge of ancestry. But there is something also about this "take-home" message that is indicative of the wider ways in which human biological difference—or, more specifically, human genetic variation—is figured within human population genetics. In contrast to the significance of inherited biological differences in the racial science that emerged in the late nineteenth century, "genetic differences" in this statement seem neutralized, just a means to something else, to knowledge of ancestry, something positive, rewarding, meaningful but politically neutral. This is a science of difference purposefully distanced from the science of race, which justified eugenics and the Holocaust. "Genetic difference" is a vital sign of something more benign; it is revelatory but in service to a more significant level of collective self-knowledge. "Our ancestry" remains semantically open; it might mean a collective of individual ancestries (mine, yours, and so on) or "our" universal human ancestry. However, it also evokes, if only implicitly, ideas of other human groups historically figured as communities of shared descent—racial, ethnic, and national. It is the potency of these collectives that underlies public interest in these accounts of difference and curiosity about how they confirm, challenge, or complicate claims about the origins, arrival, and distinctiveness of traditionally defined groups.

But while the origin stories of ethnic or national groups are being explored genetically in numerous research projects, or turned to by population geneticists to explain patterns of variation, the lexicon of human population genetics is predominantly one of relatedness rather than race, ethnicity, or nationality. The broad project of human population genetics to reconstruct genetics lineages, which are interpreted in terms of the historical geographies of early human migration, is couched in terms of reconstructing a genetic "human family tree." Contemporary patterns of human genetic variation are treated as sources for tracing the interactions between different human groups through migration and reproduction and thus how different human groups are related in terms of the nature of their shared or distinctive ancestry. While all humans are understood to share ancient ancestry in Africa (even within recent multiregional models of local evolution and interbreeding between modern and archaic humans),[19] human population geneticists explore patterns of genetic variation as a measure of different ancestries within humanity. These ancestries are the product of distinct patterns of migration and demographic histories in the millennia since the spread of early humans from that African homeland. A recent common ancestor indicates a strong degree of ancestral relatedness, while a more temporally distant common ancestor indicates a lesser degree of ancestral connection. Accounts of human genetic variation are figured through and presented as sources for knowledge of that global "human family tree" and personal (genetic) genealogies. This language of familial relatedness is mirrored in the wider culture and commerce of genetic genealogy. Genetic ancestry testing companies describe those who share particular forms of genetic similarity (or markers) as "genetic cousins." Questions of who is related to whom and how, as individuals and in terms of human groups, are central to the culture and science of human population genetics.

This idiom of relatedness is figurative as well as descriptive. The relationships between human "populations" are explored and presented in terms of relatedness, and genetic lineages are figured in diagrammatic form as branches on that human family tree. Though the phylogenetic diagrams of commonality and divergence of human population genetics are of genetic lineages rather than of individuals or human groups and their time scales are of thousands of years rather than the generational timespans of conventional genealogy, they share the dendritic form of stems and branches with the figure of the family tree. Indeed, visual parallels between these representational forms reflect past crossovers between scientific efforts to address human evolution and the cultures and practices of genealogy.[20]

This focus on relatedness offers an ostensibly positive and progressive language for framing the study of genetic variation with ideas of deep and natural familial solidarity and security, bonds and belonging, love and care that distances it from its own history of racial science. But the emphasis on relatedness is more complex than it might seem. The study of human genetic variation is no longer envisaged as a means to categorize humanity into racial groups. However, the shift from typological approaches and the language of race to population-based approaches in the 1950s was not, as Jenny Reardon has importantly demonstrated, a simple transition from racial to postracial science.[21] Debates persisted about the most appropriate models and methods for studying human genetic variation and the terminology for describing patterns of variation. Nevertheless, by the 1990s, the study of human genetic variation via molecular genetics was largely characterized by an explicit commitment to an antiracist model of human genetic unity. The study of human genetic variation, under that ideal of fundamental human unity, as Nadia Abu El-Haj insists, has shed key elements of racial science: human genetic variation is not envisaged in terms of hierarchies of difference; patterns of variation are not read in terms of genetic variants determining the traits or abilities of human groups. Instead, genetic variation is interpreted as evidence of collective ancestral histories.[22]

But while contemporary human population genetics clearly cannot be understood to be racial science in new guises, neither should the vigorous claims by human population geneticists and others in the academy and public domain—that the study of human genetic variation has profoundly antiracist effects in demonstrating the genetic unity of humanity and in the genetic nonexistence of races—be simply taken for granted. As David Skinner has argued, though social scientists often invoke science to emphasize that race is a social construction that has no basis in nature, race has a much more ambiguous and contradictory complex of meanings in contemporary science and in human population genetics, more specifically.[23] As I will discuss more fully in chapter 1, accounts of human evolution, origins, and migration can be presented and interpreted as either confirming or disrupting the idea of humanity as a family tree of biologically distinctive and relatively stable human groups, whether described as ancestral populations or interpreted as races. Antiracist statements of genetic unity coexist with contested but influential claims about the biomedical utility of race or ethnicity as the focus of studies of genetic variation. Contemporary biomedical genomic research, often drawing on human population genetics, is based on the assumption of higher levels of relatedness among people of the same socioculturally defined racial categories.[24] Relatedness is not a simple alternative to race. Instead, assumptions about relatedness draw on wider conventions of thinking about human groups.

Arguments about whether geographical patterns of variation can or should be described in terms of conventional racial categories, how-ever, take place within an overarching commitment to antiracism. Yet, as Jenny Reardon astutely points out, the pursuit of antiracist futures cannot progress by accepting early twenty-first-century efforts to forge a "liberal anti-racist genomics" as the solution to the problem of race in the study of human genetic variation and its application in genetic ancestry testing.[25] As she argues, the criticisms of the use of racial categories in studies of human genetic diversity, especially the Human Genome Diversity Project, and in biomedicine, despite claims that racial categories are social rather than biological, have led in the early twenty-first century to a new empha-sis on liberal principles of democratic participation, consultation, and inclusion in the practice of human genomics and to a new emphasis on individual agency and self-determination in the consumption of genetic technologies. These principles will, it is hoped, correct the dominating, objectifying tendencies of the science of human genetic variation. But, as Reardon argues, the emergence of "liberal anti-racist genomics" invites continued critical engagements with the ways in which race is remade in reconfigured models of agency and expertise, with the genomic making of the categories of collective identity that research subjects and indi-vidual consumers are "free" to choose, and with the individualization of race, as policies to address racism are undermined by the figuring of racial identification through genetic ancestry as a matter of individual agency and choice.

In this book, I take up this injunction to explore the making of race in the antiracist liberal science of human genetic variation. But my con-cern is not only with the making of categories of identity and difference as genetic. It is with the making of ideas of genetic relatedness, as they are entwined with, but not confined to, the question of race, ethnicity, or nation, that seem most powerful and politically problematic because of their framing as antiracist contributions to human understanding. Using the descriptor *antiracist* is, of course, not meant to be a simple characterization of the science, nor is it meant to conflate the antiracist framing of this science with the history of antiracism and ongoing antiracist struggle.[26] Instead, foregrounding this key dimension of the science and culture of human genetic variation, along with its multicultural framing (see chapters 3 and 4), provides greater purchase on the complex making of ideas of difference and relatedness.

In chapter 1, I reflect on the making of ideas of human relatedness and difference in accounts of genetic variation and in genetic genealogy through a focus on the geographical nature of the practices of producing and interpreting accounts of ancestry and origins in both these entangled domains. Here I set out a framework for addressing the cultural and political embeddedness and implications of genetic accounts of ancestry and origins. It is a critical framework that follows the shift within the idiom of the science itself from race to relatedness. But this is not to leave the making of race behind as a focus of critique, nor is it to take that broad shift from the language of race to ideas of relatedness and diversity as the end of race in science. Instead, it encompasses the important and complex question of the contradictory, simultaneous remaking and refutation of race in genetic science within a wider scrutiny of the figuring of shared ancestry (and thus genetic similarity) as the basis of different human collectives (ethnic and national as well as racial) and as the basis for senses of commonality within and across these categories. My aim is not only to problematize those accounts of human genetic variation that do configure human genetic diversity in ways that evoke older racial categories. It is also to problematize the idea of genetic relatedness itself.

Genetic Kinship

This can begin by considering genetic accounts of relatedness in relation to the social practice and categorizations of kinship. As Peter Wade has argued, a focus on kinship is a fruitful lens for considering the complex implications of genomics for understandings of race, nation, ethnicity, and nature.[27] It throws up the connections and distinctions between accounts of genetic relatedness and kinship as a social practice, but it is a comparative mode that avoids figuring science as a practice and mode of knowledge production that is removed from, but influential over, wider society. Nor does it hold to neat distinctions between science and popular science or between science and society, more broadly. Different representational forms (e.g., peer-reviewed journals or popular documentaries) and audiences (scientists' peers or the wider public) clearly do matter in terms of the making of knowledge. But these are not isolated domains given the current emphasis on public engagement and, to some degrees, the commercial application of science, and more fundamentally, the cultural embeddedness of science. The traffic in meaning is not one way, from science to society, since the making of scientific knowledge is already shaped by the contexts of its production, including the values, concerns, and perspectives that scientists knowingly and unknowingly bring to their work. This is, of course, a well-established perspective within science studies, but it is particularly vivid in the mutual imbrication of human population genetics and popular genealogy in its traditional and newly geneticized forms and the deeper shared epistemologies and models of ancestry within this science and within society. Human population genetics and the wider business and cultures of genetic genealogy, as I explore across their scientific and popular forms in the chapters that follow, are shaped by the particular configuration of the politics of identity and difference of their contexts. However, the status of science gives genetic accounts of ancestry and relatedness particular authority as they travel through their social worlds and get taken up and put to work.

It would also be a mistake to position genetic accounts of human relatedness as the straightforward antithesis to social understandings and practices of kinship. Human population genetics is a culturally embedded knowledge-making practice whose accounts of who is related to whom and how and the significance attributed to ideas of ancestry and origins both draw on and feed back into wider cultures of genealogy. Accounts of human origins—or the origins and ancestral pasts of specific people, as individuals and as members of groups—in the science and culture of human population genetics, are pursued within a particular model of identity and relatedness that informs the widely popular pursuit of genealogy or family history and underpins the broader meaning of ancestry, inheritance, and origins in Western modernity. The rapid development of human population genetics and the rapid growth in popular genealogy in conventional and technologically assisted forms since the 1990s not only coincide but also are closely entangled. This is not just through the most direct commercial application of the data and techniques of human population genetics in genetic genealogy testing but also in terms of the shared meaning attributed to ancestral knowledge, so often posed in terms of "knowing who you are and where you come from" as individuals, as groups, and as humanity.

The deeply naturalized view that "ancestry" fundamentally matters underpins both scientific research on collective human origins (or the origins and migratory history of specific groups) and group-based and personal genealogical research in the contemporary genealogical moment.[28] Human population genetics and wider cultural models of identity and relatedness in Euro-American societies share this genealogical model but not without some differences. As Nadia Abu El-Haj argues, accounts of genetic ancestry are not deterministic in the sense of inherited characteristics passed on along genetic lineages.[29] Culture is not figured as the outcome of biogenetic inheritance. This is central to her reading of genetic ancestry testing as bringing together ideas of the profound significance of ancestry and individual agency in responding to newly found knowledge. Genetic genealogy thus extends the double sense of genealogy as a matter of empirical evidence and a practice of self-fashioning, which I have described as "genealogical identities"—commonly understood as determined through the fundamental "facts" of genealogy and as produced through the social practice of genealogy in action.[30] Yet genetic lineages are presented as being imbued with special cultural significance, since they offer a scientific way of knowing what geneticist Spencer Wells describes as "deep ancestry," which has depth of meaning as well as historical depth.[31] Ancestry matters.

The pursuit of questions of who is related to whom and how in both domains also reflects the ways in which scientific and popular understandings of relatedness share a wider and deeply embedded epistemological tradition, a mode of thought and practice concerned with relations. Marilyn Strathern has argued that a way of thinking about and valuing relations—"relationality"—is a shared feature of Euro-American science and social life. Relations, she argues, are commonly understood in terms of connection and disconnection and as categorical or conceptual (and thus given and preexisting practice) or interpersonal (and thus made). These two modes of figuring connections within modern scientific knowledge systems underpin understandings of the work of science both as making or inventing connections between things and as discovering their interconnections. They are found also in the ways in which Euro-Americans think of familial and other sorts of relations with others and are not a matter of kinship alone but are part of wider ways of knowing and thinking about the world in terms of connections as doubly there to be discovered and as the product of (scientific or social) labor.[32] Understandings of relatedness may be affected by new genetic knowledges, but at the same time, they already share with science an epistemology of discovery and invention, of what is found in nature and what is made of nature. This reflects the ways in which human population genetics and understandings and practices of relatedness are both located in a culture that valorizes the discovery and making of connections.[33]

This shared epistemology is one strand of her argument against reading the implications of genetic discourses in terms of a simple contrast between social and scientific models of kinship, especially when figured as a contrast between deterministic and individualistic ideas of selfhood and identity in science and the rich and complex social relations of community or kinship.[34] This is because both Anglo-American accounts of kinship and genetic accounts of relatedness combine ideas of individual uniqueness and relationality. A focus on individual uniqueness is, she argues, part of social understandings of kinship. Within the conceptual frameworks of human population genetics, a person is genetically unique (bar the identical twin exception), but that uniqueness is the product of a set of ancestral relations defined by the intergenerational transfer of genetic material. This means that, firstly, it is the understanding of scientific practice as connections given in nature and uncovered by science that frames human population genetics, and, secondly, different models of kinship are at work despite the shared focus on uniqueness and relationality. For human population geneticists, relatedness—patterns of connection between people—is a function of patterns of genetic difference and similarity that reflect degrees of ancestral connection. Kinship is genetic; it is there to be found and made newly known.

Kinship in social practice is, however, a calculus of connections that order relationships and is itself a social practice through which the relations that matter are selectively performed. As social and cultural anthropologists have long argued, kinship is a system of ordering relations between people based on social, material, or biological ties centered on birth, parentage, and shared ancestry and is a practice through which those bonds are constituted as more or less significant in the "doing" of kinship.[35] Though kinship has conventionally been understood as the social meaning of the "natural" facts of reproduction, ideas of both what is given, fixed, and inherited (nature) and what is forged, mutable, and chosen (nurture) are routinely and flexibly used in practice.[36] The ever-extending family tree is truncated by the ways in which relatives "drop out" of the family or are "dropped." Biological links can be discovered and be the basis of new relationships—or not. So-called fictive kin—adults who are named as aunts or uncles on the basis of practiced relationships rather than kinship connections—can be very real family members.[37] It is this attention to kinship as a matter of connections both given by nature and selectively made to matter within, across, and beyond the reckoning of close and distant family ties that provides one lens through which to consider accounts of genetic relatedness.

As Jonathan Marks puts its unequivocally, "There's DNA and there are probabilities of sharing some, but no tangible genetic stuff divisible among kin and distinguishing or bounding them from non-kin. There is no genetic test for kinship. Kinship is not a genetic property."[38] Social understandings of human relatedness are not narrowly based on a genetic calculus of degrees of shared substance. Kinship involves ideas of incontrovertible bonds based on blood, biology, or genes; routine practices of choosing kin and doing kinship; and flexible senses of the significance and sometimes insignificance of shared biogenetic inheritance and connection. The everyday fluidity and flexibility of the significance attributed to inheritance and experience and nature and nurture in people's sense of themselves is nevertheless encompassed within a dominant social understanding that ancestry matters and that self-knowledge is incomplete without some understanding of the ancestral past.

This is a social understanding of the significance of ancestral knowledge that is shared with anthropological genetics. However, in human population genetics, relatedness is genetic and based on ancestry alone. All the complexity of the social and cultural performative doing and making of family is simply epistemologically irrelevant. Relatedness in human population genetics is fundamentally genealogical, and this is understandable given the nature of this scientific practice whose subject is human genetic variation and whose fundamental objects of knowledge are patterns of genetic similarity and difference as the product of the biology of reproduction and genetic inheritance. Human population geneticists would likely argue that their work is not about the social practice and meaning of kinship but about genetic variation and genetic relatedness. However, this imaginative border between science and society is breached by the claims made for the social value of the science itself by many scientists themselves. Discourses of genetic kinship and genetic connection become socially significant both through the model of the family, which is so heavily deployed in human population genetics, and through the authority of science, especially when presented as a science that can discern true relatedness—who is really related to whom—among mistaken versions in the messiness of real social relations (e.g., in paternity testing when practiced fatherhood is tested for its biological truth or when claims about specific ancestral connections to historical figures, especially members of royal families, are investigated, as they frequently are).[39]

This contrast between ideas of genetic kinship and the social practice of kinship is important, and its implications are worth pursuing as genetic accounts of relatedness pick up on some and jar with other dimensions of the ways people reckon and practice kinship. But this only goes so far toward getting at what is at stake in genetic accounts of relatedness. It is what genetic accounts of relatedness share with wider models of kinship that shows that a focus on relatedness in human population genetics is not the safe and uncontentious alternative to race that it might seem. As I trace more fully in focusing on the Genographic Project in chapter 3, the idea of the human family is repeatedly presented in human population genetics as an ideal model for thinking of humanity and as an antithesis to pernicious ideas of racial difference and antagonisms between national or ethnic groups. Finding out who is related to whom within that family tree, as individuals or as groups, via studies of human genetic variation, is presented as enriching and rewarding—the basis of senses of connection to people, places, and cultures and of new relationships between those who share ancestry. But while the social practice of kinship is performative and flexible, it is worth remembering that kinship is also a classificatory technology that assigns significance to, and orders people within, social groups in terms of degrees of biological connection and distance; that defines categories of inclusion and exclusion; and that differentiates, ranks, and naturalizes those exclusions, differentiations, and hierarchies in families and in the other collectives also defined at some level through shared descent and ancestral relatedness (nation, ethnic group, and race).

Despite their different political inflections, the social orders of family, nation, ethnic group, and race are all constituted through ideas of bonds, affinities, and shared biocultural inheritance based on shared ancestry.[40] Each is conventionally imagined as a community of descent. Though "ethnicity" is often used to refer to groups sharing a cultural heritage and is often used to avoid the biological associations of race, it is not a neat and tidy alternative, since along with ideas of the nation, both "ethnicity" and "race" encompass ideas of shared ancestry. Nation, ethnicity, and race share this imaginative familial foundation, and they are also entangled models of relatedness—as the figure of the family moves across discourses of nation, ethnicity, and race and as "natural" familial orders naturalize other hierarchies. The idea of the nation as ordered family and as a natural community of shared descent has been historically entangled with ideas of the universal human family and racial difference. In late nineteenth- and early twentieth-century Britain, for example, ideas of the nation and the universal "family of man" were naturalized through the model of the "natural" family happily and divinely ordered through the subordination of women to men and children to adults. This, in turn, naturalized social hierarchies within an organic national unity, gendered hierarchies within the family, and a hierarchical model of "racial" difference and imperial power at a global scale.[41] Beyond the imperial homeland, colonized subjects were produced as genealogically defined ethnic groups in the classifications and orderings of colonial governance.[42]

Since these categories are all premised on some understanding of similarity and affinity through shared descent, the focus on ancestry and relatedness in anthropological genetics does not escape the politics of these categories of difference but is inescapably entangled in the politics of difference. Relatedness does not provide a benign alternative to these political categories, since ideas of connections based on shared descent are already intrinsic to them. The problem is not only one of race but also one of ideas of genetic relatedness more widely. This focus on the practices of differentiation and exclusion in definitions of commonality and connection through shared descent provides a critical framework for considering the implications of genetic accounts of ancestral relatedness. This is a framework that addresses the making of difference and relatedness in an avowedly antiracist science, by focusing on the meaning and implications of accounts of shared ancestry and biological relatedness via descent as the basis of personal and collective identities and relationships across the categories of race, nation, and ethnic group, rather than race alone.

Sex and the Science of Relatedness

Human population genetics can be understood as a science of related-ness in a second sense, however. Patterns of human relatedness revealed through the analysis of human genetic variation are not only understood as sources for reconstructing historical geographies of migration and set-tlement but also increasingly central to claims that the study of human genetic variation is a source of knowledge about the nature and social organization of human life. Genetic variation is being explored in terms not only of relatedness but also of kinship—or, more specifically, in terms of the ways in which societies organize sex and marriage. A feminist atten-tiveness to the implications of accounts of human genetic variation and their uses not only means exploring the ways in which genetic accounts play upon gendered ideologies of the reproduction of race or nation, or how gendered familial ties are genetically tested, important as this is.[43] It is also attentive to the making of difference—sexual as well as racial—within the science itself. This making of difference is a matter of not only inter-preting geographies of genetic variation in terms of often conventionally gendered accounts of migration but also taking those patterns to reveal the nature of sex and sexual difference itself, especially concerning repro-duction. This is a science not about finding "genes for" putatively feminine or masculine behaviors but of studying differences in patterns of variation of portions of DNA that are figured as indicative of maternal or paternal lineages (mtDNA and the Y chromosome, respectively) and interpreting these patterns as the product of, and thus evidence for, women's and men's different reproductive natures. Human evolutionary genetics, it is argued, can "tell us who we are" through accounts of ancestral origins, migration, and settlement but, it is argued, can also be used to reconstruct the social organization and cultural dynamics of human life. Ideas of reproduction, sex, and gender are fundamental to these claims.

In human population genetics, patterns of genetic variation are taken to be the cumulative products of human reproduction, indicative of both patterns of relatedness and sources for reconstructing the historical geog-raphy of origins and migrations of humanity or of specific human groups. But kinship is also a focus of investigation itself as human population geneticists interpret patterns of genetic variation as evidence for what are taken to be fundamentals and what are taken to be variations in the nature and organization of human reproduction. This is presented as an extension of human evolutionary genetics into the disciplinary domain of anthropology. But feminist critiques within and beyond anthropology, of ways in which the so-called natural facts of reproduction and the idea of the family's fundamental basis in nature has been used to naturalize versions of sex and gender that support men's power over women and figure alternatives to reproductive heterosexuality as aberrations from nature, provide critical tools to consider this move.[44] Furthermore, feminist science studies scholars have addressed the deeply gendered practice and epistemologies of science, the scientific production of sex and gender, and how race, gender, and sex are entangled in the making of the artifacts of bioscience and molecular genetics.[45] Most pertinent to my focus here is Amade M'charek's important work on the different ways the sexual specificity of genetic material (mtDNA or the Y chromosome) is produced, foregrounded, or elided in studies of human genetic diversity.[46] I return to this in chapter 4, where I draw on and extend existing work to explore the production and implications of genetic accounts of "men's and women's histories."

These sexually differentiated historical geographies deserve critical scrutiny. While the issue of race hangs over human population genetics in the wake of racial science and more recent controversies about the Human Genome Diversity Project, there is generally much less sensitivity about the political implications of accounts of sex and gender within human population genetics and in genetic genealogy. Science may seem to be on politically safer ground here in comparison to genetic considerations of the biocultural categories of nation, race, and ethnicity while accruing the sort of public attention that meets scientific claims about sex and sexual difference. While the shadow of scientific racism hangs over human population genetics and to different degrees shapes the ways in which human genetic variation is described, sex and gender are figured as rather less dangerous and socially divisive subjects, and any possible controversy surrounding them is much less potentially damaging than the charge of racism. The relative lack of concern with the politics of sexual difference in human population genetics also reflects the different public profiles of antiracism and feminism, in which the orthodoxy of antiracism contrasts with the popular derision of feminism beyond its most tempered and unthreatening liberal strands.

Yet, just as some accounts of human genetic variation are framed by an explicit antiracism, at least some genetic accounts of gendered migration and reproduction are framed by claims that they are newly sensitive to issues of gender and redress the marginality of women in history. So how does a broadly liberal ideal of sexual equality, in some cases at least, shape accounts of gendered migration and reproduction in human population genetics? What are the implications of other accounts that are much more unreflective or simply and unapologetically certain of the "facts" of sex and social life now claimed to be proven by, and read from, patterns of mtDNA and Y-chromosome variation or that offer historically located accounts of reproduction that are deemed to reflect universal differences in the organization of sex and marriage? New genetic claims about what is natural, social, universal, and varied in relation to human sex and reproduction through interpretations of sexually differentiated geographies of human genetic variation need to be addressed, especially because their apparent political "safety" means they have largely escaped critical attention and thus remain unchallenged in scholarship and, more significantly, in the public domain.

This relative lack of critical scrutiny contrasts with the amount of attention they receive in the public domain. There is an energetic and ready exchange of ideas of sex and gender between science and society, as sex is becoming newly and explicitly visible within the research directions and interpretative frameworks of anthropological genetics. This strand of human population genetics is emerging as a new and potentially influential contributor to and source of evidence in arguments about sex, gender, and social life within public culture. Scientists' own awareness of popular interests in the nature of femininity, masculinity, sex, and reproduction and the media's eagerness for stories of sex and science undoubtedly shape the ways in which they frame their research.[47] Exploring the making of ideas of sex, genetic variation, and descent in human population genetics is thus not simply a matter of tracing the ways supposedly "pure" and "disinterested science" gets embroiled in the messiness of human social life or distorted by media reporting. To suggest that human population genetics is premised simply on the "natural facts" of life, elevated from and disinterested in the social dynamics of human reproduction, and only gets entangled in sexual politics as an accidental or unavoidable aftereffect is to misrepresent this field.

Instead, human population genetics is enmeshed, sometimes intentionally so, in the wider public field of meanings, questions, and claims about the nature of femininity and masculinity, from biological or evolutionary explanations of the social organization of sexuality and reproduction and gendered social life to attempts to denaturalize these foundational claims. Discourses of the natural and the cultural, inherited and learned, and nature and nurture continue to differently legitimize or contest conservative and alternative models of gender, sexuality, and the organization of human reproduction, social reproduction, work, and social life. These arguments are often inflected by evolutionary psychology, with its accounts of fundamental differences in the reproductive strategies of women and men and in the nature of masculinity and femininity. Geographies of mtDNA and Y-chromosome variation, it is being argued, reveal and confirm the fundamental dimensions of the nature of human sex, sexuality, reproduction, and gendered mobilities.

In this book, I extend recent scholarship on the implications of human population genetics for ideas of race and ethnicity by examining the gendered discourses of lineage and ancestry in genetic genealogy and by exploring emerging claims that studies of human genetic variation offer insights into the gendered social order, gendered patterns of mobility, and the nature of reproduction in human history. This involves considering the technoscientific centrality and cultural figuring of maternal (via mtDNA) and paternal (via the Y chromosome) lineage in accounts of humanity's ancient historical geography of origins and mobilities and in the culture and commerce of genetic ancestry tracing. "Sex-linked" lineages are, on the one hand, made to stand for humanity as a whole and, on the other, translated into double and differentiated maternal and paternal geographical origins and ancestry, sometimes drawing readily on conventional ideas of masculinity and femininity and sometimes working harder to produce accounts of gendered communities of shared descent. My focus is thus not on the efforts of behavioral geneticists to identify genes associated with particular gendered or sexual behaviors or abilities, whose work has already been deservedly criticized,[48] but on the more subtle and subtly persuasive naturalizations that run through recent accounts and interpretations of what is being figured as a gendered geography of human genetic variation.

Genetic Geographies

This attentiveness to the politics of relatedness can be developed further by drawing out the spatial dimensions of social and scientific accounts of relatedness and by exploring their relationship to geographical imaginaries of similarity and difference in models of human collectivity based on shared ancestry and multicultural diversity. In this book, I consider the science, culture, and commerce of human population genetics geographically by foregrounding the geographical dimensions of the field itself—in terms of its data, methods, and matters of interest—and pursue the nature and implications of the ways in which human relatedness is configured geographically in terms of ideas of spatial boundedness, networks, propinquity, distance, extent, stretch, scale, and origins. Spatial patterns of human genetic variation constitute the data that are produced in the practice of the science through sampling and geographically labeling genetic material. This spatial data makes it possible to pursue the field's fundamental and inherently geographical questions about the place, as well as timing, of human origins and the pathways, as well as timing, of early human migration, or the premodern migration of specific human groups. Mapping the data is analytically central, and maps, along with diagrams and narratives, are important modes of representing these reconstructed historical geographies of origins and migration.[49] These patterns may be visually figured as maps of the distribution of certain forms of genetic variation, as diagrams of phylogenetic origins and divergence, and as maps of the origin and spread of particular genetic lineages.

In this book, I explore the ways in which geographies of human genetic variation and ancestral origins are attributed significance in terms of human identity and relatedness by bringing to bear an analytical focus on the geographical specificity of the contexts of scientific and popular science knowledge making; on the significance of scale in the production of accounts of human diversity and relatedness; and on the crucial question of the construction of spatial boundaries and categories within patterns of human genetic variation. Much of the recent work on studies of human genetic variation in different national contexts highlights the ways in which the apparent universality of science is, in practice, shaped by and embedded within the particular social, cultural, economic, and political dynamics in which it is undertaken.[50] The specificity of the geographical contexts of human population genetics in the United States and the United Kingdom is fundamental to my discussion and emerges comparatively in the chapters to follow. However, context is understood not in a simple bounded sense but in terms of networks, flows, and interconnections between sites of knowledge making in this global science.

Furthermore, I explore and demonstrate the way an attentiveness to scale is key to addressing the nature and implications of the categories of identity that are evoked and reworked in the field. These range from the universal, to continental regions, countries, sub- or transnational regions, and to the family, itself imagined at different scales. Moving from a case of exploring the "global human family tree" genetically in chapter 3 to the national People of the British Isles project in chapter 4, I pursue the question of how ideas of human difference and similarity are articulated differently at different scales of investigation and description in human population genetics. Importantly, this book deploys a geographical perspective in considering the construction of boundaries and categories within patterns of spatial variation. Indeed, the question of how human genetic variation is described in terms of gradients, spatially bounded categories, or broad geographical locations is central to current scientific debate about how to describe human genetic variation in the practice of biomedical genetic research, as well as anthropological genetics, and in relation to the politics of conventional categories of difference, including, but not limited to, race.

But I also want to think spatially about relatedness itself—that is, I want to consider the relationship between ideas of closeness and distance as terms that delineate degrees of kinship connection or genealogical relatedness and actual spatial proximity and distance. This opens up a series of questions about geographical and social belonging; about membership in spatially, as well as ancestrally, defined groups; and about place as location of belonging and place as imaginative inheritance or actual territory. In everyday Euro-American accounts of family relationships, a relative may be described as close or distant in terms of the reckoning of kinship connections. The fewer links removed from an individual's immediate family of parents, siblings, and grandparents, laterally within cotemporaneous generations, and the fewer links backward in time from the present, the closer or less distant the relation. In terms of the practice of kinship, of course, degrees of emotional closeness do not neatly parallel a relative's conventional place in the reckoning of kinship. One may be much closer to a more distant relative and not, in practice, be close to an immediate relative—nor does spatial proximity correlate with emotional closeness or, in a mobile world, degrees of formal kinship. Spatial proximity and distance—while deeply significant to the practice of kinship, in both face-to-face and mediated forms (old and new—from letters and phones to new social media)—does not align with any necessary symmetry with the formal reckoning of kinship ties nor lived emotional closeness.

However, the idea of the coincidence of bonds between a group of people through shared ancestry and their geographical propinquity is fundamental to the deeply embedded imagination of a world of nation-states. The conventional idea of the nation-state as an extended family and a shared community of descent, whose senses of collective identity and culture derive from a shared ancestry and biocultural inheritance, is not only a matter of an imagined community but also that of a collective sharing of a geographical portion of the world as a natural homeland. There may be ancestral connections and genealogical links that crosscut the borders of these national units, but the conventional geopolitical map of the world of nation-states is underpinned by an assumption about the spatial and social ordering of human difference in the geopolitical map: that geographical proximity is a measure of ancestral relatedness and that the political geography of national borders marks out a mosaic of national communities of shared descent. This is a violently divisive model of ancestral closeness and geographical proximity. Much political conflict worldwide over the political legitimacy and cultural constitution of the state, from ethnic separatism to struggles to address internal patterns of political and economic inequality, involves the question of difference and inclusion within societies shaped by historical and contemporary patterns of migration or by the superimposition of national borders over preexisting patterns of ethnic difference. Models of cultural pluralism within the state and diasporic identities within states and transnationally are both defined in opposition to the traditional national equation of geographical proximity, spatial copresence, shared ancestry, genealogical rootedness, sociocultural sameness, and belonging.[51]

How, then, might accounts of the geography of human genetic variation draw on and reshape geographical imaginaries of a global mosaic of national communities of shared descent? What models of geography and ancestry do they put to work as well as work to reconstruct? How do they challenge or support, or both undermine and reinforce, ideas of the geography of natural homelands for ancestrally bound and geographically rooted groups? What largely implicit geographical imaginations about the historical and geographical organization of human genetic diversity, isolation, and mobility inform the production, representation, and interpretation of geographies of human genetic variation? There is another fundamental tenet of human population genetics to consider here. It is that human genetic variation is "geographically structured." Population geneticists agree that due to long histories of local reproduction and relatively locally limited migration, people living near each other are likely to be more genetically similar to each other than they are to people living further away. At one level, this seems an entirely satisfactory and uncontroversial account of the geographical ordering of global patterns of relatedness and one that has been used by human population geneticists, as well as social scientists, in arguments about gradients of genetic variation undermining ideas of genetically distinctive racial groups.

The tenet that people living near each other are likely to be more genetically similar to each other than they are to people living further away, of course, only holds for those who have not migrated or whose ancestors have not migrated far over the last four hundred years or so. It only holds for places with no experience of inward migration over those centuries, if such places exist. Human population geneticists seek to reconstruct the ancient migratory patterns and demographic processes that over many thousands of centuries produced a geography of human genetic variation that is taken as a stable and long-established spatial patterning of genetic difference. And though human groups or "populations," except in instances of geographical isolation, are understood to be open groupings, subject to continuous "gene flow" through sexual reproduction across socially defined boundaries, there is an assumption of the relative fixity of this pattern until early modern European expansion.

So while the idea of gradients of human genetic variation that do not correspond to human social categories of identity and difference has been frequently used in arguments about the power and value of human population genetics in dispelling ideas of the genetic existence of races, the idea of the geographical structuring of human genetic variation has a more complicated relationship to other understandings of identity and difference—national, ethnic, or indeed, racial—as a function of geographical proximity and distance. This raises crucial questions about the relationships between accounts of human genetic variation and understandings of the composition of societies shaped by the complexity and scale of migration over the last four centuries and in the much more recent past. Human population geneticists work to reconstruct ancient and premodern patterns of genetic variation and the migration pathways and demographic processes that produce them, but they do so in contemporary contexts like the United States and the United Kingdom that have been deeply shaped by recent centuries and recent decades of immigration with their particular contemporary configurations of politics of identity and difference. This relationship between the imaginative and analytical focus on a geography of human genetic variation that is a product of human migration but prior to modern mobility, on the one hand, and contemporary multiculturalism as a description of cultural diversity and contested political perspectives on that diversity, on the other, is, I argue, a fundamental dimension of the production, interpretation, and presentation of geographies of human genetic variation.

Amy Hinterberger has used term "molecular multiculturalisms" to describe the ways in which population-based medical genomic projects in Canada are shaped by a politics of ethnic inclusion.[52] This term could be expanded to capture the multicultural inflections of human population genetics, which in different contexts reflect particular national discourses of culture, diversity, and identity. The liberal antiracist character of contemporary genomics that Jenny Reardon identifies can thus also be described as a liberal multicultural science of difference and relatedness. In the chapters to follow, I trace the nature and implications of recent accounts of human genetic variation in terms of how the idea of a global geography of everyone in their natural ancestral places is informed by and reconciled with multicultural models of national diversity and multicultural imaginaries of migration and mixing. How are mobility and indigeneity figured in a science of reconstructing the ancient migration of humans from an original homeland in Africa and the subsequent interactions of human groups? When does indigeneity—being first in or original to a geographical territory—become fixed in the long time spans of human global mobility? How are old models of indigeneity resurrected to describe people in some places and new models of indigeneity applied in others, in accounts of human genetic variation? How is the term being used in science and society to describe social groups or categories of people that would not traditionally be seen to be indigenous? How does an ideal of indigeneity—of unbroken presence—shape interest in knowledge of origins and indeed get cultivated and serviced through genetic genealogy, and how does the idea of ancestral origin itself get attached to an imagined place of previous ancestral indigeneity? How are ideas of indigeneity, as rooted in a single original place of native purity, reconciled with or reworked in terms of a multiplicity of origins, mobility, and hybridity in personal and scientific accounts of ancestry? Addressing these questions means considering ancestry spatially and exploring them in relation to the contemporary cultures, politics, and geographies of indigeneity.[53]

Thinking about relatedness spatially is a matter of thinking of ancestry spatially also. Family trees are diagrams of connections arranged in a temporal sequence of descent. But given their historical and contemporary geographies of immigration, much popular genealogy in the United States and the United Kingdom is about family trees whose ancestral lines stretch back in time, toward multiple places of origin, and across complex geographies of migration. Genealogy is commonly described as a means of "knowing who you are" through knowing "where you came from." This is the notion of personal and collective self-knowledge enhanced and enriched by knowledge of ancestral origins that is central to human population genetics and to genealogy in its conventional as well as genetic versions. As I have explored in previous work, these geographies of ancestry can themselves be considered spatially, both in terms of the historical and geographical specificity of what it presented as a naturalized human concern and in terms of the different temporalities and scales at which ancestral origins are defined (when origins are presented as potentially traceable beyond genealogical records and potentially refined geographically from broad to more precise locations).[54] Indeed, in this book, I consider the idea of ancestry not only in terms of historical intergenerational links between individuals but also geographically, in terms of imaginative geographies of connection between people and between people and places—both in the sense of the scale of webs of ancestral connectedness and the geographical reach or extent of ancestral connections.

I do so also by considering the relationship between ideas of geographical origins and indigeneity—that is, between the idea of a former foundational place, "where you came from first," and the idea of "being first" and still present in that place. There has been considerable critical attention paid to how the first wave of human evolutionary genetics in the 1990s, typified by the Human Genome Diversity Project, treated the genetic material of indigenous people as data for scientific investigation and figured indigenous people as isolated relict populations frozen in an early stage of human history, despite the complex historical geographies and contemporary transnational political and cultural geographies of indigenous people.[55] As I discuss in chapter 3, there are dimensions of human population genetics that deserve a reiteration of those critiques.

But an expanded critical focus on ideas of indigeneity in the science and culture of human genetic variation can include attention to the politics of discourses of indigeneity in new as well as contrasting social contexts, in which the idea of indigeneity has quite different political inflections—in the United Kingdom, for example, where the majority of the population could be defined as native, or in the United States, where a minority is conventionally defined as native. While human population geneticists set themselves the task of exploring the origin stories of human groups that have long been defined by others and identified themselves as indigenous, the idea of indigeneity is also being evoked in projects exploring genetic variation in Europe and, differently, being taken up in or distanced from the wider turn to ideas of indigeneity or autochthony in anti-immigration nationalisms.[56]

At the same time, in the differently multicultural contexts of the United Kingdom and the United States, those who are defined according to the most conventional biocultural configurations of natural rootedness or national belonging, and through genetic ancestry, as "nonnative"—the majority of Americans and black and ethnic minority groups in Britain—are offered new genetic knowledges of their place or places of origin and prior indigeneity. Celebrations of ethnic particularity and cultural pluralism in societies shaped by complex geographies of migration coexist with the cultural and, indeed, spiritual significance attributed to the idea of an authentic, deep, unbroken, and harmonious relationship between the place of ancestry, birth, residence, and cultural inheritance. In the U.S. context, the appeal of being indigenous—of *not being* from elsewhere—and the significance of ethnic distinctiveness—of *being* from elsewhere—are entangled. It is the combined potency of ideas of ethnic diversity and the ideal of indigeneity and origins that produces the appeal of personalized genetic ancestry tests. And it is the power of the national and ethnic model of geographical origins and genealogical relatedness that produces scientific interest in investigating the genetics of human groups at different scales and produces public interest in the scientific refutations, reinforcements, or revisions of collective origin stories. A focus on race alone does not get at the making of these geographies of identity, belonging, and difference—nor does it address the ways in which ideas of sex and gender are drawn into and emanate from accounts of human genetic variation and genetic kinship and are entangled with other versions of human difference and relatedness. Genetic accounts of the sexual specificity of "gene flow" between human groups and across space—that is, women or men migrating, reproducing in the new location, and thus "bringing their genes"—for example, can suggest gendered national imaginaries based on the different origins, incorporations, and reproductive combinations of women and men. My focus on the making of ideas of difference includes the making of ideas of sexual difference, sexually differentiated historical geographies of migration and settlement, as well as ideas of the supposed fundamental nature of women's and men's reproductive strategies via accounts of the geography of human variation.

The term "geographies of relatedness" thus points to my concern with the ways in which geographies of human genetic variation are attributed significance in terms of human identity and relatedness and points to the book's geographical interpretative framework, which orders the chapters to follow. In chapter 1, "Genome Geographies," I focus on the production and meaning of geographical ancestry and origins in human population genetics and genetic genealogy, addressing how portions of genetic material are read as indicative of ancestral origin places and examining the relationships between ideas of cultural and genetic distinctiveness, genetic relatedness, and geographical categorization at different scales across biomedical genetics, anthropological genetics, and genetic genealogy. This exploration of the making of ideas of genetic ancestry sets out the key strands of recent critical engagements with the question of race, geography, and genetic variation and argues for a critical engagement with ideas of genetic ancestry that is attentive to the politics of the making of difference at different scales and to the relational ethics of genetic genealogy. In chapter 2, "Mapping the Global Human Family," I consider the geographical imaginaries of the avowedly antiracist Genographic Project—a project global in its claims and aims but shaped by the particular multiculturalism of its U.S. context—to map "the human family tree" and trace its negotiation of the tensions between its liberal multicultural celebration of diversity, discourse of global unity, and effort to reconstruct to a premodern geography of genetic variation. The genetic "human family tree," as I will argue, suggests particular models of relatedness based on genetic similarity that sit uneasily with its antiracist discourses of shared ancestry and its multicultural discourse of diversity. The focus on the global scale in human population genetics is paralleled by national projects. In order to track the different ways in which themes of genetic unity and diversity, sameness and difference are articulated differently in relation to differently scaled collectives—global or national—I turn to the national People of the British Isles project in chapter 3, "Our Genetic Heritage." In this case, studies of genetic variation in the United Kingdom are also notably inflected by multicultural models of diversity and refigure the genetic composition of the state not in terms of an indigenous "gene pool" now complicated by immigration but in terms of different sorts of diversity within a "mongrel nation." Nevertheless, as I will explore, ideas of "genetic heritage" differentiate between those that do and do not have a genetic and genealogical connection to and thus "natural" relation to the ancient history of Britain. But, as I have begun to show, accounts of human genetic variation are not just a matter of categories of shared descent and difference—global, national, racial, or ethnic. They are being interpreted in terms of sex, sexual difference, and sexually specific mobility. In chapter 4, "Finding the 'Truths' of Sex in Geographies of Genetic Variation," I address gendered geographies of human genetic variation and sex, gender, and descent in genetic genealogy, thereby expanding critical engagements with human population genetics as the field expands its interpretative range. Together these chapters offer a critical analysis of the making of difference and relatedness in these strands of the liberal antiracist and multicultural science of human genetic variation.

1

Genome Geographies

The Making of Ancestry and Origins

What does it mean to say that part of an individual's genomic sequence indicates the place of ancestral origin of that person? What is genetic ancestry, and how are places of ancestral origin defined and located through the analysis of genetic material? How and to what end is knowledge of this kind being produced in the scientific study of human genetic variation and in the business of genetic ancestry testing? What cultural understandings and scientific practices come together to locate an individual within a global geography of differentiated ancestral origins? What makes this a meaningful form of personal knowledge? Posing these questions in this way draws attention to the relationship between the molecular, individual, and global scales in accounts of genetic ancestry. But pursuing them means attending to the fundamental question of the social categorizations that fall between the individual and the universal and between ideas of individual genetic uniqueness and the shared human genome—the categories of race, ethnicity, and nationhood that each encompass ideas of a common ancestral past and shared geographical origin in a foundational region or homeland at different scales. It means addressing how global geographies of human genetic variation and genetic lineages are scientifically produced and described.

This chapter interrogates the making of ideas of genetic similarity, shared genetic ancestry, and differentiated geographical origins as meaningful sources of collective and personal knowledge in terms of the cultural categories of human identity, difference, and relatedness that inform them and are reworked through them. I do so by considering the practices and approaches that produce accounts of the geography of human genetic variation or that attribute geographical ancestral origins to bits of genetic material, in relation to the politics of producing, classifying, and naming spatial patterns of genetic variation within those global geographies of human genetic diversity. I do so also by considering how genetic ancestry, origins, and relatedness are produced as desirable and meaningful commodities. This provides a broad context for the engagements with themes of the global human family, national genetic heritage, and sex and genetic histories in the following chapters. But it also puts a geographical perspective to work to track the dimensions of scientific, public, and academic debates about the production, identification, and naming of patterns of genetic variation in relation to conventional categories of identity and difference by descent—especially, but not only, race.

In their work on the different approaches of biomedical scientists to human "population" differences in their search for genetic variations that may be associated with common complex diseases, Joan H. Fujimura and Ramya Rajagopalan examine what they describe as "genome geography." The term refers to "how, through the tools and practices of human genetics, bits of genomic sequence become associated with specific geographic locations, posited as the place of origin of people who possess these bits."[1] Their focus is on genome-wide association studies that seek to identify genetic variations that might be linked to common complex diseases by comparing the frequency of particular sorts of genetic variation of a sample of people who have a specific disease with those who do not (the control population). But, as they point out, biomedical genetics and human population genetics are entangled fields, both of which involve the making of categories and subcategories of people whose genetic material is to be studied—a "population"—and the naming of those categories in relation to place of contemporary residence and/or ancestral origin. The value of international projects to gather and analyze genetic samples and map human genetic diversity, such as the International HapMap Project, is argued to be the potential medical usefulness of the knowledge they produce.

Here I want to borrow and pluralize this term to consider the "genome geographies" at work in the making of accounts of human genetic diversity at different scales, which are sources for reconstructing ancient human migrations as evolutionary processes and reconstructing the migrations of and relationships between human groups in the premodern and historic past. "Genome geographies" stands for the particular geographical methods, understandings, and imaginaries that are put to work in producing, describing, and interpreting patterns of human genetic variation and that, in turn, inform the making of ideas of genetic ancestry and genetic origin in the domain of ancestry testing. Geographical categories, bound-aries, and distributions, as analytical tools and objects of knowledge, and geographical imaginaries of origins, settlement, and migration underpin the entanglements of race, "genetic ancestry," and population in the sci-ence and culture of human genetic variation. Studies of human genetic diversity are about the "structure" of genetic variation in itself, its geo-graphical dimensions, and that geographical structure as a window to the past and as a resource for future genomic medicine. But, as I will explore, geography is also bound up in claims about human collectives shar-ing ancestry and ancestral places of origin and evoked as an apparently neutral term beyond the troubled issue of categories of race, ethnicity, or nation. Attributing geographical designations to samples or to bits of genomic sequences serves practical purposes in producing accounts of genetic variation but, as I will argue here, cannot be detached from geog-raphies of identity, difference, and belonging. Human population genetics and genetic genealogy are entangled in the science and culture of ancestry and origins. Here I consider the making and meaning of geographies of human genetic variation first before turning to their application in genetic ancestry tests.

Geographies of Genetic Variation

Human population geneticists study human genetic variation at dif-ferent scales: sometimes seeking to contribute to knowledge of human evolutionary history through studies of human genetic variation at a global scale; sometimes working at the level of continental variation (e.g., across Europe) or within and between smaller regions within or across national boundaries. The focus may be on these global, continental, or regional patterns or on the patterns of differences and similarities between specific ethnic or national groups that are interpreted in terms of their demographic histories and historical relationships. Its investigative and explanatory range thus encompasses the universal and the particular, homogeneity and difference, different orders of collectivity, and degrees of genetic similarity. Across these scales and starting points is the shared methodological issue of sampling—the procedure by which a portion of a whole is studied as representative of the larger whole. This applies both to the genetic material itself and to the process through which it is generated as the basis for analysis.

Though advances in the speed of analysis and reductions in the cost of analysis suggest that the sequencing of entire genomes—the totality of genetic material in an individual—will become more common, studies of human genetic variation have hitherto been based on studying patterns of variation of selected genetic material that has been identified as variable and on using these indicative "markers" as proxies for wider patterns of genetic variation. Geneticists have identified chromosomal regions, or loci, that are highly variable and feature alternative variants (or alleles) of nucleotide sequences on a gene. These include base-pair differences, known as single nucleotide polymorphisms (SNPs), as the result of single substitutions of nucleotides, which commonly occur. In SNP-based studies, several hundred or thousands of these SNPs will be examined in the genetic material sampled as measures of genetic variation. In addition, patterns of variation of segments of DNA sequences identified as polymorphic—known as short tandem repeats (STRs) or microsatellites—are similarly analyzed within and between human groups. Useful markers are both stable and highly variable. A series of linked alleles on a chromosome or region of a chromosome that are inherited together is called a haplotype.[2]

Many studies of patterns of human genetic variation, especially anthropological genetic studies, focus on two specific sorts of genetic material: the nonrecombining portion of the Y chromosome, inherited unchanged from fathers to sons, and mitochondrial DNA (mtDNA), passed on unchanged from mothers to daughters and sons. The occurrence of mutations leads to distinctive forms of mtDNA or Y-chromosome markers, which, because of the direct maternal and paternal inheritance of this genetic material, are common to those sharing direct maternal or paternal descent, respectively. This combination of variability and direct inheritance that furnishes a measure of ancestral relatedness through matrilines and patrilines is fundamental to their use in genetic genealogy as well as human population genetics. While the term "haplotype" refers to the particular pattern of markers on genetic loci on an individual genome, the term "haplogroup" usually refers to a set of mtDNA or Y-chromosomal haplotypes indicative of a broad genetic lineage or phylogeny.[3] Both terms are used to refer to forms of genetic similarity that suggest a shared ancestry.

The geography of these lineages is derived from sampling the genetic material of different groups across the world, establishing the proportions and predominance of different markers within those groups, and comparing these patterns between groups. By being able to work out the order in which mutations accumulate and by estimating the relative and absolute timing of mutations, population geneticists attempt to reconstruct the relationships between different lineages and postulate migratory histories that have led to contemporary geographies of genetic variation. These particular ancestral lineages only reflect direct maternal or paternal descent and only focus on a very small proportion of the already very small portion of genetic material that differs among humans (less than 0.01 percent), but they are used as proxies for patterns of similarity, difference, and ancestry, more generally. This is a lineage-based approach. Much research is also conducted on human genetic variation by studying the pattern of allele frequencies across the genome more widely, rather than mtDNA or the Y chromosome alone, within and between populations. Human population geneticists thus examine selected, albeit more and more extensive, parts of the genomes of the individuals whose genetic material is included in their studies. But what is the basis for inclusion?

This clearly depends on the nature of the research. Studies of human genetic variation at the global scale do not, and clearly cannot, undertake a total project in which the genomes of the world's population are compared. Instead, comparisons are possible by sampling—gathering genetic material from a selected sample of the world's population made up of individuals who are taken as representing a pattern of variation shared with a wider group. This issue of selective sampling is at the heart of debates about the practice of human population genetics. Individuals are meant to stand for their wider population. But what is a "population"? What is the relationship between populations as objects of scientific study and as social and cultural groups? How are populations selected as relevant or suitable for study? How are individuals selected as representatives of those samples? These questions are central to the debates and criticisms that have surrounded human population genetics since the Human Genome Diversity Project was first proposed in the early 1990s. Even before the issue of interpreting and ordering the data on global human genetic variation arises, there is the issue of how the data are produced through the ways in which research projects conceptualize their sources of genetic material.

The study of genetic variation of human populations constitutes human population genetics as a discipline, but the definition and identification of populations has itself long been a subject of debate within the field. Close readings of the refiguring of studies of genetic variation from a typologi-cal tradition concerned with the identification of races to populations as new objects of study have challenged accounts of the straightforward turn from race in the 1950s. Rather than discarding race, approaches to human genetic variation continued to be contested in terms of the validity and meaning of race.[4] Jenny Reardon's work has been especially significant in tracing how typological versions of race were replaced with populationist approaches, which continued to combine an interest in groups that seem to conform to the model of population as a small group of geographically isolated, interbreeding individuals who share genetic distinctiveness with an understanding of human groups as open and dynamic. It is now widely agreed that the geography of human genetic variation is of continuous gradients of gradual variation over space (or clinal) and that populations are dynamic and overlapping. This is central to the argument that pat-terns of variation do not correspond to conventional racial categories. Indeed, many population geneticists use this to demonstrate the value of their research in dispelling ideas of races as biologically distinct groups, even if groups judged to be genetically distinct are routinely used in sam-pling strategies. But though "population" may seem a more neutral term than "race" or "ethnicity," populations are delineated in many ways in human population genetics and often through region, nation, continent of origin, ethnicity, or race. As Amade M'charek has shown, populations are not found in nature but are constituted in diverse ways through laboratory practices, technologies, and routines and in terms of race, national bound-aries, and genetic markers.[5] Her ethnography of the scientific practices "consisting of individuals, technologies, language and theories" through which "population" is "enacted or performed rather than discovered, analyzed or animated" challenges the realist ontology of "population" or "human group."[6]

The practical problem of selecting, naming, and categorizing samples within what is understood to be a geographically graded pattern of genetic variation is always a political issue of human categorization and differen-tiation and the power of doing so biologically. This is the case in studies that take social and cultural groups as units of analysis whether as sources of data on global genetic variation and human evolution or for specific histories of ancestry, origins, and relatedness. It is also the case in those that seek to avoid ethnic or racial categories in the production and inter-pretation of accounts of human genetic diversity. Different approaches to naming and categorization occur in three broad strands of research: (1) studies whose starting points are culturally defined human groups, whether the purpose of the study is to reconstruct the global premodern pattern of human genetic variation and the migratory, demographic, and evolutionary processes that produced this pattern or to explore the demographic historical geographies of, and degrees of, ancestral connection between these ethnic or national groups; (2) research that draws on accounts of genetic variation of what are taken to be broad categories of human diversity to ascertain the relative ancestral contribution of these "populations" to groups understood to be of mixed ancestry (these admixture studies are a feature of biomedical rather than anthropological genetics, but I consider them here because of their significance in the making of race and geographical ancestry, especially via their application in genetic genealogy); and (3) projects that seek to explore the "structure" of human genetic variation at different scales—global or continental— whose analytical starting points are not culturally defined groups but whose methods of data collection and interpretation are shaped by culturally embedded ways of thinking about categories of genetic, bodily, and cultural distinctiveness. I consider each in turn here.

Cultural Groups as Populations

For the Human Genome Diversity Project, the populations to be studied as sources of knowledge about human evolution were those taken to be most representative of the pattern of human diversity that preceded the migration and human mixing of human modernity: indigenous people imagined as both isolated and facing extinction. The ethics and implications of the practice and assumptions of the project were quickly and severely criticized.[7] These criticisms included the ways in which the selection of "populations" for investigation—on the basis that their linguistic and ethnic traditions and geographical isolation make them genetically interesting as sources for knowledge of the evolution of human genetic variation—assumes a correspondence between genetic and cultural difference from the start. Using ethnic groups as the organizing principle of genetic surveys and collecting genetic material from them even under the most stringent ethical protocols—and despite the wide agreement about the clinal nature of genetic variation and of the shared origins of humanity—still suggests that the boundaries between sociocultural and political communities correspond to patterns of genetic diversity.[8] There were serious concerns about this within the field as well as among critics.[9] Some human population geneticists and anthropologists, alert to this problem, argued for a geographical grid as an alternative sampling strategy. In this strategy, sampling would be driven by the collection of an equal number of blood samples from areas corresponding to each square of a uniformly sized sampling grid covering all areas of human occupation—an expensive, time-consuming but more neutral and comprehensive starting point.[10] It was not adopted.

Instead, the selection of populations through linguistic and ethnic criteria is routine in studies of human genetic diversity at the global scale and intrinsic to attempts to reconstruct the evolutionary and demographic histories of, and relationships between, named human groups. If the aim is to study the genetic variation within and between two ethnic or national groups or between people from different regions for the purpose of elucidating their degrees of relatedness and historical relationships, then these groups constitute the populations. However, this also entails, as I will discuss in relation to a national genetic project in chapter 4, selecting individuals who best represent that population and thus raises similar issues about representation and inclusion. Projects of this kind take the genetics of a cultural, ethnic, or national group as the object of analysis and take their existence as social and cultural entities as something to be tested against their degree of genetic distinctiveness in comparison to wider patterns of variation.

Biomedical Ancestry

In the case of admixture mapping, the "population" whose mixture is to be delineated is composed of those groups understood to be of mixed ancestry in the United States: African Americans or Hispanic Americans. This research is often undertaken by biomedical researchers who are committed and self-defined members of these groups and underpinned by their concerns about the neglect of these groups in biomedical research and their health disparities. They are conducted with the aim of identifying ancestral components, or "risk alleles," linked to the prevalence of illness. It is done so by means of what are described as ancestry-informative markers (AIMs), which are markers identified as having distinctive frequencies in three ancestral "Old World," "parental" populations (i.e., Africans,

Europeans, and Native Americans), and statistically comparing their frequencies in the "admixed" population to derive percentage components of these ancestries in the "New World" population. This is described as "biogeographical ancestry." As Duana Fullwiley argues in her ethnography of admixture mapping, AIMs are based on taking the traditional Euro-American categories of race to be distinct ancestral populations. These assumptions drive scientists' decisions about where, across the world, genetic material is collected from "populations" and what data are deemed relevant to admixture mapping. So, as Fullwiley argues, "New genetic technologies that link geography and 'ancestry' do not necessarily depart from older notions of 'race,'" since the making of "racialized genomic fractions" depends on producing "parental populations" as genetically distinct and recognizable categories that divide up the "Old World" into old categories and geographies of race.[11]

As Ramya Rajagopalan and Joan Fujimura argue, geography plays a major role in the constitution of race and ancestry in admixture mapping—in particular, the idea of continental categories as indicative of ancestry and relatedness.[12] As with much work in human population genetics more widely, a few selected contemporary inhabitants are taken to represent ancient ancestral populations that are imagined to have been geographically isolated and thus homogenous. Thus "alleles and even chromosomes are labelled with continental descriptors" and "acquire geographical qualifiers, via a vernacular that pins down their origins to (and collapses the genetic histories and diversity of) entire continents," and "markers acquire genealogies that are rooted in place."[13]

Ancestry, as Fujimura and Rajagopalan make clear, means different things in different strands of medical genomics. In admixture studies, ancestry refers to these continental racial ancestral populations; it means something different and more plural in genome-wide association studies in which ascertaining ancestral fractions in a population is not the aim. In contrast, differences due to geographical ancestry, or "population substructure," have to be dealt with in order to make meaningful comparisons between the genomes of those with common complex diseases and the genomes of the nondisease control group, to avoid genetic similarities due to geographical origins being mistaken for potential gene–disease associations. In this form of biomedical research, the "genome geography" of the individual sample is derived from its labeling in terms of race, ethnicity, nationality, or sample location by those gathering or donating the genetic material. The identification and/or "ancestral" differentiation of the sample population relies on ethnically or racially labeled patterns of genetic variation and theories of human migration produced by population geneticists who interpret existing geographical patterns of genetic variation in terms of historical, archaeological, and wider cultural accounts of the origins and mobilities of particular human groups. Ancestry, in this case, refers to a single geographical origin rather than genomic fractions. But as Fujimura and Rajagopalan argue, tracing the ways in which genetic similarity is interpreted in terms of "shared ancestry" and "ancestral" geographic locations that can be read as genetic distinctions between racial or ethnic groups, often despite the scientists' intentions, also makes the three concepts of "population, race, and 'genetic ancestry' . . . difficult to untangle."[14]

These technical and epistemological entanglements that biomedical researchers work with, around, and produce are themselves entangled with the politics of race, genetics, biomedicine, and diversity, especially in the United States, where approaches to addressing diversity in human genome research have been heavily shaped by U.S. federal policy regarding race and ethnicity in health care.[15] Much of the debate about the genetic validity of racial categories has revolved around the question of whether or not racial categories are helpful in the prediction and treatment of disease, both in light of what Steven Epstein describes as the "vexed history of attending to, or ignoring differences in medicine" and in light of pharmaceutical interests in developing ethnically or racially targeted drugs.[16] The degree to which real disparities in health between socially identified racial and ethnic groups justify their treatment as genetic populations is challenged by those who argue that these disparities are the health consequences of the experience of racism and the intersections of racial discrimination and socioeconomic deprivation rather than a reflection of genetic racial differences.[17] These debates shape biomedical genomics whose accounts of race and ancestry both draw on and feed back into anthropological genetics.

Producing the Global Structure of Human Genetic Variation

Other research projects do not start with sociocultural groupings but with an interest in broad spatial patterns of human genetic variation. Exploring the "structure"—distinctive patterns of variation—within the global geography of human genetic variation is central to human population genetics. The aim is not simply to record variation but to consider how variation is patterned geographically and to devise ways in which that pattern can be described and categorized. Researchers may or may not consider this in terms of exploring the relationship between structure and ethnic or racial categories. But the shared starting point at least is to look at variation across the world or across a region to see what patterns emerge. Sometimes the relationship between these patterns and categories of race is an overt research question; sometimes it arises through the practices of categorization. In either case, it continues to be a focus of deeply fractured and fraught debate about the significance, meaning, and modes of conceptualizing, classifying, and representing human genetic variation. It is a contentious issue within the field and a theme of wider public interest and debate avidly taken up by media commentators. Between those population geneticists who argue against the validity of race through genetics and those who argue for its genetic reality is a spectrum of intensely contested, often ambiguous, and sometimes inconsistent approaches to understanding, exploring, and referring to what are variously called ethnic groups, races, or human populations.

These competing perspectives do, however, share a frequently reiterated common ground. Human genetic diversity is currently widely understood to be a matter of continuous geographical gradations. These clinal patterns of allele frequencies gradually changing over geographic space are described as "geographically structured." The term "isolation by distance" refers to the way in which "the farther two populations are from each other geographically, the more genetically different they will be from one another."[18] Setting aside the effects of modern migration, this means that degrees of genetic similarity correspond with geographical distance: genetic similarity decreases with increasing geographic distance—that is, to put it another way, "genetic distance," which is a measure of genetic dissimilarity, positively correlates with geographical distance. People near each other are more genetically similar to each other than they are to those further away because of localized patterns of "gene flow." As Deborah Bolnick explains, "because geographic distance limits migration, individuals tend to mate with those who live nearby and geographically close populations tend to exchange more genes than geographically distant ones."[19]

Contrasting perspectives on the validity of race reflect the degree to which scientists are inclined to draw boundaries within and construct categories from this global geography of genetic gradients.[20] For some, describing this diversity in terms of continental races can only ever be a reductive and dangerous simplification. For others, it is a functional shorthand that knowingly overlooks groups on the edges of these imagined clear geographies of race that do not fit these continental divisions. There is also a general consensus among those in the field that the degree of human genetic diversity is relatively low; that the small proportion of the human genome that is not identical between individuals does not correspond to racial categories; that there is more genetic diversity within rather than between human groups; and that variant alleles found to be common in one human group have also been found to be common within humanity as a whole. But this consensus coexists with significant differences of opinion whether continental descriptions of the geography of human genetic variation (such as African or Asian) are adequate even as proxy indicators of more complex patterns or are dangerously reductive.[21]

For some influential commentators, the results of statistical efforts to categorize diversity that appear to correspond to conventional categories of race are welcomed and promoted as proof of a new scientifically validated common sense of race free from the inhibitions that followed an earlier history of racial science. Science and society, it seems, can come to their senses and talk sensibly about race free from the charge of racism. Reports that geneticists had tested and proved the invalidity of the idea of genetically distinct human racial groups frequently appeared in the 1990s. But they have been followed by reports that patterns of human genetic diversity do follow the old schema of five continental races and that race is real after all.[22] This position is typified by Nicolas Wade, science reporter for *The New York Times*, who celebrates human population genetics for proving that the patterning of human genetic diversity in continental races is a matter of fact, a product of the dispersal of groups from Africa, subsequent isolation, separate evolution, and local interbreeding.[23]

This matter-of-fact science of race is, however, as critics have argued, the product of a series of methods and assumptions, from sampling strategies to statistical algorithms. First, these studies frequently construct their sample of human genetic diversity by collecting blood in places that are far from other sample locations, usually chosen as representative of a continental region. They do so also by including individuals who are thought to typify their continental region—especially the "extremes" of human difference based on old criteria of hair type and especially skin color—rather than including those who occupy more ambiguous positions on the boundaries between what are imagined in advance as continental divides. In addition, samples from "intermediate" locations that would demonstrate genetic continuities rather than discontinuities are discounted in the analysis or in the published results of influential studies of global genetic diversity.[24]

Second, the genetic clusters that are identified in the studies are not found in nature but produced through computation. Deborah Bolnick has traced the ways in which two influential studies of human genetic diversity produced accounts of genetic clusters that lent credence to the idea that genetic variation does correspond to a geography of continental distinctions.[25] Both used a statistical program called Structure to model genetically distinctive clusters and to allocate individual samples to those clusters or populations. But the number of clusters it produces to do so is set in advance by the research team. Thus an account that human genetic diversity falls into three clusters and that these correspond with traditional racial categories—Africans, Europeans, and East Asians—is a product of setting the program to produce that number of clusters. Choices in the analysis and in its interpretation are shaped by preexisting assumptions about a continental geography of genetic variation. So while there is widespread agreement on the clinal pattern of human genetic variation, accounts like these suggest a geographical mosaic that takes the continents as natural units of human difference, perhaps hazy at the edges where "gene flow" is acknowledged, but reflecting a deep stable pattern of continental genetic difference. Though, as Bolnick argues, the data itself and its analysis support established geographies of clinal variation, they are "described and interpreted in ways that both reflect and reinforce traditional racial views of human biological diversity and the evolutionary history of our species."[26] Implicit within this is a deeply persistent geographical imagination that locates the "true" genetic character at the center of "natural" geographical regions assumed to be places far enough from the influence of other groups to constitute a heartland of genetic distinctiveness. At the global scale, the continents provide the long-standing racial framework for locating these centers, but there is no transhistorical reason for assuming that the clinal pattern of human genetic variation is structured in ways that correspond to continental genetic heartlands. At stake in this is that deeply geographical and profoundly political question of determining patterns and boundaries within continuous variation.

Of concern here is the slippage between ideas of ancestry, geographical origin, race, and other biocultural categories of nation and ethnicity within the science and culture of human population genetics. Again, it is not a case of seeing in these developments a simple return to those older versions of race. As Nadia Abu El-Haj points out, the most fundamental difference is that these accounts of human genetic variation are not framed by a hierarchical understanding of racial difference.[27] Genetic variation is not figured in terms of rank and relations of superiority and inferiority. But the problem of new accounts of human genetic variation lies in the way in which ideas of categorically and geographically bounded distinctions between groups are produced and popularized despite the broad scientific agreement on clinal geographies of genetic variation. Maps are powerful visual devices in this production and popularization of genetic geographies of human similarity and difference, ancestral interconnection, and distinction (as I discuss, through a focus on the Genographic Project, in chapter 2).

"Geography" and "Ancestry" after Race

How might projects that are designed from the start to avoid the problems of producing racial, ethnic, or national groups as genetic categories deal with the issues of sampling to produce accounts of human genetic diversity and of naming the patterns of variation they produce? Jenny Reardon has traced how the International Haplotype Map Project—which began in 2003, with the aim to sample the world's genetic variation, and whose HapMap was completed in 2005—sought to include the views of the group (the "people") whose genetic material was being gathered, in contrast to the Human Genome Diversity Project (HGDP), but did not adequately address the way in which the "people" in this project and human groups more widely are being reconstituted in novel ways through studies of human genetic variation.[28] The question of the making of populations thus encompasses not only the increasingly recognized issue of the making of familiar social categories as genetic but also the making and unmaking of new communities. In practice, donors can be constituted as a community in sampling and consultation strategies and can be deconstituted by those studies if their contributions are later deemed unsuitable. This, Reardon argues, challenges the assumption that science simply needs to be further democratized by consulting and engaging with those whose genetic material is gathered, since genomic science is implicated in the making of familiar and new social categories of the "people" it seeks to enlist as donors and as active agents in the ideal of democratic science. Rather than see democracy as separate from and applied to science, as Reardon agues, "democratic ideas and practices are made along with scientific ideas and practices"—in this case, "the people," as a constituency, constituted through the science itself.[29]

Her analysis also clearly demonstrates the ways in which questions of sampling, representativeness, and definitions of groups and categories in relation to ideas of race, ethnicity, and nation dog this project despite the organizers' deliberate intentions to avoid race and avoid "defining populations." The HGDP took human cultural groups—indigenous people, more specifically—as the basis for its sampling. This continues in other projects that are constituted as global studies (as I will discuss in chapter 3). In contrast, the HapMap project was devised to produce a map of the world's human genetic variation that the project organizers did not want to be interpreted as starting from racial categories. Nor were indigenous groups sampled. But samples still have to be chosen and named, and for population geneticists, these samples, since they are samples, have to be chosen in a way that best captures the range of human diversity within the world. Taking samples from people who are thought to be genetically similar due to their shared genealogical presence in a place could pick up on fine-grained genetic differences among them but not the broad patterns of variation on the global scale that these projects seek to map.

In light of this, the HapMap project gathered samples and analyzed DNA from "populations with African, Asian, and European ancestry" thus relying on conventional continental racial categories, even if, as Reardon reports, most "project organisers resist the suggestion that racial categories played any role in shaping the initiative's sampling strategy."[30] But samples have to come from somewhere and have to be located in order for any geographical patterning of variation to be derived. Rather than take up the geographical grid sampling approach, researchers gather a group of samples in specific places. These are places taken to be good choices in terms of capturing that variability. But what do the samples stand for beyond the individual donor?

As Reardon asks, "What did researchers come home with when they went to Africa and collected blood from 90 people in Ibadan, Nigeria? The DNA of the human species? Of a race? Of Africans? Of Yoruba? Of

90 people who lived in Ibadan, Nigeria?" Making them stand for humanity is meaningless in a study of worldwide diversity, but making them stand for any wider grouping raises the issue of producing a genetic account of a social group whether that is a newly constituted "community" of genetic donors or an ethnic, national, or racial category. Researchers may try to specify the particular source and nature of the sample but, as Reardon argues, oscillate between, on the one hand, denying that the samples represent broad categories and, on the other, claiming their representativeness and thus their scientific value. Despite the organizers' concerns about how a group, consulted and sampled under the project's ethical protocols, could be taken to stand for a wider national group—Japanese, for example—as she argues, the danger of invigorating genetic constructions of nationality, ethnicity, or race remain.

In this antiracist science of difference, both "geography" and "ancestry" are being increasingly evoked as ways of describing patterns of genetic variation without recourse to the language of race. In an effort to avoid the term "race," human population geneticists have argued that "ancestry" is a less loaded and more objective term. As Bolnick argues, though it is not precisely defined, it is used to refer to the "geographic region or regions where one's biological ancestors lived" and thus to locate an individual genealogically and geographically.[31] Though ancestral origin can encompass multiple regions and these can be defined at different scales, in practice, ancestral regions in individual ancestry studies are usually based on continental geographies of difference and thus evoke Euro-American definitions of race without using the term. This sort of semantic slippage has been identified by social science critics who have highlighted how those working on human genetic variation fall back on the lexicon of race or inconsistently alternate between or collapse the terms "race," "ethnic group," "human group," or "population," even if they claim not to mean "race."[32] Even terms such as "population" or "human group" as alternatives to "race" or "ethnic group" are not natural or neutral. So while the terms in current use to describe human genetic variation sometimes distinguish between ideas of race, ethnicity, geographical ancestry, population, or human group, in practice the terms do not remain semantically distinct.

Describing ancestry or geographical ancestral origin through the categories of the continental model of difference is most obviously problematic in terms of its racializing effect. But describing ancestry genetically at other scales is also problematic, since to identify ancestry genetically at other scales also raises the issue of implying that cultural geographies of difference—national or ethnic groups—have some sort of genetic constitution. To describe a portion of genetic material—a haplotype, for example—as if it comes from somewhere or is associated with a particular region is to imply a distinctive genetic pattern for that region. Again, this might seem most obviously of concern if it implies that a national category is genetic, but there is a politics to differentiation at any scale. This applies to subnational or transnational ethnic groups associated with particular regions or differentiation between adjoining localities. Human population geneticists may celebrate the increasingly precise genetic spatial differentiations—between nearby villages, for example—that are possible, but the problem of scientific differentiations and categorizations still remains. New accounts of genetic variation, even those that turn to geographical labels to avoid race and that work at subcontinental scales, still have implications for imaginations of social and cultural difference—local, regional, and national identities—and for the practice of social relations. The continental scale has been profoundly entangled in the making of race, but this is not the only scale at which scientific categorizations inform and crosscut social practices of identification, inclusion, and differentiation.

The identification of ancestral geographies for individuals or groups cannot be seen as an objective and apolitical alternative to race, since descriptions of geographical ancestry cannot escape the risk that they reinforce ideas of genetically identifiable groups that correspond with sociocultural collectives, whether racial, ethnic, or national. This is because geographical labeling is not neutral. Any naming of a location or region as a place of ancestral origin comes with the implication that that place and the people there can be characterized in terms of genetic distinctiveness. Similarly, the labeling of genetic samples in biomedical or human population genetic databases in terms of geographical origin, whether self-described or attributed at the point of collection, cannot avoid the implication that saying that bits of genetic material come from somewhere evokes an imaginative geography of bounded genetic distinctiveness at different scales in contrast to geographical gradients of genetic variation. Like ancestry, geography, as Reardon notes, is often evoked as an apolitical answer to how to name groups in genomics, but, as she asserts, it is "right to question whether geography acts, as it is implied, as a neutral arbiter of complex and consequential questions about identity."[33] Geneticists turn to geographical identifiers to avoid the inadequacy or misleading effects of conventional racial categories of human variation. But geography can only be imagined as neutral if the potency of geographically constituted collective identities and ideas of difference—local, regional, national, racial, and ethnic—are somehow overlooked. These collectives are a matter not only of shared and inherited cultures or ancestries but also of shared ancestral locations and boundaries of belonging, and in the case of nation and ethnicity, political and cultural geographies of natural homelands. It is the cultural potency of ideas of geographical ancestry and origins, rather than the supposed neutrality of geography, that is central to the production of genetic ancestry as a commodity in genetic genealogy.

Genetic Ancestry and Geographical Origins

So what is meant by genetic ancestry in genetic genealogy? How are questions of identity and origin—of who you are and where you come from—posed and answered in this domain of "science, profit and kinship"?[34] How are sequenced bits of an individual's genome made to mean anything? In their most basic form and in the most common sort of lineage tests, an individual's results are a set of numbers that represents their pattern of nucleotides on specific segments of the nonrecombining portion of the Y chromosome and/or hypervariable region (HVR) of mtDNA. Y-chromosome results are presented as numbers that indicate the allele at a specific location (marker) on the Y chromosome and via a haplogroup name. In the case of mtDNA, results are presented as a set of numbers corresponding to the nucleotide position and as letters indicating specific nucleotide differences between that of the individual and that of a standardized mtDNA reference sequence, the Cambridge Reference Sequence (CRS). A result, for example, could be reported as 16311C for HVR1. It would be explained that, unlike the CRS, the individual has a cytosine nucleotide instead of a thymine nucleotide at position 16311. This may be described in terms of an alphanumerical haplogroup name and presented diagrammatically as a set of letters alongside the nucleotide patterns at accompanying points on the HVR. The production of results is thus a comparative process. The comparison between these genomic sequences and wider reference data also characterizes the subsequent inscribing of their cultural meaning through named groups and geographies of origin.

Though companies are providing increasing amounts of information to help customers make sense of these results, on their own and as numbers alone, the results mean very little. Genetic ancestry tests are made meaningful and desirable commodities through their entwined scientific and cultural production. While these tests are generally framed as meaningful in relation to wider cultural discourses of the significance of origins and ancestry to personal and collective identity, in practice, companies figure genetic ancestry and genetic origin with different degrees of definitiveness and exactitude and through different temporalities and geographies. Running through these processes of meaning making are those issues of collective categories of identity and difference—in the marketing of the tests, in their appeal as confirming or revealing ethnically specific ancestry, and in terms of different approaches within the sector to genetic descriptions of ethnicity and race. Tracing the different geographies and temporalities of genetic ancestry and origin informs a critical sense of the relational ethics of these tests not only in terms of the figuring of race and ethnicity but also in terms of the making and implications of ideas of genetic relatedness more widely.

The results of genetic tests are imbued with significance not only through the authority of science but also through the material culture of genetic genealogy. Test results are often presented as elaborate certificates, graphically framed by the conventions of records of achievement—signed, embossed, and, of course, personalized—often accompanied by maps, diagrams, and additional explanatory text. They are also culturally framed on company websites, in promotional events, and through their wider media presentation on television, radio, and newspapers since the first companies were set up in the United Kingdom and the United States in 2000 by enterprising population geneticists who recognized the commercial potential of the data and techniques of their field, and that have proliferated since.[35] The appeal of genetic tests in the U.S. context lies in the central and deeply valorized place of ethnic distinctiveness in American national imaginaries and public culture. Within discourses of American multiculturalism and within genetic genealogy, the United States is only the ancestral origin place of Native Americans; everyone else has origins elsewhere. Family Tree DNA, for example, advises customers entering their details into an online searchable customer database that "unless you are a Native American or of Native American Ancestry, your Country of Origin is not the USA. It should be the country where your ancestors came from." Everyone else is diasporic in that sense, with ancestral ties to other places. All people, except the indigenous, are diasporic.

Genetic genealogy is marketed as a scientifically enhanced form of genealogy that serves a naturalized need to know "where you came from" beyond recent generations and beyond the places of birth, upbringing, or residence. Like the newly digital domain of conventional genealogy in which sources and contacts can be accessed online and whose growth has paralleled the turn to studies of human genetic variation and evolutionary genetics, these companies use these new information technologies as well as the technologies, methods, and research findings of human population genetics as they seek to build on the popularity of reconstructing family trees and family histories. The genetic ancestry tracing sector capitalizes on and encourages what Donna Haraway has called "epistemophilia, the lusty search for knowledge of origins"—human, collective, familial, and personal.[36] The desire to know "where you are from" through knowledge of where immigrant ancestors came from appears self-evident. It only has to be evoked to be understood.

This is especially the case in the marketing and media attention given to genetic tests that offer to provide African Americans with a region and ethnic group of origin in Africa. The promise of genetic ancestry tests to recover knowledge of specific ancestral places and ethnic ancestries for the descendants of slaves has dominated American media coverage of this sector because of the deeply symbolic meaning of this recovered knowledge within the politics of race, belonging, and multiculturalism in the United States. The television documentaries that have been most prominent in the media representation of genetic genealogy in Britain as well as the United States—*Motherland: A Genetic Journey* and *African American Lives*, respectively—have framed these new technologies through narratives of both the deeply desired and the deeply meaningful restitution of knowledge of African origins that was violently erased by slavery. Recovering this knowledge is figured by African Ancestry, the company solely devoted to this strand of genetic genealogy, and by many customers, in terms of its profoundly healing relation to the violent severing of social and kinship ties and genealogical rootedness through enslavement and as a means of making new connections with people, cultures, and places via shared ancestry and ancestral identifications. Individuals are offered not simply haplogroup names but a certified, shared genetic ancestry with specific "people" or "tribes" in specific countries.

While, as I will argue, race is variously evoked, reworked, and renounced within the genetic ancestry industry, race, or at least a specific historical experience of racialized violence and trauma, is also put to work in the wider marketing of genetic ancestry. The significance of knowing ancestral origins is intensified in some marketing strategies by extending the personal, cultural, and political significance of recovering lost knowledge of origins for those tracing slave ancestors to anyone who cannot name an ancestral origin except in a broad sense. In the promotional materials of genetic genealogy, the theme of recuperative rediscovery is drawn on and extended. In an earlier iteration of their website, the British company GeoGene used Bob Marley's words as their strapline: "If you know your history, then you would know where you are coming from."[37] The Sorenson Molecular Genealogy Foundation, a not-for-profit project that extends the Mormon contribution to genealogical research by building a global database of combined genealogical data and Y-chromosome and mtDNA results, includes the words of Alex Haley among the quotes on its website: "In all of us there is a hunger, marrow-deep, to know our heritage—to know who we are and where we came from."[38] Companies deploy these direct and inferred references to the cultural politics of memory, commemoration, and restored historical knowledge of origins within the Black Atlantic diaspora to create wider desires to ameliorate senses of lack or incompleteness through buying these new genetic tests. By suggesting that a lack of knowledge of ancient ancestry is a lack to be addressed, companies strive to produce a formerly unrealized absence of knowledge as a new deficiency. In this way, the new tests are sold to assuage a newly worked-up sense of genetic ignorance. The specific history of racial slavery and displacement is thus evoked, extended, and erased in the effort to promote a generalized sense of genetic ignorance of origins that can be ameliorated by buying these tests.[39]

Where Did Your Ancestors Come From? Answering the Question

But if evoking a naturalized need to know where immigrant ancestors came from and working up the idea of genetic ignorance, even for those who have some genealogical knowledge already, makes the question of where your ancestors came from have considerable purchase, how is the question answered through test results? It is answered in multiple ways. The general promotion of this sector suggests clear and authoritative answers. In practice, the answers to where your ancestors came from are presented as more or less definitive, as more or less probabilistic, and as more or less corresponding to ethnic or racial categories. Genetic ancestry can be associated with differently sized regions, as single or multiple locations of ancestral connection, and with migration routes as well as regions. Answers involve different sorts of temporalities. This is the case in the presentation of individual results and in comparisons between how different companies present the results in relation to currently agreed knowledge about human genetic diversity and in relation to their proprietary or shared databases on the geography of genetic variation. Tests may offer what are presented as clear indications of specific ethnic ancestries, or the geographies of where particular patterns of variation are associated, or percentages of different continental ancestries contributing to an individual. Genetic ancestry is both broadly figured as ancestral knowledge beyond known generations and differently configured in test results.

At one end of a spectrum running from the categorical and definitive to the more open and ambiguous are tests that offer customers genetic answers to the question of whether they have Jewish or Native American ancestry or offer customers specific, named ethnic and regional origins in Africa where ancestors were enslaved.[40] These tests are based on surveys of "populations" that are assumed to have distinctive patterns of genetic variation and on the association of particular genetic variants with ethnic groups. This is so despite the repeated criticism by other human population geneticists, as well by anthropologists, that genetic variants exclusive to ethnic or racial groups do not exist and that specific genetic variants are not found uniformly within groups.[41] The labeling of particular haplogroups as indicative of particular ancestral origins or groups produces the idea not only that human genetic diversity corresponds to ethnic or national groups but also that contemporary ethnic groups have patterns of genetic variation that define them as representative of the ancestral groups of a customer, across the extended geographies of historic human migration.

As critics have argued, African genetic ancestry services rely on databases that are constructed on the basis of treating "ethnic groups" or "tribes" in Africa as both genetically identifiable units and long-standing entities—in the tradition of colonial administrators and early anthropological studies, which continue to inform human population genetics—rather than as dynamic and fluid categories shaped by continuous movement, historic relationships, and political, social, and cultural transformations.[42] Contemporary ethnic categories are projected into the past, as if the name and cultural traditions of a contemporary cultural group represent those of a group existing several hundred years ago. The nature and implications of accounts of ethnically specific African genetic ancestries are, as Katharina Schramm argues, found in the interplay between individual interpretations, wider discourses of ethnic belonging in American multiculturalism, cultural heritage projects in the "origin" countries, and charged (and neither always successful nor sustained) encounters between genetic roots tourists and local people within a genetically defined culture of origin.[43]

Companies offer not only tests for specific ancestries but also more general lineage tests of varying levels of detail (and cost), which also use ideas of ethnic specificity and ancestral origins to make the results meaningful but in different and sometimes, in comparison at least, less categorical ways. Some tests purport to identify male descent from named individuals—semimythological or historic heroic men, most notably Genghis Khan. (I turn to the figuring of sex and gender in this strand of genealogy in chapter 4.) But this sort of test is unusual. Most customers receive results in terms of diagrams of their nucleotide patterns that are labeled in terms of broad Y-chromosome and/or mtDNA haplogroups, which use an internationally recognized standardized alphanumeric code, such as the Y-chromosome ones (e.g., J2 or R1A) or the mtDNA haplogroups (e.g., D, HV1, or K). These are patterns of variation that human population geneticists have mapped in terms of their geographical distribution in the present and in terms of the historical geography of their emergence and spread. Results are thus often accompanied by descriptions and maps of where a customer's particular haplogroup is geographically concentrated, what human evolutionary and migratory histories it is associated with, and the contemporary ethnic or broader regional groups within which that haplotype predominates. As geneticists commenting in the sector have pointed out, standard genetic genealogy tests can produce "at best, a very approximate sub-continental origin at a point of time with very large uncertainty, typically somewhere between 5,000 and 40,000 years ago."[44] These geographies are often at very broad scales. For example, an American man may be informed that his Y-chromosome haplogroup is associated with western Europe. This offers very little to a man of known European ancestry. However, it can have much deeper implications in cases where African American men are informed of hitherto unknown European paternal ancestry. The significance of differently scaled regions of genetic origin depends on what an individual already knows, assumes, or suspects about his or her family history and on the wider politics of race and ancestry.

Genetic testing companies and the geneticists involved are also working to develop data and tests with finer powers of differentiation and geographical exactitude to deal with the risk that, for many customers, the results might just be too broad, too general, and too shared to be worth buying or recommending. An alternative scheme, specific to geneticist Bryan Sykes and his Oxford Ancestors company, is to try to make general, widely shared, and geographically extensive results more meaningful by fostering ideas of shared identity based not on existing collective categories—of race, ethnicity, or nation—but on shared haplogroup and shared descent from founding mitochondrial "mothers." I address this strategy and its place in the wider figuring of sex and gender in human population genetics in chapter 4, but this is clearly an effort to produce new forms of distinctive shared relatedness—shared haplogroup identities—out of semantically empty results and out of shared haplogroup collectives that would include millions of people.

Genetic ancestry is thus presented not only as a matter of straightforward evidence for descent from or ancestral connection to specific ethnic categories but also as a suggestive resource for imaginative identification. But answers to genetic tests for ancestry are also not spatially singular or fixed for several reasons. They are not spatially singular because knowing where you come from via genetic lineage testing is potentially to know of two lineal ancestries and two places of "genetic origin"—maternal and paternal. Women are encouraged to seek a paternal relative to be tested also if they want to know about their paternal ancestry. This is, of course, a deeply selective and reductive model of ancestry that only addresses a tiny fraction of an individual's ancestors.

But each of these two haplogroup ancestries are themselves not spatially fixed. The global maps that show lines of haplogroup "migration" extending and branching from east Africa that often accompany results and that feature on company websites offer customers a particular historical geography for their haplogroup, one of movement as well as regional "destination." The geography of genetic ancestry is not fixed, since these maps feature specific global pathways rather than regional ancestral origin places. A distinctive haplogroup history is suggested as an addition to customers' sense of "where they come from" but only by producing the odd fiction of haplogroups as human groups. Maps of the spread of highly specific and selective versions of lineage seem to stand for groups sharing a haplogroup, traveling together in one direction. This is an imaginative fiction, since human groups are never homogenous genetically; migration is not a matter of the unilineal movement of genetically homogenous groups.[45] But these maps pose other problems if they are meant to provide knowledge of genetic ancestry, since they are maps not of fixed locations but of routes. They might offer the end point of the line as the place of origin, but as maps of movement and spread, all lineages ultimately coalesce in east Africa. Even though the account of shared human origins frames these products with the wider associations of liberal antiracist genomics, customers are being offered something more specific. But where along the way from Africa to the place identified with a present-day predominance of a haplogroup might an individual's origin lie? Where on that pathway is the origin place? When is the foundational time?

However, customers are also offered much more specific information about potential ancestral connections to people and places, often alongside haplogroup names, descriptions, and maps. Many companies also inform their customers that their results "match" those of other people in the company database. In the case of African Ancestry, this match is interpreted in terms of ancestral connection to the ethnic group that the person's genetic material in the database is taken to represent. More commonly, a person is simply informed of the country or countries from where that matching sample comes. These matches are, implicitly at least, meant to be at some level informative. The implication is that the individual shares an ancestor with the person who supplied the "matching" genetic material. These "matches" are also entirely dependent on the size, content, and geographical coverage of the database. These databases are derived from the work of human population geneticists, directly or indirectly associated with the company, amalgamated from new and commonly available published data, and in many cases, supplemented by the addition of the genetic data and locational information of previous customers.

For example, a customer of Roots for Real might be informed that, according to a table and accompanying map, their mtDNA genetically matches with individuals in France, Spain, Switzerland, Germany, Russia, Poland, Slovenia, and Austria but has six identical matches in Iceland and in Bosnia-Herzegovina. This presents some interpretative conundrums if anything more than a broad regional origin—such as Europe—is desired. Large numbers of matches might be more indicative of the presence of large numbers of samples from particular places than indicative of an ancestral location. In this case, work on the genetics of Bosnians and Slovenians, and Iceland's special place as a field site in human population and medical genetics, has contributed to the database and thus produced that number of matches. Similarly, reports of a large number of African Ancestry customers with matches in Nigeria may, as Katharina Schramm suggests, reflect the volume of genetic data gathered there by company director and geneticist Rick Kittles.[46]

"Matches" themselves are not a matter of definitive relatedness: "matches" vary in degree from exact (when all markers examined are the same as another individual's) to partial. A person may be told that they "match" with another and so are likely to share ancestry. But from more detailed explanations, or from their more detailed reading, the customer may realize that this is an estimated statistical probability and that chances of sharing ancestry increase the further back in time one goes. Probabilities increase but only with decreasing distance in time from recent generations, and thus further from potentially meaningful genealogical connections. Family Tree DNA has developed a system of estimating the number of generations or time to the most recent common paternal ancestor (TMRCA) of two "matching" male customers. They may be told, for example, that they have a 10 percent chance of sharing an ancestor within the last two hundred years or a 74 percent chance within the last six hundred years. Exact genetic matches are indicative of shared ancestry, but when and how this has arisen simply cannot be assumed. For example, as Charmaine Royal and her coauthors explain, if someone in North America matches someone living in Indonesia, from the result alone, "it is impossible to say whether this match arises via recent Indonesian ancestors in the North American's family tree, whether both share distant ancestors who lived in an entirely different part of the world, or whether the Indonesian match has recent North American heritage."[47] This match still suggests something worth considering, but millions of other matches would be possible if databases were more comprehensive and if other ancestors could be traced genetically other than those direct maternal and paternal lines.

"Matches" between customers also vary in terms of precision—with the cheaper tests looking at fewer markers producing more general results than more expensive tests, which look at more markers. Results can thus generate suggestive but unsatisfying results that may disappoint but also potentially generate more desire and more company income as customers seek the results of more detailed tests on offer or promised as under development. The advance of science itself promises precision, but under the rules of scientific knowledge making, no truth is absolute. Scientific advancement creates new or anticipated commodities for existing and new customers.

In contrast to these haplogroup lineages (with their different degrees of direct association with ethnic groups and different geographical scales of origin and different geographies of ancestral location and ancestral migration) are tests whose results are presented through broad "biogeographical ancestries" and through the idiom of statistical precision—that is, as percentages of different ancestries that have contributed to an individual's genome. Though less common in terms of the number of companies offering these tests, they have been quite prominent in terms of public interest reporting and in critical debate. A small but growing number of companies, such as AncestryByDNA, offer tests based on "autosomal" (i.e., non–sex linked) markers known as ancestry-informative markers (AIMs), derived from admixture mapping in biomedical genetics, which have been identified as showing differences of frequency across populations that are differentiated as four major groups based on continental origins—European, Asian, sub-Saharan African, Native American, or variants of these categories. A customer's genetic material is analyzed focusing on these AIMs and in relation to their frequencies in these groups, and the results are presented in terms of the relative contributions of these ancestries to the individual's "biogeographical ancestry"—that is, the "aspects of PGH [personalized genetic histories] that can be computed using the ancestry information contained in AIMs" and expressed as percentages of different ancestries.[48]

Geneticists Mark Shriver and Rick Kittles, who have been developing, promoting, and applying "biogeographical ancestry" analysis, recognize that these ancestral categories could be "misinterpreted as indications of 'real' racial divisions."[49] However, they suggest that this means that companies need to work against the public's tendency to do so rather than more fully acknowledge their own role in producing genetically recognizable continental races. The explanatory material on the AncestryByDNA website addresses the question of race directly and at length. While earlier versions challenged the idea that race is "merely a social construct" by insisting that genetic variation does correspond to the "major population groups defined by anthropologists," more recent versions insist that the tests "are measuring a person's genetic ancestry and not their race" and draws attention to "the recent common origin of all populations and strong connections between populations throughout history."[50] But though the tests are presented through the idea of hybridity and human genetic interconnection—"the rich diversity of your genetic heritage"—their concept of admixture is based on correlating the old continental categories of race with patterns of genetic variation. AncestryByDNA tests are cloaked in an apparently evenhanded, level-headed, and liberal approach to race that nevertheless racializes human genetic variation. Biogeographical ancestry tests are presented as if they challenge the idea of genetic purity, but they are based on statistical and survey techniques premised upon the idea of the former genetic neatness and real genetic nature of races.

The conjunction of genealogy and human population genetics in genetic genealogy brings together different and sometimes incommensurate models, scales, and temporalities of ancestry. Lineage tests, which predominate, focus only on direct maternal and direct paternal descent in contrast to the potentially endlessly ramifying thicket of the conventional family tree. Company logos entangle images of the double helix and the family tree, but genetic genealogy hard prunes that tree back to two unbranching lines. Family history or genealogy works on the time scale of generations—unusually, only back to the point of the emergence of written sources, usually three or four hundred years at the very most for nonnobles (i.e., most people). Genetic genealogy, unless applied to specific historical cases, offers results that describe ancestry in terms of tens of thousands of years. This includes accounts of the timing of the emergence and spread of a particular haplogroup or explanations that the probability that two customers share ancestry increases the further back in time from the present and far removed from the time scales of ordinary genealogy. The value of genetic genealogy is widely claimed to be its usefulness in overcoming the limits of documentary sources. But in most cases of individual tests, there is a considerable temporal gap between conventional and genetic genealogy.

The idea of geographical origin itself has a range of scientific and social meanings. The term "origin" is evoked in genetic genealogy as the object of discovery and as profoundly significant in terms of collective and personal knowledge and identity. But as Sandra Soo-Jin Lee and her coauthors point out,

> to a geneticist, origin might refer to ancestral populations inferred for an individual on the basis of specific genetic markers, specific algorithms for assessing genetic similarity, and specific reference populations. To a casual consumer, origin might mean "the country where I was born," "the country (or countries) where my grandparents were born," "the place or language group where my last name originated," or "the place and/or time when my family narrative begins" . . . To a Native American, origin might also signify the landscape feature or event where his or her people emerged or acquired their identity.[51]

Despite the promise of discovering something profoundly meaningful and definitive, in genetic genealogy, origins are figured as both spatially fixed—but at different scales—and vague, multiple, and indeterminate. The answers that seem most fixed have been challenged by critical human population geneticists, as well as social scientists, for eliding the limits of these models of ancestry, the contingencies of their comparative analysis, and the probabilistic nature of the results. However, those results that seem more open to interpretation also need to be more deeply problematized. While some population geneticists are behind the development of genetic genealogy, others can be its most effective critics. The opening chapter of the main textbook for human population genetics in the United Kingdom cautions against seeking answers to "meaningless questions." They include, "What was the ancestral biological homeland of population X?" and "Where did my ancestors live a thousand years ago?" The first is a meaningless question, they insist, since it is impossible that "all genetic diversity in a population could be traced to a single time and place." Unless ancestry is defined through matriline or patriline alone, the answer to the second question is, they argue, "everywhere."[52]

Do-It-Yourself Genetic Genealogy

For companies, there are risks that their products will not live up to their promissory marketing and that they will not provide satisfying solutions to genetic ignorance, fill new senses of lack, or resolve mysteries. There are risks also, however, in results that in contrast do seem too definitive in terms of ethnic or racial ancestry in a context where the geneticization of ethnic and racial groups is so deeply political and contested. Faced with the double risk of results being too indeterminate or too determining of ethnic ancestry, companies, especially the largest lineage-based companies, not only offer a range of interpretative resources to customers—haplogroup histories and geographies—but also defer interpretive work to them. Customers are encouraged by companies to make of the results what they will, and customers do so with different levels of interest, investment, and expertise. There is a growing refiguring of the distribution of expertise between company scientists and genetic genealogy enthusiasts. While the technoscientific and statistical making of results remains unclear to many, and while many may have neither the time nor inclination to pursue their interpretation, other customers become lay experts. They do so with the help of increasingly detailed explanations on company websites and by reading the work of human population geneticists. They are active in online discussion boards, reading and contributing to journals like the *Journal of Genetic Genealogy*, or, along with industry professionals, they may be members of the International Society of Genetic Genealogy and often take up the role of educators for other consumers. Distinctions between academic science, culture, industry, and consumers blur, as scientists develop commercial applications of their work and as some customers enter into dialogue with scientists or start their own companies.[53]

In practical terms, this redistributed interpretative work is promoted by companies like Family Tree DNA in specific ways. Customers are encouraged to interpret their results themselves through practices of identifying genetic "matches" with other customers in company databases. They are invited to enter their results into a collective searchable database along with brief details of the place of origin of their earliest known ancestor so that customers can explore the origins and potentially exchange genealogical information or form relationships as "genetic cousins" with those to whom they genetically match. Many companies host searchable databases or e-mail message boards with the promise of the possibility of customers making connections with others and exploring the meaning of genetic similarity. In addition to online discussion forums organized on the basis of haplogroup and hosted by the commercial companies, databases are available for customers to search for and contact those who are genetically similar according to their Y chromosome or mtDNA. Ybase:

Genealogy by Numbers is a searchable database to which men can submit their Y-chromosome results, their contact details, and the details of their oldest known direct paternal ancestor and can search for near matches or "genetic cousins." Family Tree DNA offers similar public searchable databases—Ysearch for men and MitoSearch for men and women—to which people can submit their results, search for matches, and upload their genealogical records in the form of standardized digital files formats.[54] Genetic genealogy providers draw on the wider culture of digital social media and "reuniting" to promote and provide new forms of electronically and genetically assisted kinship that will give meaning to test results that are not readily explained by documented genealogy or family memory or through ethnic or racial categories. This is reflected in a recent guide to "genealogy in the twenty-first century," which helps readers engage with the two "revolutions" that have transformed what was once a solitary and documentary practice: "the genetic genealogy revolution" and "the social networking revolution."[55]

New genetic collectives or new forms of genetic relatedness are encouraged so that individual results can be of more value. Groups based on already existing interests in shared ancestry are also encouraged to make use of genetic ancestry tests. These include the strand of popular genealogy concerned with tracing genealogical connections among people with the same surname. Because of the parallel between the wide, but not universal, patrilineal inheritance of family names and the patrilineal inheritance of the Y chromosome, many existing surname-based projects are being encouraged to explore patterns of genetic variation within the group as the basis for establishing degrees of genealogical relatedness and different ancestral branches within the group. Many do so. At the time of writing, the Family Tree DNA website states that they support 7,560 Y-chromosome group projects listed in their surnames database library.[56] These genetic surname projects have not been subject to much critical scrutiny, despite being a significant dimension of genetic genealogy.[57] Though they appear to be less contentious than genetically identifiable racial or ethnic ancestry or origins, the reckoning of relatedness via genetics in genetic surname projects intersects with the wider issue of constructing collective identities—national, ethnic, racial, or diasporic—via genetic similarity and difference. Genetic surname projects are also cases in which genetic ancestry tests have most immediate and personal effects, as people may find their claims to their membership undermined or members may be ranked in terms of degrees of relatedness within existing groups—familial or genealogical—on the basis of the results.[58]

Self-Fashioning in a Field of Relational Ethics

But what do people make of these tests? The relatively limited but growing research on the meaning of test results for those who undertake them challenges critiques of these commodities as genetically deterministic in their effects. Instead, customers are active agents of meaning making who negotiate and evaluate different sorts of evidence and authority in relation to existing identifications, relationships, and specific genealogical questions and wider social formations. Alondra Nelson uses the term "affiliative self-fashioning" to point to the way in which "individual desires for relatedness" shape "evaluations of the reliability and usability of scientific data."[59] Customers—in her case, African American and Black British people buying tests for specific ethnic or tribal origins in Africa or those enlisted in media features like the *Motherland* television documentaries—may experience what she describes as "genealogical disorientation" when results confound expectations or conflict with other sources of genealogical knowledge but are received as part of an ongoing, active, evaluative, and selective process of incorporating genetic accounts of ancestry into family history or life story.

In this way, genetic genealogy shares the character of conventional genealogical practice. As I have explored in previous work, the self in popular genealogy is similarly there to be both "found" and "forged" through self-exploration. While genealogy stands for the immutable facts of a genealogical past that is taken to be the foundation of identity, genealogy is a practice of self-definition and self-making, of choosing which apparently determining ancestries matter most, and, through the sharing and keeping of genealogical knowledge and skills, a practice of making relations within and beyond those genealogically related.[60] This combination of determination and choice, foundational identity and self-fashioning, as Nadia Abu El-Haj has also argued, is fundamental to the contemporary appeal of genetic genealogy.[61]

Attending to what people do with test results and the test results' implications for their sense of themselves and for existing and new social relationships is, of course, an important strand of recent critical engagement with genetic genealogy. People are not simply subject to the definitions or determinations of the science despite its authority. However, the focus on the consumption of genetic ancestry tests should not be seen simply as a corrective to the predominant critical focus on the technologies and discourses of genetic genealogy. This is because a focus on consumption can reinforce the idea of individual freedom, agency, autonomy, and self-determination that has become incorporated into what Jenny Reardon astutely identifies as "genomic liberalism." Early twenty-first-century genomics is, she argues, characterized by efforts to "transform genetic studies of human beings from a racist, totalitarian force to an anti-racist democratic one."[62]

This is by means of a liberal vision of the dangers of concentrated power and of the importance of the rights of individuals—that is, the basis of a new emphasis on and strategies to ensure some degree of democratic redistribution of power and authority to research subjects. This is a vision that also underpins the wider making of advanced liberal subjects as agents of individual self-fashioning. The emphasis on research subjects' rights and this ideal of self-making, Reardon argues, problematizes the idea of "genomic renderings of human identity" as a matter of scientific dominance and a matter of the objectification of passive subjects, which can and should be reformed by ensuring the individual freedom to self-fashion. This figures science and society as ideally separate spheres and does not acknowledge the role of science in shaping the constraints and categories through which groups and individuals constitute and define themselves. While people engaging with genomics, in biomedicine, and in genetic genealogy are not passive subjects but hold and assert varying degrees of expertise and interpretative authority, genomics, as Reardon argues, is profoundly implicated in the making of categories through which people have "autonomous" power to make themselves.

As Reardon argues, this "liberal understanding of genomics—as a domain of truth that exists apart from the subjective realm of desires and political and economic interests—inhibits accounting for the material and symbolic conditions that shape genomic explorations of human origins and identity." Furthermore,

> a liberal approach that locates the power to self-identify with
> the individual . . . allows genome scientists to continue to offer
> their subjects new powers of self-identification, while remaining

unaccountable for the uncertainties and often dis-empowering
effects of these new powers. It places the blame for these new
uncertainties and injustices introduced by genomic constructions
of race and ethnicity on individuals . . . while making it difficult for
genomic scientists to recognise and respond to the role their ideas
and practices play in re-making racial and ethnic categories, even
when theses scientists explicitly set out to do this work of recognition (as in the HapMap case).[63]

Furthermore, the language of choice, as well as individualism, is incorporated into accounts of genetic ancestry as another way genetic human
geographies can be presented as resources for antiracism and antiracist
subjectivities. The liberal idea of choice conceals a fundamental lack of
choice that is the product of the science, of wider social models of ethnic
or racial belonging, and of the ways these models inform and are reinforced in and through genomic science. There are interpretative limits to
tests results. They cannot, at least within the logic of the science itself, be
seen as interpretatively indeterminate. Interpretative possibilities exist,
but they are not endless if some adherence to the authority of the science
is maintained. More fundamentally, the freedom to choose is not evenly
distributed. Some may be afforded many different options for identification, but options are curtailed for others through the cultural logics of
ancestral belonging that are themselves consolidated through genetic renderings of ancestral origins.

The television documentary featuring genetic research on the ancient
settlement of Ireland, *Blood of the Irish: Who Are the Irish and Where
Do They Come From?* (screened in Ireland in 2009), for example, ended
with the suggestion that viewers could decide who they wanted to be from
the choices on offer—in this case, Irish, European, African, or all three.[64]
This works against a celebration of a single unique identity and singular
sense of rootedness and lifts the program out of its obsession with ethnic or national distinctiveness—"who are the Irish?" But figuring identity
as happily multiple and ideally incorporating a sense of global humanity both depend on the choices on offer as a function of this "genomic
rendering of identity" and masks the documentary's production of a deep
lack of choice. According to the logics of identity and belonging as a function of ancestry, the choice to be Irish is not open to all in Ireland but
only to those defined via ancestry as Irish. Similarly, racialized ideas of

belonging mean that the choice to be seen as European is not open to all in Ireland, nor the rest of Europe.[65]

The emphasis on individual agency and self-determination as an ideal in "genomic liberalism" also does not take into account the relational ethics of genetic genealogy. Accounts of genetic ancestry are never a matter of personal genealogical interest alone, since by their very nature they are about relatedness. Tests are sold to individuals, but an individual result is marketed as means of knowing "where you come from" in relation to collective identities based on shared geographical origins and shared descent, or roots and relatedness. While tests are sold to individuals, the ancestral information they receive is intrinsically about relatedness, whether within ethnic groups, to individuals in the past and present, within newly constituted genetic communities, or within living families. Genetic genealogy is not a neatly bounded domain in which the tests for ancestral knowledge remain a matter of personal genealogical interest alone. Genetic ancestry information is increasingly being incorporated in quite different and consequential practices of identification and categorization, from legal cases for reparation to forensic identification of suspects or victims.[66]

But even within the domain of genetic genealogy, an individual's results enroll and entangle other people who may have a range of perspectives on the legitimacy, meaning, and significance of the tests, test results, and ancestry itself. They do so because an individual's results are never simply individual. They not only situate or invite consumers to situate themselves in relation to their "deep ancestry" or "biogeographical ancestry" or in finding "matches" to establish some sort of genetic relatedness. But more immediately, as in conventional genealogy, the results of research pertain not only to the person who has undertaken the test but also to other family members. Just as there is a complex ethics to informed consent in the gathering of genetic samples when individual consent is taken to stand for the consent of a wider group, and in the disclosure of the risk of inherited disease to wider family members, there is also a complex relational ethics to genetic genealogy.

Most of the companies involved now include terms and conditions that outline the company policy on the retention or destruction of the genetic sample for information after the customer has received the result. They include statements that protect the company from liability for any harm caused by the information and guarantee the privacy of the customer's data. These provisions reflect companies' concerns about possible litigation and customers' concerns about the ownership and control of what are presented as personally unique and significant forms of identification. However, questions about the ethics of this form of genetic self-knowledge are not resolved by these guarantees. This is because, despite the emphasis on results as unique and personal property, results are always about relatedness: about who is or isn't related, about inclusions and exclusions, commonalities, and distinctions. One person's mtDNA results are shared with siblings and maternal line relatives but not with a father or paternal relatives. Y-chromosome results link paternal line relatives even more exclusively. When those who are logically deemed irrelevant to an individual's genetic ancestry are still alive and interested in their daughter's, grandson's, or nephew's results, the discovery that they don't share the haplotype in question can cut across their bonds of care and affection. A man who has had a close relationship with his mother's father may have to explain to him that, actually, his Y-chromosome results are only relevant to those men on his father's side and define his "deep ancestry" in this way alone. The relational ethics of genetic genealogy encompass intimate and extended family relations, wider categories of identity and identification, and the entanglements of both.

As this discussion of the making of ancestry and origins in human population genetics and genetic genealogy has made clear, the questions of what it means to say that a portion of genetic material comes from somewhere and of how that material is taken as evidence of geographical origin involve the technical and cultural making of ideas of genetic ancestry. Running through that making are different sorts of approaches to studying and effectively producing accounts of the geography of human genetic variation that are implicated in the politics of human categorization and not in terms of race alone. This includes those approaches that seek to avoid ethnic or racial categories but whose use of geographical descriptions cannot be simply detached from the implications of taking a sample of genetic material from someone who stands for a geographically located and ethnically defined human group. Geography is never neutral. At the same time, while genetic ancestry in human population genetics (and biomedical genetics) and in genetic genealogy means different things in terms of its scale, temporality, exactitude, and resolution, this is not to say that the overriding message about genetic relatedness should not be challenged given the relational ethics of individual but always also shared genetic ancestry results.

In the next chapter, I turn to a project that constitutes a liberal "genomic rendering" of identity and relatedness under the banner of antiracism and through the image of a global human family made newly known through human population genetics. This is a project in which imaginaries of an original premodern geography of human genetic variation and models of genetic relatedness meet multicultural celebrations of contemporary diversity. The complexities and contradictions of definitive results and indeterminate interpretations, of multiple geographies and time scales of origin, might make customers dismissive of the claims of genetic genealogy. It also shores up the authority of science, since for many people the complexities seem beyond lay understanding. But overriding these complexities and contradictions there is a prevailing message about the significance of shared ancestry as constitutive of relatedness and of genetic similarity as an index of degrees of relatedness. In the next chapter, I explore that fundamental issue of genetic similarity as the basis of a sense of relatedness as it plays out in a global antiracist project to explore human genetic variation worldwide. This is a case in which this model of relatedness is articulated and implicated in a context where that central tenet of decreasing genetic similarity with increasing geographical distance is complicated by the conjunction of genetic dissimilarity and geographical proximity in multicultural modernity.

2

Mapping the Global Human Family

Shared and Distinctive Descent

In August 2009, a documentary titled *The Human Family Tree* was broadcast on the National Geographic Channel in the United States as a popular presentation of the National Geographic Society's Genographic Project. This five-year collaborative international research project in the field of human population genetics (launched in 2005 and funded through an alliance of charitable, educational, and corporate interests) is described as an "effort to understand the human journey—where we came from and how we got to where we live today" by studying contemporary patterns of human genetic variation.[1] *The Human Family Tree* documentary focused on the genetic ancestries and stories of six participants who donated genetic samples on a single day, on a single street in Queens, New York. Making use of that familiar trope of reading information about the past in the genes, it was heavily framed by a message about contemporary ethnic diversity and collective human ancestry:

> The Human Family Tree travels to one of the most diverse corners of the world—Queens, N.Y.—to demonstrate how we all share common ancestors who embarked on very different journeys. Regardless of race, nationality or religion, all of us can trace our ancient origin back to the cradle of humanity, East Africa. What did our collective journey look like, and where did it take your specific ancestors? At what point in our past did we first cross paths with the supposed strangers living in our neighborhood? Now, in The Human Family Tree, the people of this quintessential American melting pot find out that their connections go much deeper than a common ZIP code.[2]

With its interweaving of ideas of "our collective journey" and "very different journeys," "our ancient origin" and "your specific ancestors," "deep connections" and "supposed strangers," this extract is indicative of the Genographic Project's geographical imaginations of shared origins and human genetic diversity, commonality, and difference. It foregrounds its simultaneous celebration of urban multicultural diversity and its emphasis on the significance of shared ancient origins that override racial and cultural difference. A progressive, antiracist, scientific refutation of ideas of race and nationality, perhaps?

This chapter considers this question through a focus on the geographical imaginaries, discourses, and techniques of mapping human origins and human genetic diversity, as they are presented on the Genographic Project's website, television documentaries, popular science books, magazine features, and other elements of its media strategy—or what Marianne Sommer calls the "Genographic network."[3] This extends beyond the science and popular cultural products of the project to include its close relationship with the largest and most well established of the genetic genealogy companies: Family Tree DNA. The location of the project within the wider National Geographic Society of America shapes the nature, scale, and power of this network. Making use of the sophisticated multimedia entertainment and educational expertise of the National Geographic Society and borrowing the established reputation, prestige, and authority of this unofficial national institution, the Genographic Project is arguably one of the most publicized and most well-known research projects in the field of human population genetics.[4] It is global in its focus and international in terms of the regional locations of the researchers funded by the project. And it reaches beyond the domain of science through an intense strategy of public engagement and, through the National Geographic, educational work. The Genographic Project is heavily promoted as a resource for the teaching of geography to American schoolchildren through the extensive online resources that are part of the National Geographic Society's Xpeditions educational program.[5] Detailed lesson plans and links to further resources suggest ways to use the project in teaching geography pupils about migration, genetics, and the project's approach to indigenous groups. Its website and newsletters feature children and college students, in the United States and other countries, undertaking the project's genetic tests as part of these lessons or in response to guest talks by project representatives. Its reach continues to expand—from school pupils to heads of government. In June 2013, the Irish Taoiseach Enda Kenny, along with other public figures and volunteers, had his genetic material collected by Genographic Project researchers who were invited as part of the yearlong "gathering" festival to encourage tourism to Ireland and appeal especially to those of Irish ancestry worldwide.[6]

The Genographic Project thus represents a striking case of the blurred boundaries between science and culture in the field of anthropological genetics. However, it is also an unusual case in being funded through charitable support from the Waitt Foundation and privately funded by IBM, rather than by public research funding, and undertaken under the auspices of the National Geographic Society, with its nonprofit and commercial dimensions, rather than within higher education. Though a collaborative project, it is also distinctive in the degree to which it is so strongly associated with the director of the project and National Geographic "explorer in residence" geneticist, and now popular science star, Spencer Wells. In addition, public engagement was built into the project from the start.

The project is described as having three strands. The first—field research—makes up the core of the project and involves "the collection of blood samples from indigenous populations whose DNA contains key genetic markers that have remained relatively unaltered over hundreds of generations making them reliable indicators of ancient migratory patterns." This has involved an international network of scientists based in universities and carrying out local field and laboratory research in the project's nine geographic sampling regions. The second component, its public participation and awareness campaign, invites "the general public" to participate in the project by paying to have their own genetic material analyzed by Family Tree DNA in association with the project to discover their own "deep ancestral history" and to be located on the project's developing map of human genetic diversity.[7] The net proceeds of the sale of the Public Participation Kits will fund the third strand: the Genographic Legacy Project, "which will build on National Geographic's 117-year-long focus on world cultures" by supporting "education and cultural preservation projects among participating indigenous groups."[8]

The project also both represents wider developments and is distinctive in terms of its relationship to the critical reception of the Human Genome Diversity Project (HGDP).[9] While these controversies have profoundly shaped what Jenny Reardon identifies as antiracist genomic liberalism more widely, the Genographic Project's relation to the HGDP is a fundamental factor in shaping the project's approach in terms of both continuities with and difference from its predecessor. This is explicit in the project's information material. The Frequently Asked Questions section of the Genographic Project website includes the question, "How does the Genographic Project differ from the Human Genome Diversity Project (HGDP) proposed over 14 years ago?" The answer given acknowledges the overlapping goals of both projects but stresses the differences between their aims and methodology. The website material emphasizes the Genographic Project's basis in "true collaboration between indigenous populations and scientists," voluntary participation, and, through the Genographic Legacy Project, plans to reward cooperation with funding for "educational activities and cultural preservation projects." The website states that the genetic material will not be patented, the project is a non-profit-making venture, it is not linked to medical research, and no pharmaceutical or insurance companies are involved. These assurances indicate a degree of awareness of the criticisms of the ethics of the HGDP. In particular, they try to avoid the charge that the extraction and patenting of biogenetic material from indigenous groups is a form of biocolonialism in which the value of their genetic material as a source of knowledge of human migratory history, potential usefulness to medical genetics, and commercial value for the pharmaceutical industry is detached from any concern for the rights, welfare, or livelihoods of those being sampled.[10]

Nevertheless, there are clear continuities both in terms of those involved—Luca Cavalli-Sforza, who proposed the HGDP, chairs the Genographic Project's advisory board—and in terms of the project's approach. Wells himself recounts witnessing "first-hand the passionate discussion" surrounding the HGDP as a young geneticist studying under Cavalli-Sforza at Stanford in the 1990s.[11] This experience clearly informs his attempt to avoid the criticisms of the HGDP by enlisting public support through the public participation strategy and by emphasizing the value of the Legacy Project for indigenous groups. It also shapes the degree to which antiracism is so heavily used in describing the project and articulating its value.

But it is not only the politics of race that can be traced in the Genographic Project but also the politics of multiculturalism. The location of *The Human Family Tree* documentary in the New York borough of Queens—"one of the most diverse corners of the world"—and its message of common origins and shared ancestry but also "specific ancestors" and "different journeys" point to its antiracist figuring of genetic unity and its multicultural figuring of genetic diversity that I explore in this chapter. This is figured as a global project, but it is also an American one that reflects and intervenes in the politics of both race and multiculturalism in this context. The Genographic Project's simultaneous discourse of antiracist human ancestral and genetic unity and scientific focus on and cultural figuring of (often racialized) diversity reflect a politics of race and multiculturalism in which racism is normatively denounced and ethnic difference is deeply valorized culturally and central to the politics of biomedical inclusion. In response to new concerns about ethnic difference and inclusion in health care, especially in the United States, as well as in cultural politics more widely, multicultural norms of group recognition and inclusion are increasingly incorporated into biomedical genomics in terms of how their value, ethics, and legitimacy are framed.[12] This is the case in biomedical genetic projects, which as Amy Hinterberger has argued, require both the identification of populations as objects of research and the approval of ethnic groups in order to prove their ethical legitimacy.[13] Hinterberger's term "molecular multiculturalism" identifies the politically contradictory ways in which particular models of multiculturalism constitute studies of human genetic difference.

But the term also usefully encapsulates the ways in which accounts of human genetic variation are shaped by not only the multicultural politics of social justice and inclusion but also the multicultural politics of cultural diversity. Describing human genetic variation as "human genetic diversity" not only distances this science from the language of racial difference but also evokes an association between studies of genetic difference and the deeply valued principles of inclusive multicultural pluralism. At one level, diversity in human population genetics simply refers to genetic variation. But accounts of genetic variation are both based on particular ideas of the geography of human cultural diversity and, in the case of the Genographic Project, presented through celebratory and overtly antiracist accounts of urban cultural diversity. This reflects a public and political culture in which diversity is associated with the ideas of respect for and positive appreciation of social and cultural difference. Diversity, it has been argued, "has become virtually a sacred concept in American life today."[14] It remains a dominant discourse despite the recent decline of state-sponsored support for and the public endorsement of multiculturalism.[15] Yet as many on the left have argued, the pervasiveness and orthodoxy of the multicultural language of diversity should not be read as simply progressive. While the language of diversity emerged from struggles against racism and other forms of discrimination, the discourse of diversity has been characterized by critics as a distraction from the inequalities of class.[16]

However, the critical perspective most pertinent here is that discourses of diversity reify categories of social difference, including race.[17] Diversity, it is argued, is an ostensibly antiracist and antiassimilationist discourse that perpetuates race as a foundational social category and privileges the normative status of whiteness.[18] Inhering in the bodies of "others," cultural diversity is a coded language of race that denies racism and racial inequalities.[19] The problematic politics of diversity are entangled with the idea of tolerance of difference that consolidates the dominance of the "tolerant" over those who are "tolerated" within and beyond the nation-state.[20] This is not to diminish the significance of the multicultural challenge to the model of the racially and culturally pure nation but to point to the racisms and racializations that persist within an ostensibly antiracist public culture.

With its celebrations of diversity, central focus on human genetic difference, and simultaneous insistence on the progressive value of its explicitly antiracist message about shared human origins, unity, and interconnections, the Genographic Project, as I explore here, exemplifies liberal antiracist *and* multicultural genomics. This becomes clear through tracing how the project both celebrates contemporary ethnic diversity shaped by human migration and repeatedly conveys anxiety about the loss of an older pattern of human genetic diversity through migration. What imaginative geographies of indigeneity and premodern human genetic diversity does it suggest, and how are its research subjects and its "public" constituted through a contrast between the modern and the indigenous? How does its model of the global human family frame familiar and newly configured geographies of difference and relatedness?

"The Story Is in the Differences": Picturing, Mapping, and Producing Difference

In his book *The Journey of Man: A Genetic Odyssey* (2003), Spencer Wells explains that patterns of prehistoric human migration can be traced by analyzing genetic samples taken from contemporary people. Comparisons between the genetics of individuals or groups are central to this work. As Wells explains, the work of reconstructing the migration path-ways of early humans depends on studying genetic difference: "It is not the code itself that delivers the message, but rather the differences we see when we compare DNA from two or more individuals. These differences are the historical language of the genes. In the same way that you wouldn't include 'water dwelling' in a classification of fish, because all fish live in water, the identical bits of our own genetic code tell us nothing about our history. The story is in the differences and this is what we study."[21] Thus the project's story of collective human origins and migration is one that can only be constructed through studying human genetic differences. This practical methodological focus on genetic difference is framed by an argument about global human interconnectedness and genetic unity. The study of genetic differences is presented as a route to the construc-tive understanding of other sorts of cultural or physical differences. For example, the Waitt Foundation, which is funding the project's field and laboratory research, argues that understandings of difference can create harmony. As Ted Waitt of the Waitt Foundation has stated, "Our hope is that by improving the world's collective understanding of human-ity's shared beginnings and similarities, we can reduce the tendency to emphasize our differences. That is an extremely powerful and important message, especially given the state of the world today."[22] This idea of study-ing genetic difference to understand and thus diminish the significance of differences is framed by an explicit antiracism. The Public Participant Kit contains a set of swabs for collecting a customer's cheek cells for analysis, an explanatory leaflet, a map, and a DVD that includes an introduction to the project and the documentary titled *Journey of Man* first screened in the United States in 2004. At the end of the documentary, Wells artic-ulates the project's position on race. For Wells, one "lesson stands out" among those he has learned through his genetic and field research: "It is a lesson about relationships. You and I and in fact everyone all over the world, we are all literally African under the skin, brothers and sisters sepa-rated by a mere two thousand generations. Old fashioned concepts of race are not only socially divisive but scientifically wrong. It is only when we have fully taken that on board that we can say with any conviction that the journey our ancestors launched all those years ago is complete."[23]

The implication is of genetic unity "under the skin" of racialized epi-dermal difference, a unity that can only be known through exploring the genetic differences also "under the skin" in the body's interior of cells and

DNA. The analysis of genetic variation is used to reconstruct an account of shared origins *and* genetic differentiation that supplants "old fashioned concepts of race." In the book *The Journey of Man* (2003), which effectively served as advance publicity for the Genographic Project, Wells locates this exploration of human genetic difference at the progressive end of a historical trajectory, beginning with accounts of racial typologies, and moving forward through anthropological and scientific schemas of race to what is presented as a contemporary enlightened postracial era. It is a trajectory of both shifting perspectives on human diversity and changing technologies of investigation. Wells outlines a history of racial thinking from eighteenth-century racial hierarchies such as Linnaeus's classifications of human "subspecies," to nineteenth-century proslavery assertions of innate and divinely ordered white racial superiority, to early twentieth-century eugenicist schemes of racial fitness and anti-immigration policy, and finally, to the racial science of the Holocaust.[24] It is also a narrative of changing forms of measurement from broad descriptions of human morphology to the use of blood types as surrogates for genetic difference and to the late twentieth-century sequencing of genetic material itself.

Wells foregrounds two key moments in the shift from using surrogates of genetic difference to studying genetic material directly that have come to be paradigmatic moments in a new science of human diversity. The first is biologist Richard Lewontin's statistical account of the patterns of human variation published in 1972, which famously showed, as Wells recounts, that "the majority of the genetic differences in humans were found within populations—around 85 per cent of the total. A further 7 percent served to differentiate populations within a 'race,' such as the Greeks from the Swedes. Only 8 per cent were found to differentiate between human races."[25] The second is the publication in 1987 of the work of Rebecca Cann, Mark Stoneking, and Allan Wilson using mitochondrial DNA to explore the structure of human genetic diversity. Their findings that most genetic diversity exists within African populations and that all human mitochondrial lineages ultimately derive from an early African ancestor are the basis of subsequent genetic accounts of humanity's shared African origins and shared descent from a genetic or mitochondrial "Eve."[26] These two findings—of greater genetic diversity within rather than between groups and of shared descent from ancestors in Africa—are central to arguments against the biological existence of races within and beyond human population genetics (even if this account elides the debate about human origins and evolution that the research then provoked and continues to provoke).[27] In Wells's account, the science that underpins the Genographic Project exemplifies the best of a new era of posteugenic genetics that has left race behind.

However, the project's publicity material makes the question of not just genetic but also visible, physical differences central. It poses two "puzzles"—"Why do we appear in such a wide array of different colors and features?" and "If we share such a recent common ancestry, why do we all look so different?"—even though the project's research is focused not on questions of morphological difference but on patterns of genetic variation.[28] This suggests that the focus on morphological questions may primarily be a publicity device, a way of enlisting public interest and public support that is based on the assumption both that it resonates with public curiosity and that this curiosity is a natural inclination that can be dissociated from the politics of race. Foregrounding these questions both presupposes a universal, natural, and innocent curiosity, detached from the history of racial classification, and reinscribes race (in the guise of "diversity") as a focus of fascination and a legitimate subject of social interest and scientific study. Answering these questions with already well-known accounts of human adaptation and morphological evolution in response to different environmental contexts, and with already familiar accounts of human genetic similarity, serves to present the project as firmly on the side of ethically sensitive and socially responsible science.

Yet the project's cultural modes of representing human difference suggest the limits of this sensitivity. Like its website and the book *The Journey of Man*, the television documentary *Journey of Man* features an array of figures of human diversity that unmistakably reproduces the National Geographic's tradition of representing the "exotic" bodies and material cultures of non-Western people for the edification and entertainment of the West.[29] Glossy photos of unnamed individuals that stand for various named ethnic groups appear in the book, as they do throughout the project website. In the documentary, this tradition of exoticized difference, set against the image of Wells as the white, Western scientific explorer, is supplemented by another representational mode borrowed from fashion photography and the trope of youthful racial diversity famously adopted in the advertising campaigns of the clothing company Benetton that were first launched in the mid-1980s.[30] The documentary ends with a staged photo shoot of cosmopolitan, young, smiling women and men who, unlike the predominantly voiceless figures of indigenous exoticism, recount their mostly "mixed" ancestries as the camera captures their beautiful difference. Here difference is presented as what Wells describes as "dizzying diversity," but in other instances, difference is sorted in more overtly racialized ways. Those who bought the original Public Participation Kit received a folded map that includes explanatory material on human genetics on its reverse side. Above the text is a frieze of the heads and upper bodies of children arranged in a spectrum from light skinned to dark—the old racial schema of epidermal difference.[31] The complex politics of diversity in the U.S. context underpin the way in which the Genographic Project both proclaims its antiracism and foregrounds human bodily difference as a natural and innocent curiosity, both celebrating "dizzying diversity" and producing racialized representations of that diversity.

The Public Participation Kit map itself exemplifies one form of the cartographic figuring of human genetic variation that dominates both scientific and popular accounts of the origins and spread of humans and culture of genetic ancestry testing. The ideas of human difference it encodes are more subtle than the photographic and filmed representations of human diversity in the project. But they are no less significant given the deeply authoritative power of maps to communicate truths about the human past, human groups, and human migration. Human population geneticists use a familiar range of cartographic techniques to represent patterns of human gene frequency variation: shaded or color-coded maps that figure gradients of the occurrence of specific allele frequencies over space, sometimes in the form of graded or differently colored bands (or isopleths) that indicate a range of values (> 10 percent, 10–20 percent, and so on); proportional symbols (such as pie charts) located on the regions whose frequencies they represent; or distributions maps in which color-coded dots represent samples with specific genetic variants and their geographic location. Researchers have also identified patterns in diagrammatic representations of statistical analysis of genetic variation that appear to mirror the broad geography of western Europe, thus graphically visualizing the geographic structuring of genetic variation.[32]

However, the form of map that is used more heavily in the Genographic Project, and more widely, is a global map that does not feature variation in gene frequency over space but features cartographic renderings of phylogenetic representations of the relationships between different mtDNA and Y-chromosome lineages and their geographies of emergence and migration: "the passage of a distinct genetic lineage."[33] They are hybrid forms in which the genetic phylogeny of haplogroups, which stands for human genetic variation more widely (via either the mtDNA or the Y chromosome) and exhibits greater differentiation over time, is overlaid on global maps to represent not just lineage relationships but also geographies of dispersal. They are phylogeographic maps that figure mtDNA and Y-chromosome haplogroups (usually on separate maps) as lines with the oldest beginning in east Africa and radiating out from this origin point to the rest of the world, splitting as they do so into separate haplogroup lines, which themselves divide to represent more recently emerged haplogroups, color coded and labeled with haplogroup names. Much of the research on human evolution has been communicated to scientific and wider audiences through these maps, and they are central devices in the marketing of genetic ancestry tests and in the presentation of results. In comparison to the history of racial mapping, these maps appear relatively benign. They are not maps of racial contours nor of the dispersal of early humanity and the evolutionary emergence of named races in their racial zones; they use a nomenclature of haplogroups, not racial groups, and feature lines of migration and ancestral connections rather than lines of spatially bounded and genetically distinct human groups. Nevertheless, as David Livingstone has argued, they are part of that long and persistently political tradition of mapping human origins and human difference with its striking continuities of cartographic tropes and concern and share the power of that cartographic mode of knowledge production to construct models of human origins, identity, and difference.[34]

It is worth considering the models of human origins, identity, and difference and of human migration and "gene flow" that these maps suggest. Though it is made clear in the labeling of these maps that the lines represent the emergence and spread of haplogroups, they can be easily read as maps of the migration of particular human groups who are defined by these haplogroups. Obviously, genetic variants do not travel alone, so the spread of a haplogroup has to imply the movement of people. But those people cannot be imagined as genetically homogenous bands defined by a single haplogroup. This, of course, highlights a potential misreading, but one not unlikely to occur as people are encouraged to consider shared haplogroup identities and ancestries. More significantly, the unidirectionality of these lines misrepresents the nature of human migration, which is the accumulation of the millions of movements of different ranges, directions, and timing. The dispersion of a single haplogroup similarly cannot stand for the multitudinous direction and nature of "gene flow" between humans nor of human migration itself. And as spatialized phylogenies, they share the effect of the phylogenetic diagram itself whose dendritic structure suggests singular instances of genetic differentiation through mutation and the subsequent isolation of distinct populations. Critics argue that the phylogenetic trees that are used to represent the branching of different human groups fundamentally misrepresent human evolution, as they imply the isolation and separate evolution of human groups rather than continuous genetic flow between groups that would be better represented diagrammatically by an interlaced trellis rather than brachiating trees.[35] The primary representational device of the Genographic Project is these maps depicting linear branching haplogroup migration routes rather than dendrograms of named racial or ethnic groups. Nevertheless, the branching lines on the project's maps similarly suggest a process of the division, migration, and isolation of genetically distinct groups rather than gradients of genetic differentiation and complex and multidirectional movements of people and the "exchange" of genes. These phylogeographic maps include traces of older models of human differences and human groups—branching, separation, and isolation—that have been central to racial evolutionary trees even if these groups are newly defined through explicitly nonracialized haplogroups.

It is also the process through which these maps are produced that raises the problematic issue of the genetics of human "groups." The project's repeated public presentation of non-Western people as exotic and objectified is paralleled by the way ethnic and genetic differences are correlated in the project's methodology. This is a matter of sampling. The project's approach to genetic and cultural categories of difference is fundamentally founded on a particular strategy of selectively sampling global genetic variation based on the assumed genetic distinctness of those sampled. It is to focus on or screen out prospective groups or individuals in advance on the basis of whether they fit the project's criteria of being "indigenous"—a cultural distinctiveness that indicates supposed isolation and thus genetic distinctiveness. Thus, despite Wells's insistence on the difference between the Genographic Project and the earlier HGDP, and the antiracist and ethical ethos of his work, the Genographic Project follows its central and deeply problematic strategy. As Jonathan Marks argued in his critique of the

HGDP, using cultural categories as the basis of sampling strategies effectively treats culturally defined human groups as genetic units.[36]

The Genographic Project is not alone in adopting this approach. The selection of samples on the basis of a prior assumption that sociocultural categories such as ethnic identities correspond with genetic distinctiveness is commonplace in human population genetics. Even though many geneticists do not set out to prove that there is a direct correlation between genetic and cultural difference, and even though most do not describe these groups or "populations" in racial terms, the implication is that ethnic categories correspond to categories of genetic difference. Though in most cases the term "race" is avoided, the senses of shared ancestry that coexist with the much more fluid and negotiated constitution of collective identity and membership in ethnic groups are reduced to a much more essentialist, clear-cut, and scientifically authoritative equation of biology and culture. The absence of the signifier *race* does not mean that these approaches do not replicate the idea of race understood as groups defined and differentiated by fixed and immutable biological differences. These "genetically significant" populations are also produced through the screening of potential donors to exclude those family histories of migration that might have led to a genetic profile that is anomalous with the rest of the "indigenous" group. These screening and sampling strategies are thus fundamentally involved in producing the distinctive patterns of genetic variation as objects of analysis. Using ethnic groups as the organizing principle of genetic surveys—despite reminders of the graded nature of genetic variation and of the shared origins of humanity—still suggests that the boundaries between sociocultural communities correspond to patterns of genetic diversity.[37] In the Genographic Project, this is deeply tied to its imagination of a world of human diversity arranged through a particular version of prehistoric migration and isolation and now divided between the increasingly mixed and the last of the genetically pure.

"Where Do We Come From?": Human Mobilities, Old and New

The aim of the Genographic Project is to reconstruct the geographies of early human migration. However, this geography is based on an imaginative global geography of genetic variation shaped by, but now under threat from, human migration, whose authority is conveyed through familiar and largely unreflexive images of scientific exploration. The television documentary *Journey of Man* is an account of Wells presenting the "key puzzles" in human population genetics, an introduction to the science involved, and a report on his travels to the "farthest reaches of the globe" in search of knowledge of "our shared human journey." This drama of masculine, heroic, noble exploration in the service of science and humanity follows a long and persistent Western narrative of exploration and encounter, certainty and self-sacrifice, danger and discovery in pursuit of knowledge.[38] Wells sets out to "walk in the footsteps of our ancestors," from Africa to Australia via southern India, from Africa to the Middle East, from the Middle East to Europe via central Asia, and from central Asia to Siberia and on to North and South America. This is a narrative device rather than a literal retracing; it links his filmed field encounters with people in Namibia, Australia, southern India, central Asia, northern Siberia, and the southwestern United States.

The account of his work in the *National Geographic Adventure* magazine—"risking life and limb to collect DNA from the most isolated peoples on the planet" that has "taken him to some of the world's most extreme climates"—presents his work through the unmistakable hyperbole of explorer heroics. It describes his trials of extreme cold and dietary deprivation visiting the Chukchi people in Siberia and other risks whose names and locations—"difficult and dangerous" fieldwork near the "stronghold of the terrorist group Hezbollah" or near encounters with the Taliban, for example—evoke the terror of inexplicable violence.[39] Undaunted, he is reported as viewing the project as "a carte blanche for five years more of travel and adventure," visiting each sampling center, and making annual "expeditions from one of those centres into the rugged terrain of one or another isolated, indigenous peoples."[40] In *Journey of Man*, we see him meeting those people defined as indigenous research subjects, far away in time and space from Western modernity, and explaining to them the nature of the research—sometimes after long, difficult journeys punctuated with tense moments of danger. The documentary's visual images, which also appear in the project's other publicity materials, and its narrative of Wells's heroic adventure as a self-defined "lab-rat" turned anthropological field worker following the "ancient genetic journeys of humanity" presents a familiar account of the heroic explorer-scientist set against unfamiliar peoples in exotic locations. Following National Geographic's long established and visually luscious, primitivist celebration of human diversity, unfamiliar peoples in exotic locations deemed to be beyond the modern world are foils for Western, masculine, scientific exploration.

This image of the intrepid explorer-scientist sits alongside the project's representations of the nature and implications of different forms of human mobility. The story line of both *Journey of Man* the book and the documentary is of prehistoric human groups struggling in their environments and setting out to new lands. Prehistoric human migration out of Africa is explained in terms of early human responses to environmental change in ways that evoke a pioneering spirit pushing back the frontiers of the New World. The Old World, in this case, is Africa. Despite Wells's caveats that Africa should not be imagined as a place left behind by the forward march of history, the documentary and website versions of the project suggest an evolutionary narrative in which those most able to respond to environmental change leave Africa.[41] *Journey of Man* opens with a family story of ancestors who had the "speed, strength, and resilience to conquer the world"; it tells of "modern man's ability to imagine worlds beyond his horizons that drove him forward." Behind this image of progressive evolution through migration is the implication that those who remain are the less able. Thus Africa is presented as the original home of us all but also the place left behind in the narrative of human migration and the place of the contemporary primitive. The "public" that is invited to share the human journey back to "our" origins is a public that is unmistakably Western, defined against Africa as well as against the indigenous groups that are the sources of genetic data in the project.

This image of collective human achievement in peopling the globe through migration is also combined with the project's emphasis on particular forms of immobility. It is the supposed immobility of the groups who "stayed put" in the places they settled during the course of early human dispersal that makes them so important as sources of information about those patterns of prehistoric expansion that have produced what Wells describes as the "patchwork quilt that is modern humanity."[42] This is a world composed of regionally distinctive patterns of genetic variation that are initially the product of population movements and subsequent long continuities of presence. Though Wells acknowledges the exchange of genes across what he describes as "regional unities," an image of an early modern world of local, genetically distinctive groups that are the product of thousands of years of isolation, permanent presence, and endogamy after the prehistoric journeys of their ancestors is central to the project.[43]

This is an imaginative geography of everyone in their natural places that directly reproduces the perspectives that informed the HGDP.[44] As Wells himself makes clear, the graded nature of human variation and the process of gene flow between "populations" are standard tenets of human population genetics. Nevertheless—and in contrast to anthropological, archaeological, geographical, and historical accounts of continuous human contact and mixing and the fluidity of social groups—the Genographic Project regenerates ideas of the isolation and ancient longevity of indigenous groups prior to Western "discovery."[45]

In this, the Genographic Project reproduces a particular imaginative historical geography based on a "thoroughly Eurocentric image of a precolonial world as a mosaic of cultures and territories that was already fixed in perpetuity before history began."[46] The aim of much of this work is to reconstruct the migrations that shaped global patterns of human genetic diversity. But these patterns of genetic variation are imagined as having been shaped by those migrations and then to have largely stabilized into an unchanging geography of variation up until the advent of European expansion in the late fifteenth century. As Alan Goodman notes, contrary to archaeological evidence, it is imagined that people "did not move around much before 1492."[47] This imaginative geography underpins the significance of indigenous groups who are imagined as remnants of that old pattern. It informs choices of sampling regions in studies that do not only focus on indigenous groups. It shapes sampling criteria within those regions. It is the basis of admixture mapping and the "biogeographical ancestry" testing. It shapes the figuring of indigenous people in the Genographic Project's public science.

The !Kung San people, for example, are presented in the *Journey of Man* as if their ways of life are a direct window into those of "our ancient ancestors" in Africa. This is despite the "fierce revisionist ethnohistorical battle" of the 1980s that challenged their characterization as isolated and archetypal hunter-gatherers by highlighting long histories of "contact with pastoralists, European traders, colonial and economic exploitation."[48] In contrast, Wells describes being led to investigate these people by his "genetic time machine." On the website, they are visual icons of ancient ancestry. Thus, though it is claimed that the project will help undermine racism by exploring genetic similarity, the project clearly inherits the HGDP's construction of genetically isolated, pure, and homogenous groups whose genes supposedly hold clues to particular events in the prehistoric geography of human migration. It reproduces the HGDP's paradoxical "celebration of modern technoscience applied within the framework of archaic racialist language and thought, clearly loaded with astonishing archaic assumptions of primordial division and purity of certain large segments of the human species."[49]

Also echoing the HGDP, the Genographic Project is presented as working against time to capture the remaining evidence of that older geography before it is too late by collecting blood samples from those who are deemed to still live in isolated areas of this former "patchwork quilt." Wells closes *The Journey of Man* with an account of what he describes as a "Final Big Bang" in human evolutionary history: "The Mobility Revolution"— the extent and degree of human migration over the past few centuries and increasing in intensity in the recent past. Globalization and the "mixing" or "admixture" it entails is figured as a menace to the task of mapping human prehistoric migration: "Time is short. In a shrinking world, mixing populations are scrambling genetic signals. The key to this puzzle is acquiring genetic samples from the world's remaining indigenous peoples whose ethnic and genetic identities are isolated. But such distinct peoples, languages, and cultures are quickly vanishing into a 21st century global melting pot."[50] The Genographic Project is thus deeply shaped by a sense that the patterns of human demography shaped by prehistoric migration are being disturbed by contemporary globalized migration and mating.

Deep Ancestry, Wells's account of the Genographic Project's origins, scientific basis, key research questions, and preliminary findings one year in, opens with the narrative of cultural loss that ends *The Journey of Man*. We are told again of the rate of loss of languages, which, for Wells, is indicative of the loss of the last old patterns of indigenous genetic isolation. The world, he claims, "is currently experiencing a cultural mass extinction similar to the biodiversity crisis."[51] Like the HGDP, the Genographic Project borrows from the language of biodiversity to stress the urgency of preserving human diversity while cloaking the project in a liberal humanitarian concern for cultural rights, identities, and diversity.[52] Wells frames the "loss" of indigenous groups in terms of the erosion of cultural identities and the engulfment of the "isolated" by the wider world. Indigenous people feature as sources of special genetic material that is vulnerable to the effects of contact with the wider world: "Ancient, local populations are key, and the less admixture they have the better. [Yet] these are the groups that are now being lost."[53] This framing cannily cloaks the project in all the associations of liberal humanitarian concern for cultural rights, identities, and diversity in an attempt to deflect the criticisms that the HGDP encountered. Yet it unknowingly reproduces the HGDP's rhetoric of genetic salvage, of threatened "isolates" as subjects of urgent genetic testing, and the deeper geneticization of human social groups. In this case, the concern to preserve the genetics of indigenous people as a source of information about the human past is supplemented with a discourse of cultural preservation. The Genographic Project is presented as not only a scientific resource but also one whose "anthropological genetic" work will, just in time, save details of the "cultural context" as well as genetics of indigenous populations. This work will result in "the creation of a global database of human genetic variation and associated anthropological data (language, social customs, etc.). This database will serve as an invaluable scientific resource for the research community. Many indigenous populations around the world are facing strong challenges to their cultural identities. The Genographic Project will provide a 'snapshot' of human genetic variation before we lose the cultural context necessary to make sense of the genetic data."[54]

Thus a multicultural celebration of global diversity and a discourse of minority group rights to recognition and respect are welded together in an apparently progressive concern with cultural erasure. Yet, with its primitivist fetishization of purity, the project contrasts a Western world of modernity and regrettable assimilation and a non-Western world of tradition and threatened isolation, reproducing the long-established trope of the "vanishing indigene" as the last representatives of an old world before mixing.[55] In contrast to recent accounts of the complexity and diversity of indigenous mobilities, from the dated perspectives of this project, the indigenous cannot, by definition, be mobile.[56]

But how can this concern with threatened purity be reconciled with the project's celebration of modern multicultural mixing? Wells's accounts of the project are caught in a tension between a multicultural celebration of diversity and anxiety about the impacts of reproductive interconnections or "mixing" for genetic research on human origins and migration, celebrating cultural interconnection while searching for isolated research subjects. The cities of Los Angeles (in the book *The Journey of Man*) and New York (in *Deep Ancestry*) are used to foreground Wells's liberal appreciation of diversity. But these cities are also used to explain the problems of the genetic "mixing" they represent to the work of reconstructing that "patchwork quilt" of humanity. Urban cosmopolitanism is figured as the counterpoint to ancient and pure indigeneity. While human prehistoric migration is the subject of the Genographic Project, modern and contemporary migration is figured as a threat to its attempts to reconstruct those early human journeys. The "Mobility Revolution," Wells argues, is a new geography of genetic diversity and of new generations who are the product of the "jostling together of people, who historically speaking would never have met." Though, he suggests, this "is certainly a good thing socially, leading to the breakdown of racial stereotypes," it is leading, more problematically, to "a new genetic landscape": "The patchwork quilt of diversity that has distinguished us since human populations started to diverge around 50,000 years ago is now re-sorting itself, blending together in combinations that would have never been possible before."[57] Wells writes that "while we hope that this will lead to a new sense of interconnectedness among the world's peoples, it also means that the genetic trails we follow will become hopelessly intertwined. When this happens we will no longer be able to read the historical document encoded in our DNA."[58]

This sense of interconnectedness is thus ideally between people arranged in that old imagined "patchwork quilt" that, for Wells, is being torn apart by the scale and extent of human migration. Thus while the location of *The Human Family Tree* in Queens, New York, reiterates this celebration of metropolitan multiculturalism, it is underpinned by an anxious imagination of an older geography of difference that soon will no longer exist. The project thus combines a multiculturalist celebration of global diversity, a discourse of minority group rights to recognition and respect, a concern about both cultural erasure and the salvaging the genetic material of indigenous "isolates," and an imaginative historical geography of genetically distinct human social groups.

It is those who are most valorized in the project who are reluctant to be enlisted in what Wells envisions as a global collaboration between indigenous populations and scientists; indigenous rights groups have strongly challenged the project despite its ethical intentions.[59] *The Journey of Man* ends with Wells's case for a sensitive acknowledgment of the histories of colonial exploitation, scientific experimentation, and the desire of indigenous groups for "cultural privacy" and their "suspicion that the scientific results may not agree with their own beliefs." He calls for scientists to take responsibility and rebuild trust by explaining the relevance of their work to the people they hope to study.[60] Considerable efforts were made to avoid the controversy surrounding the HGDP from the start by emphasizing that it is a genuinely collaborative, independent, and non-profit-making venture. In particular, the Legacy Project is designed to present it as a more enlightened and more sensitive version of the HGDP, offset potential criticisms, and garner public support.

However, the limits of the Legacy Project have been exposed by critics who point out the lack of indigenous consultation in decisions over funding and highlight the very small proportion (1 percent) of income derived from the sale of the Public Participation Kits that actually funds "cultural education and preservation projects."[61] More fundamentally, they have highlighted the lack of prior effective consultation with indigenous peoples in the planning of the project and questioned the ethics of using its promise of funding in seeking indigenous consent. Indigenous critics assert that education and cultural preservation are rights that should be independent of any involvement in the project and argue that there are better ways of promoting indigenous people's culture than those tied to the collection of genetic material.[62] Running through all statements of protest is the criticism of the project's insensitivity to indigenous knowledge and belief, its potential effects in undermining indigenous origin stories and thus political rights, and its assumptions of the greater authority of science over collective oral histories of ancestry and origins. As expressed in the statement submitted to the UN Permanent Forum on Indigenous Issues in 2006, "Indigenous peoples oppose this kind of research because our creation stories and languages carry information about our genealogy and ancestors. We do not need genetic testing to tell us where we come from."[63] Indigenous people represented by the Indigenous Peoples Council on Biocolonialism resist both the geneticization of their identities and the legitimacy of asserting the truth of science over collective knowledge of origins.[64]

In response, the project's publicity material emphasizes the support of its three "indigenous representatives," who featured in the project's launch event as authoritative voices for wider indigenous groups, to legitimate the project and forestall and undermine the indigenous resistance that followed.[65] These criticisms have resulted in the development of a revised ethical protocol for the project but one mostly confined to more detailed guidelines for ensuring informed consent, both individual and collective. But the authority of science is not blithely asserted. Instead, it is both relativized and reinforced. Wells presents contemporary human population genetics as a source of narratives of prehistoric migration that serve as the "songlines" of the West. Acknowledging the significance of Aboriginal Australian accounts of the "journey taken by their ancestors during the Dreamtime, a period in the distant past, before collective memory," Wells proposes an analogous function for the results of research in human population genetics:

> In a sense this is precisely what we are trying to do with our studies of DNA—resurrect a global songline for everyone alive today, describing how they reached this current location and what the journey was like. As secular Westerners we have lost our traditional songlines to a greater extent than other peoples around the world, so it is perhaps appropriate that Western science has developed the methods for rediscovering them. However, our research does not take place in a vacuum, and science can sometimes run rough shod over cultural beliefs. I would hope that this book might be a small step towards changing the field into what it really is—a collaborative effort between people around the world who are interested in their shared history.[66]

However, in the Genographic Project, this collective story of origins has to be a scientifically verified global song line. Despite Wells's appreciation of the danger of science running "rough shod" over cultural beliefs, he does not hesitate later in *The Journey of Man* to point out the inaccuracy of one indigenous attempt to use the results of new technologies for dating biological samples to support an account of Australia rather than Africa as the homeland of humanity.[67] Though more recent accounts of the project now suggest that the scientific accounts will complement rather than replace people's stories,[68] when it comes down to it, only science holds the truth about "where we come from and how we got to be where we are today." This rests, as Jenny Reardon and Kim TallBear argue, on assumptions that the genetic material of indigenous bodies is the rightful property of those who seek to produce useful knowledge for the collective good of humanity. Following a long colonial tradition of whiteness as a privileged property and white claims to property, the DNA of indigenous peoples is claimed in the "name of the civilizing project of antiracism"—the "cosmopolitan anti-racist world promised by genomics."[69]

Getting to Know the Global Human Family

The resistance of indigenous organizations to the project has significantly affected its ability to solicit samples of genetic material from indigenous people. Yet considerable numbers of people in the United States and western Europe have paid to have their genetic material analyzed through the project's public participation and awareness campaign. These are not the people whose genetic material is of primary interest in the project. Nevertheless, this public engagement strategy devised to garner public support and forestall the criticisms the HGDP encountered deserves attention because of its considerable significance in shaping ideas of human connection, difference, and relatedness. Those who pay to participate have their genetic samples analyzed by Family Tree DNA, which is undertaking the analysis of "nonindigenous" participants for the Genographic Project. Women receive a description of their mtDNA and men of their Y chromosome in the form of standardized haplotype alphanumerical codes, along with maps and broad accounts of the geography of their lineage's origins and dispersal prior to the last ten thousand years and its contemporary relative predominance. In 2012, the Genographic Project entered a new phase—Geno 2.0—and launched a new version of its participant kit, which now includes the analysis of other genetic markers—ancestry-informative markers—and offers results also in the form of the percentages of an individual's ancestry from different global regions.[70]

In the Genographic Project, as in the commercial sector of genetic genealogy more widely, the naturalness and authority of this model of genetic ancestry and relatedness are constructed by presenting genetic genealogy as a technologically extended and scientific version of conventional genealogy. The Public Participation Kits, Wells's "nifty and novel idea"[71] for enlisting widespread public support as well as generating income, offer customers individual "genetic lineages" and knowledge of the "ancient genetic journeys and physical travels of your distant relatives." The explanatory material is careful to make clear that this is not conventional genealogy: "Your results will not provide names for your personal family tree or tell you where your great-grandparents lived." Yet the project is presented through the familiar trope of the human family tree. Participants who allow the results of their tests to be added to the global genetic database will "help to delineate our common genetic tree, giving detailed shape to its many twigs and branches."

This figure of the genetic family tree is part of a wider familial discourse. The project's insistent message—repeated again and again in newspaper reporting and throughout the project's various media outputs (documentaries, books, websites, and *National Geographic* magazine features), and reproduced in accounts of its progressive potential—is that it will track a collective human history that will lead to an understanding that all people are connected together as relatives in a globally extended human family.[72] In the Genographic Project, the broadly positive conventional associations of the family—as a sphere of affection, intimacy, and care sheltered from the world of economic competition, social struggle, and political conflict—are extended to an image of humanity as fundamentally bound together by bonds of ancestral connection. Fostering a sense of global family connectedness is presented as unquestionably constructive, progressive, valuable, and worth pursuing. It assumes a collective global appreciation of the meaning of personal bonds with immediate relatives and extended familial connections. In one video clip available on the project's website, Wells summarizes the project's "take home" family story:

> I think the take home message from all of this is that if we trace far enough back we all share ancestry with each other. We are all part of an extended family and we all originated out of Africa within the last fifty to sixty thousand years. At that point there was a relatively small group of people living there, literally an extended family, trying to make it through the worst of the last ice age. And the story of how they succeeded, how they were able to conquer adversity and go out and populate the world is the story we are trying to tell. And that's a pretty cool story. I think that most people are interested in that ultimately.[73]

Everyone knows and no one can legitimately argue against the value of the family or the idea of the shared ancestry of all humanity. Or at least, this is only possible by overlooking how the family is a sphere of power, hierarchy, and subordination as well as love, care, and nurturance and a focus of social anxiety and normative, conservative models of gender and sexuality and by not keeping in mind the exclusions and differentiations in the reckoning of familial relatedness. And despite its positive connotations, the idea of a global human family is not unambiguously progressive. Nineteenth- and early twentieth-century imperial and racial discourses of the "family of man" naturalized hierarchies of power and difference within a paternalistic model of the global human family.[74]

Furthermore, underlying this image of a genetic human family tree as the basis for a progressive collective human identity is a fundamental conviction in the authority of science to determine relatedness and a fundamental assumption of the universality of the model of genetic relatedness that is central to the project and the wider field of human population genetics and geneticized genealogy. This is a geneticized version of kinship. Only genetic connections count as real family, and only direct maternal and paternal lineages constitute the branches of the family tree. This is reductive even if accepting that the focus of human population genetics is necessarily on genetic connections, since it implies that an individual's ancestry is defined through the very small portion of genetic material that is directly inherited, maternally and paternally. But it is even more reductive when considered in relation to how biological connection is both foregrounded and decentered in the social practice of Euro-American kinship,[75] and even more so in light of the global diversity of understandings and practices of relatedness.[76] As Pricilla Wald points out in her criticism of the HGDP, "implicit in the very conviction that genetics can refute the logic of racism is an assumption about the authority of genetics—not just population genetics, but genetics broadly conceived—to establish definitive terms of relatedness."[77] A specifically Western model of kinship is assumed, and then a more specifically geneticized version of that model is asserted.

Or perhaps, it is less asserted than assumed as truth—but a truth that needs to be translated or made meaningful for those operating with less scientific versions of kinship. The project's media outputs assume a universal interest in family and personal family connections but have to work to make a genetic account of a global family tree sit easily alongside that natural interest. One device used heavily within the documentary *The Journey of Man* is that of the family album. Wells is shown setting off on his travels after parting from his wife and children on a train station platform, a family good-bye that serves to emphasize both the solitary heroics and sacrifice of his journey. But he also imaginatively brings his family with him as he explores the genetic lineages of what is described as the human family and its migrations. Wells is filmed breaking the ice with !Kung San men by showing them the photo of his daughters in his wallet. In a later scene, he shows Navajo people photographs from what he describes as his "family album" of other people he has met en route and sampled. They are meant to make the idea of a global family tree real, even though the images of largely unnamed "relatives" are more like photographs of anthropological "types" representing the groups identified as of genetic interest rather than family snapshots. Like domestic family photographs, they are an attempt to produce a "stretched, integrative" space linking people over distance but also, in this case, to produce an integrative global familial space composed of unknown (but through the photographs, somehow knowable) distant relations.[78]

The "truth" of genetic relatedness at a global scale is also conveyed through individualized accounts of genetic ancestry. The promise of meaningful self-knowledge and the ability of science to reveal that vital but hitherto hidden knowledge is dramatically illustrated by the project's presentation of individual tests, expectations, results, and reflections—a drama of suspense and scientific revelation common to other popular television depictions of genetic genealogy. The *Journey of Man* documentary features Wells in Kazakhstan telling a man named Niazaroff that he represents the direct descendant of one man living in the region two thousand generations (or forty thousand years) ago from whom all European, Native American, and many Indian men descend. There is little explanation of what this means or how it is contrived as a "discovery" through a complex combination of sampling practices, suppositions, statistical techniques, and speculative reconstructions. The reductiveness of this construction of personal patrilineage is masked; Niazaroff also descends from thousands of other men and women, and this line of descent is also logically shared with many, many others. Similarly, the launch of the project featured Wells revealing the result of their genetic tests to the project's "indigenous representatives" and in each case underemphasizing the cultural and scientific production of the results as meaningful accounts of ancestry.

In *The Human Family Tree* documentary, the focus is deliberately on more ordinary "deep ancestries" in line with the emphasis on the everyday multiculturalism of its New York location. The accounts of the geographies of the ancestries of the six people whose genetic and personal stories it featured are necessarily highly generalized and widely shared, since these haplogroups are extremely broad and, in most cases, add little sense of depth to their existing understandings of origin. The Irish-born New Yorker, Eamon, for example, is told that he "belongs to one of the most common European lineages. His ancestors were among the first modern humans to settle Europe more than 30,000 years ago. They spent the last ice age—when enormous ice sheets covered most of northern Europe—wintering near the Mediterranean in present day Spain. From this base they expanded northward after the ice melted, re-populating northern Europe. The highest frequencies of his haplogroup, R1b1, are found in Ireland."[79]

There is an awkward relationship between the Genographic Project's emphasis on direct maternal and paternal descent and the documentary's emphasis on cosmopolitan, multicultural mixing. Though *The Human Family Tree* and the Genographic Project, more widely, celebrate (albeit ambivalently) the "melting pot" of this multicultural metropolis, an individual ancestry is reduced to one or two lineages rather than the tangle of connections, inheritances, and heritages of many American genealogies shaped by the country's long and complex history of immigration. This may obviously be the appeal. But this simplified and effectively purified personal ancestry suggests the multiculturalism that the project celebrates is the copresence of people with identifiable and distinctive genetic lineages rather than a meaningful, effective, critical multiculturalism that challenged the imaginative geography of difference implied in that "patchwork quilt" model of human cultural and genetic variation. Any hope that the project might indeed suggest ways of overcoming resistance to relationships across the boundaries of race or ethnicity cannot be fulfilled, since its genetic family tree is more about divergence and difference than entanglements that cross these conventional categories. Eamon is described as hoping to find that his and his Korean girlfriend Hanna's DNA may "reveal that their ancestors crossed paths at some point along the way" because of her family's disapproval of their "mixed-race relationship," but he and Hanna would be assigned quite different places on a genetic human family tree.

This is because the project grafts a geneticized model of ancestry onto the powerful and pervasive cultural resonances of family connection and ancestral origins for its "public," but its model of the family is as much about differentiation as connection. Despite the rhetoric of shared origins and interconnectedness, the project focuses on specific genetic lineages that do coalesce in the very distant past but are shaped by divergence and characterized by difference. Stories of making connections and revealing personalized and shared "deep ancestry" do not work on the basis of generalized human genetic ancestral interconnection. People do not buy tests to be confirmed as members of the global human family but buy them in search of ancestral origins that are specific to them and shared by those with the same particular rather than generalized human ancestry. The tests do not simply say "we're all related"—nor do they confirm human African origins. Instead, they depend on a science of difference and the social meaning of difference and are constituted as a technology of difference. They promise specific ancestral origins and specific lineages, which necessarily distinguish between people on the basis of different ancestries. Genetic genealogy, like conventional genealogy, is a practice of differentiation as much as identification but, like the Genographic Project, framed by an ideal of global familial unity, shared ancestry, and origins.

The marketing of genetic ancestry tests makes much of the potential of customers to make connections through "matches" with fellow customers. The publicity material for the Genographic Project and the wider media engagement with genetic ancestry similarly foregrounds the possibility of finding out who is related to whom and the promise of surprising connections with newly discovered "relations." This can be understood in terms of what Marilyn Strathern identifies as the value placed on making and finding connections in Euro-American society and science and in terms of how that is currently intensified through digital social media in which the number of "friends," "hits," and "followers" is a measure of popularity and value.[80] Connectedness is valorized. And in light of the wider discourses of globalization, the more connected the better. But there is a specific value attributed to ancestral connections, since they are figured in terms of ideas of affinity, commonality, solidarity, and care of familial relatedness. The marketing of genetic genealogy plays heavily upon the value of finding "matches" and connecting with "genetic cousins" and with the senses of bonding, mutual recognition, and reciprocated interest that may follow new relationships based on shared ancestry and assumed genetic similarity.

But this emphasis on the significance of shared ancestry and genetic similarity implies the thinness and weakness of other sorts of social relationships. Foregrounding shared haplotypes as the basis of senses of connectedness suggests diminishing empathy with increasing biological difference. Implying that genetic connectedness is the basis for meaningful and rewarding social relations or imagined commonality undermines alternative versions of empathy and care across distance and across conventional categories of identity. This is clearly not the intention of the Genographic Project organizers, but it is the inadvertent implication of an unconsidered celebration of genetic relatedness. There are also those who are more keen to articulate the idea of the natural bonds between the genetically related, explaining nationalism, ethnicity, and warfare through the supposedly innate drive of humans to succeed in reproducing their own genes or those most similar to them in a competitive struggle with genetically different groups. This idea is not only found on the fringes of serious scholarship. Writing in a well-established and scholarly journal most associated with work on the historical, geographical, and cultural making of ideas of the nation, nationalism, and national identity, evolutionary psychologist Phillippe Rushton has claimed that "at the core of human nature, people are genetically motivated to prefer others genetically similar to themselves."[81] Genetic similarity theory, Rushton argues, explains the altruistic sacrifice that individuals make for those to whom they are most genetically similar within ethnic, racial, or national groups and predicts that many "seemingly purely cultural divides are, in fact, rooted in the underlying population genetics."[82] Altruistic self-sacrifice, he argues, is a strategy for ensuring the reproduction of the collective gene pool. The logic of this theory suggests that the focus of social and governmental concern should not be racialized versions of nationhood nor patterns of racism and ethnic discrimination that shape inequality but should be the management of "natural" antagonism of the genetically, ethnically, and racially dissimilar through policies that could include residential segregation or the curtailment of immigration.

Central to this new strand of evolutionary psychology is a vision of human antagonism and affinity as fundamentally genetic and thus racial and ethnic. Racism and ethnic conflict are natural, biological, and genetic. Thus, though the trope of the global human family may be intended to discredit ideas of race, promoting "natural" interests in making connections via ancestry and the natural bonds of shared ancestry produces a model of human connection and affinity based on degrees of genetic similarity. The project's statements of the scientific invalidity of race are not matched by a critical perspective on the implications of emphasizing genetic ancestry as the basis of human relatedness.

At the same time, the idea of a global genetic family may simply provide a new means of reproducing accounts of the exotic physical and cultural diversity of humanity in the tradition of Western travelers' tales but now couched in terms of an apparently enlightened sense of global family connections. The October 2005 issue of *National Geographic Traveler* featured an illustrated account of journalist Donovan Webster having undertaken the Public Participation Kit test and then traveling to meet those who are described as the present-day descendants of his distant ancestors in Tanzania, Lebanon, Tashkent in Uzbekistan, and Spain's Basque Country.[83] Webster describes how the results of his Y-chromosome genetic test suggest that his "life was a lie." Having been "comfortable with [the] truths" of his family history as "old-line Anglo-Saxons," he got a "fateful shock" in the discovery that his R1b Y-chromosome haplogroup traces an ancestral line that goes back in time and space from the British Isles to Northern Spain, to central Asia, to the Middle East, and ultimately, to east Africa. This is that Y-chromosome haplogroup that geneticists estimate characterizes a very high percentage of men in western Europe and of western European ancestry who also share the ancestral lineage and is an ancestral line that, according to the Genographic Project logic, links millions of people in Europe and Asia and ultimately, when traced back to earlier lineages, the entire world of men.

However, following a route clearly contrived through Wells's research contacts in specific research sites and iconic groups in the culture of human population genetics such as the Basques, Webster sets off "in search of my genetic family" and for a series of "family reunions" beginning with Julius Indaaya Hun/!un/!ume, the chief of those Webster describes as his "extended family," the "Hadzabe Bushmen of East Africa," who has already been enlisted in Wells's efforts to present examples of indigenous support for the project. The account that follows, illustrated by photographs of those he has encountered, reproduces the familiar tropes of travel writing: the wonder of difference; the quaintness of other people's ways; colorful and ancient customs, costumes, and buildings; and the beauty of feminine youth. Its reflections on people's different physical appearances, ordered in a journey and description that go from dark-skinned to light, are legitimized by Webster's expressions of the "joys of reuniting with family." Getting to know the global human family through the project and its individual customer's kits reinforces an idea of both genetic similarity and, by implication, difference as the basis of senses of connection and distance. It also produces a depoliticized notion of humanity as an extended global family that is easily incorporated into the tradition of Western exoticism.

Since the screening of *Journey of Man* in 2004, with its follow-up piece by Webster the year after, a new hybrid documentary form is appearing, albeit with some mutations and local adaptations. Part travel documentary, part popular science, and part family history feature, this form is being developed by program makers, often in conjunction with the scientists behind genetic genealogy companies, to win audiences and win over customers, respectively. The tropes of individual results are joined to the trope of traveling to meet "ancestral groups" back along a lineage to Africa, a particular Africa that is happily framed by ideas of family reunion and personalized global interconnectedness.

In February 2013, comedian, actor, and transvestite Eddie Izzard (who in an earlier documentary, as we will see in chapter 3, championed the idea of Britain as a mongrel nation) was featured in a two-part documentary on BBC called *Meet the Izzards*. Echoing the device of the personal journey retracing ancestral migration routes and "meeting his modern DNA cousins from the African bush to the shores of the Red Sea," in the first episode, "The Mum's Line," focusing on his mtDNA lineage, he "discovers how humans populated the globe, why he has blue eyes and how the Izzards ended up in Europe." The second episode, "The Dad's Line," involves another journey—this time based on his Y-chromosome lineage. The documentary is meant to be another story of an individual exploring his place within a global human family—"We all come out of Africa, and we come from the same people." It is also about Izzard's attempt to feel closer to his mother, who died when he was a young boy. This is thus a very personal genetic family history. Yet much of the documentary reproduces the figuring of contemporary people, the oft-visited !Kung San here also, as if they are ancient ancestors even if this is framed again by ideas of a familial bond across difference. As described in the program notes, "Eddie begins on the outskirts of Namibia's Kalahari Desert where he meets the San Bushmen and learns to make fire. He might set tongues wagging with his painted nails, but Eddie is also moved to discover how at home he feels with his most distant ancestral cousins."[84]

Given the documentary's affective power in Izzard's efforts to, in some way, know his mother through "mum's line," it also is troubling to see this personal emotional authenticity being commercially exploited. The documentary is the work of one of the geneticists who is most energetic in developing ways to gain publicity and buyers for the tests he and colleagues are marketing through a suite of ethnically and geographically specific genetic ancestry tests: Jim Wilson, cofounder of BritainsDNA, ScotlandsDNA, IrelandsDNA, and YorkshiresDNA, who with his colleagues pursues media attention with knowingly well-chosen efforts to make headlines.[85] This includes, in June 2013, his widely reported claims to have proven an Indian maternal ancestor for future British king Prince William, nicely timed to just precede a royal birth.[86] It is clear that this apparently postcolonial refiguring of ancestry in the unashamed pursuit of publicity and profit, cloaked in progressive liberal associations of entangled histories and genealogies, is designed to shore up the political as well as the scientific credentials of an industry that is as much about differentiation as connection and as much about disassociation as affinity through degrees of genetic similarity and difference within the global "human family tree."

The science and commerce of "genography" are often entwined. Though the Genographic Project is a not-for-profit venture, it is closely associated with Family Tree DNA, and the National Geographic Society puts the project to work in commercial enterprises. For most members of the specific "public" that are sought as enthusiasts for the "shared" global project, traveling the world to visit those deemed to be the Genographic Project's significant populations would be an imaginative exercise in genetic familial exoticism. But in 2012, those who could afford it were offered, for the cost of $66,950, a National Geographic Expeditions *Journey of Man* trip via private jet. Led by Spencer Wells, this twenty-four-day journey to four continents was promised to "trace the paths of human migration around the world." "Following an itinerary based on Spencer's groundbreaking book *The Journey of Man*," customers could "travel to ten incredible destinations that tell the story of our shared history." The trip's highlights included the chance to "get acquainted with people who live much as our ancestors did." Each traveler was offered a Genographic Participation Kit in advance with Spencer "on hand to analyze your DNA and the path of your own early ancestors, placing your own genetic history within the context of this larger odyssey."[87] This is a model of global family not only differentiated into lines of ancestry and degrees of relatedness but also fundamentally stratified in terms of economic inequality. A well-established tradition of Western travel in search for the exotic—in this case, a luxury version—is reproduced but with the added feature of a legitimating model of relatedness across economic as well as cultural difference.

The Genographic Project—as an avowedly antiracist project to measure, map, and interpret human genetic variation—is thus a striking example of the remaking of ideas of human difference and origins in human population genetics that is heavily framed by discourses of the scientific invalidity of race and of human interconnectedness through shared membership of a genetic global human family. An apparently progressive language of multiculturalism, diversity, global human harmony, and indigenous rights frames its reductive versions of relatedness, unreflexive assumptions of scientific authority, and primitivizing accounts of exotic and isolated indigeneity. The Genographic Project celebrates modern multiculturalism but at the same time is fundamentally informed by its vision of a premodern world of people and genes arranged in a mosaic of difference. It draws on images of cosmopolitan cultural diversity as a progressive alternative to ideas of national purity while expressing its anxieties about the admixture of those who represent human ancestry in the present as the last remnants of that mosaic of culture and genes. Similarly, its model of a human family tree depends on reducing relatedness to biology and reducing ancestry to lines of direct maternal and paternal descent. Its discourses of genetic connectedness as the basis for social relations or imagined commonality undermine alternative versions of empathy and care across distance and across conventional categories of identity.

These dimensions of the project deserve criticism, but I have also sought to demonstrate the tensions and contradictions of the project's antiracist approach to the geography of human genetic variation, rather than simply pit unenlightened or unwittingly racist science against critical social science. Wells's historically informed approach and ethical efforts clearly do not stand for a robustly unreflexive science of human diversity. Nevertheless, the predominantly liberal politics of human population genetics do not mean that its accounts of human genetic variation are either politically neutral or automatically progressive. Instead, these accounts are powerful because their overt antiracism masks their problematic geographical imaginaries of genetic difference and genetic relatedness. The idea that "we are all related" leaves much room for delineating degrees of relatedness along familiar lines of difference.

3

Our Genetic Heritage

Figuring Diversity in National Studies

"What does being British mean to a scientist?" This is the opening line of the text accompanying a short video that appeared in December 2010 featuring the People of the British Isles project on the website of its funding body, the biomedical charity the Wellcome Trust.[1] This project was initially granted £2.5 million in 2004 and was extended through funding for a further five years in 2010. It is led by the eminent geneticist Sir Walter Bodmer at the Weatherall Institute of Molecular Medicine, University of Oxford. In its first phase, the project aimed to produce a "genetic map of the British Isles" by taking 3,500 blood samples from selected volunteers in thirty locations across England, Wales, Scotland, and Northern Ireland.[2] The case for doing so rests on the biomedical value of knowledge of regional genetic diversity in the United Kingdom and on the wider cultural and historical significance of studying the "genetic heritage of our present day UK population."[3]

The question "what does being British mean to a scientist?" evokes the possibility that this category of collective identity might be understood scientifically or, more specifically, be addressed through studies of human genetic variation. Most population geneticists (the sort of scientists in question here) would argue that the meaning of Britishness is not something that can be scientifically addressed, but many often do argue that genetics can contribute to understandings of a collective past. The question is more of an engaging gambit than strictly representative of the People of the British Isles project, since the project is not formulated with the scientific meaning of Britishness as its object of study. But it does foreground the ways in which this project and studies of human genetic variation in human population genetics and biomedical genomics, more widely, call on and reconfigure conventional categories of human similarity, difference, and collective identity—in this case, the nation. The figuring of human population genetics as a tool of collective self-knowledge and collective self-understanding for humanity as a whole is paralleled by the framing of national genetic studies as ways of understanding a collective national past and contemporary collective identity.

This framing by population geneticists themselves, science correspondents, and the popular media means that the idea that accounts of genetic variation are sources for addressing questions of collective national identity is becoming entirely orthodox and naturalized. A 2011 BBC Radio Four documentary focusing on research on human genetic variation within and between the United Kingdom and Ireland posed the question of identity in its title—*British, More or Less*—and in its focus on "what the results of such studies might tell us about ancient Britons and how this is reflected in the multi-cultural British Isles of the 21st century . . . Should we be prepared to draw further lines of difference between the four nations or will we be forced to accept a shared ancient heritage?"[4] This question suggests that new forms of genetic knowledge can be used to address common assumptions about "lines of difference" within Britain and the British Isles, assumptions about the biological basis and distinctiveness of and relationships between Irish, Welsh, Scottish, and English categories of identity and difference.

Here I want to interrogate the genealogical and geneticized model of the nation that underpins the posing of these questions by addressing the way in which the "genetic heritage of our present day UK population" is constituted in a project that takes the population of the United Kingdom as its unit of analysis and is heavily framed by discourses of collective heritage and collective self-knowledge. How do scientific and popular accounts of the human genetic variation in the United Kingdom evoke— and in different ways, rework—ideas of a collective, national ancestral past? What counts as "our present day UK population"? What is meant by "genetic heritage" and to whom does it belong? How are accounts of national genetic variation or "gene geography"[5] inflected by and embedded within wider debates about diversity, integration, and multiculturalism in Britain and British national identity? Engaging with this project and this wider field of scientific projects and popular accounts involves exploring the intersections between the science of human genetic diversity and the politics of national belonging not only in terms of how these studies may contribute to the wider debates and discourses—supplying resources for different models of identity and belonging or providing a new lexicon for their articulation—but also in terms of how they are already embedded within these contexts and undertaken by geneticists already attuned in different ways to the climate of British cultural politics. Those involved are often aware of both the popular appeal of genetic "truths" of origins and identity and the politically sensitive nature of these categories.

Addressing a project in which the "population" whose genetic variation is to be studied is defined in terms of a state's boundary and framed by ideas of collective self-knowledge provides a way of exploring human population genetics as a multicultural science, shaped by and intervening in the particular politics of belonging, identity, and inclusion, in different national contexts. Moving from a global project to a national project makes it possible to consider how the nature of scientific messages about genetic variation (homogeneity and diversity) and genetically identifiable groups depends on the sort of geography being analyzed and described (i.e., national, continental, global, nearby, or distant) and the politics of invoking human genetic unity and difference at different scales. What would it mean to evoke ideas of genetic unity at the scale of the nation-state? How do ideas of diversity work in relation to ideas of national, racial, or ethnic difference in projects focusing on genetic variation within a country? How is indigeneity differently configured and located geographically and temporally in studies of human genetic variation in different national contexts? Before turning to the figuring of indigeneity and settlement in accounts of genetic variation in Britain, it is worth considering the relationship between the category of national population as a political, social, and cultural collective and the category of population as unit of genetic analysis.

The Genetic Nation-State

As we have already seen, much of the most vigorous debate about human population genetics has focused on questions of race and ethnicity.[6] Yet nationhood is also a biocultural category, traditionally understood in terms of shared descent, and is entangled with, rather than neatly distinct from, the similarly biocultural categories of race and ethnicity. While ideas of ethnicity based on shared history and culture and ideas of race based on shared genealogy and blood are commonly distinguished in social science scholarship, they do not remain distinct discourses of collective racial or ethnic identity. Discourses of nationhood frequently combine ideas of ancestral connections between members of the national community and ancestral connections to soil, land, and landscape.[7] Concepts of nation, race, and ethnicity all evoke the notion of a community—or, more specifically, a kinship—of shared descent and shared geographical origins that underpins ideas of identity and difference, inclusion and exclusion, but with differing degrees of explicit emphasis on bodily or genetic difference within and between these categories.[8] While concepts of ethnicity and to some extent national identity are often used in the British context as alternatives to a problematic language of racial difference, the terms slip in their referent and intended distinctions. Ethnicity is sometimes presented as a subcategory or transnational category of collective identity or, alternatively, as synonymous with nationhood; ideas of national identity can be racialized subtly or overtly. This slippage in society and in science complicates efforts to pin down the nature and implications of the figuring of race in human population genetics.

However, addressing the category of the nation in relation to accounts of genetic variation can productively extend recent work on genetics, race, and ethnicity. This is not only by exploring the slippage between race, ethnicity, and nation as they are configured through accounts of human genetic variation but also by considering the particular political and imaginative geography of the nation. While ideas of both ethnicity and race are constituted through ideas of difference based on geographies of origins and shared descent and, in the case of race, the classic continental cartography of difference, the category of nationhood is intrinsically geographical. Whether aimed for or realized, nationhood is distinctive in being fundamentally constituted in terms of an ideal coincidence between the community of shared culture and descent and the political boundaries of the nation-state. Nation-states may work to make those boundaries also align with categories of race, but concepts of race do not fundamentally depend on this political geography. References to a national population evoke both the formal political boundedness of the state's territory and the cultural imagination of the nation as an idealized symmetry of geography, identity, and belonging.

This raises particular issues for studies of human genetic variation that take the national population as their unit of analysis. It brings together the question of the making of the "population" in human population genetics and the politics of national belonging. In this chapter, I consider the ways in which a population for genetic analysis and a national population sharing "genetic heritage" are mutually constituted in studies that structure their research in terms of the national population and national boundaries and interpret patterns of genetic variation in terms of national origin and settlement stories.[9] The idea of the national population is, of course, itself not timeless and unchanging but historically and geographical constituted and currently being reworked along with the political rationalities and forms of citizenship and subjectivity emerging with bioscientific developments especially in relation to biomedicine. One of the most influential readings of the implications of recent advances in the life sciences is that the late twentieth century is characterized by the "molecularization of life"—the new configurations of ethics and politics that have followed the profound shift of focus from the "unified clinical body" to the "genetic body" visualized, analyzed, and mobilized for modification on the molecular scale.[10] For Nikolas Rose, an old biopolitics of state concern with knowing and improving the national population has been replaced by an ethnopolitics of individual responsibility, informed choice, and active self-management of risk. The state continues to be concerned with "the nation's health" but as the aggregated health of individual citizens and not in terms of the fitness of the "population as an organic whole [in a] struggle between nations" nor in terms of an exclusionary biopolitics of race.[11] New forms of collective identity are emerging through shared genetic conditions or susceptibilities—as in patient advocacy groups—rather than around old models of biological membership in a national family of shared blood and belonging. Terms such as "biological" or "genetic" citizenship highlight new forms of political mobilization around genetic risk and new forms of distributed authority and ethical deliberation and thus highlight different relationships between the individual and the state (at least for the affluent in the West).[12] More broadly, Rose argues, the "idea of 'society' as a single, if heterogeneous, domain with a national culture, a national population, a national destiny, co-extensive with a national territory and the powers of a national government has entered a crisis."[13]

Much of the work that has followed this diagnosis has traced the ways in which new practices, knowledges, and technologies operate through and rework, rather than displace, established imaginaries and categories, including the national population and the national territory. Despite the crisis in the idea of national culture, an older imagination of the nation as a community of shared descent continues to matter in the configuration of collective belonging. And despite the emergence of new forms of biosociality,[14] conventional ideas of shared descent and shared ancestral origins, as the foundation of collective identities, are mobilized and reworked in studies of human genetic variation and genetic genealogy. The national population remains significant in state-led biomedical and public health policies and is evoked as the category of collective interest in the geopolitics of biosecurity.[15] National biobanks and national biomedical research projects, for example, are often framed in terms of collective benefit but raise questions about difference, identity, and inclusion, including racialized ideas of "genetic particularity."[16] The attempt to produce a genetic, genealogical, and medical record database for all Icelanders is the paradigmatic case.[17] However, most national genetic projects involve constructing a representative sample rather than a total archive. Thus decisions about how to construct a data set from a sample of all the people that live in a state raise the question of how the national population is defined both through formal citizenship and through cultural models of belonging. Techniques of genetic identification and categorization in human genome projects are, in turn, being taken up by the state to order and delimit the national population in forensic genetic databases and in family unification immigration cases. The state does not explicitly define its national population in genetic terms, but genetic technologies and knowledges can be used to produce categories and boundaries of belonging that are inflected by old and new configurations of an imagined national community. The crisis of the idea of "national culture" thus does not mean the irrelevance of the idea of the nation to new genomic practices and knowledges but that they need to be made sense of in relation to, and as enmeshed within, the particular ways in which ideas of nationhood and multiculture are configured and contested in different national contexts.[18]

The increasingly common idea that human population genetics can contribute to understandings of collective national identity is shaped by, and significant in terms of, the particular ways identity, belonging, and difference have historically been configured and continue to be refigured in the United Kingdom. The *British, More or Less* radio documentary's reference to "lines of difference between the four nations" and question of what genetic accounts of ancient lineages "might tell us about ancient Britons and how this is reflected in the multi-cultural British Isles of the 21st century" points to the two broad conventional strands of the politics of belonging, difference, and commonality within the United Kingdom.

First, one relates to the history of British state formation and the politics of national identity within the United Kingdom in terms of the national identities encompassed within or defined against Britishness. Questions of national identity in the United Kingdom involve the long-standing issue of the complex historical relationships and asymmetries of power between English, Welsh, Scottish, and Irish categories of identity, the contested and shifting status of Britishness as an overarching identity in relation to Welsh and Scottish national identities and separatist aspirations, the complexities of Irishness or Britishness in Northern Ireland, and ideas of a late twentieth and early twenty-first-century crisis of Englishness.[19] The nature of this crisis—which is argued to involve its problematic associations with racist English nationalism and British imperialism and reactions to the robust assertions of identity in the devolved regions of Wales and Scotland (Northern Ireland is a more complex case)—is itself complicated by the class-based demonization of white working-class Englishness.[20]

Second, the reference to the "multicultural" in the *British, More or Less* documentary evokes long-standing and continuing debates about ethnic diversity and immigration, including the significant ways in which immigrant groups have critically addressed and appropriated the category British and challenged assimilationist models of belonging.[21] The term "multiculturalism" in this context stands for a range of positions and perspectives, which include the embeddedness of ideas of cultural pluralism in British public culture, that have resulted from a history of critical engagements with ideas of cultural purity and racialized models of belonging and the continued legacy of New Labour discourses of cultural diversity. The term is also the target of more recent criticisms of multiculturalism as a policy of ethnic segregation (criticisms that preceded but intensified following the London bombings of July 2005). Multicultural discourses of respect for difference coexist with the rise of Islamophobia and anti-immigration attitudes over the last decade.[22]

These two strands of identity and differentiation in the United Kingdom are deeply entangled, politically and culturally. Ideas of internal difference and commonality prior to twentieth- and early twenty-first-century immigration shape perspectives on contemporary ethnicity and national identity in the United Kingdom. In turn, contemporary discourses of diversity and complex migration histories that reflect recent patterns of immigration are sometimes extended back into the distant past. But as I will explore here, different temporalities of indigeneity and immigration are central to how ideas of identity and belonging are figured in popular culture, political discourse, and in studies of human genetic variation in Britain and their commercial enterprises and media features. How are national genetic projects constituted through and contributing to competing understandings of collective identity and difference in a context not only in which the idea of a genetically defined nation-state is widely viewed as politically suspect but also in which genetic knowledge is increasingly turned to as a means to address collective identities via descent?

A "Family Tree of the UK"

The full text of the Wellcome Trust feature on the People of the British Isles study explains that the project is concerned with studying regional genetic variation in relation to historical accounts of the premodern settlement of Britain and with aiding biomedical studies of the genetic contributors to disease. Human genetic variation is figured through the language of relatedness:

> What does being British mean to a scientist? How does someone from Kent differ from a native of the Hebrides? People of the British Isles is an ambitious project aiming to catalogue the genetic basis of the entire United Kingdom.
>
> By doing so, Sir Walter Bodmer and his team will amass information enabling them to mine the UK's genetic heritage, following lineages back through time.
>
> But the genetic information gathered provides much more than just a detailed family tree of the UK. To researchers hunting for DNA changes, or variants, responsible for diseases, this information provides researchers with an essential genetic backdrop for comparison, allowing them to see which differences are simply due to history and geography.[23]

In publicity for the project, the value of this "genetic map of the British Isles" is presented both in terms of its biomedical usefulness and in terms of how it will reveal the genetic legacy and reconstruct the demographic impact of "successive waves of colonisers—Celts, Romans, Angles, Saxons, Jutes, Vikings, and Normans—in various parts of Britain."[24] The aim is to produce an account of regional genetic variation—a geographical and genetic "family tree"—that can be considered in relation to historical accounts of settlement and that will enable other biomedical researchers to see beyond "differences due to history and geography" in their search for genetic variants linked to common complex diseases. In this strand of the project, the mapping of regionally distinctive patterns of genetic variation is a means to confirm, revise, or refine historical accounts of the premodern settlement in Britain and Northern Ireland. However, these accounts of regional genetic variation are also being produced to help biomedical research projects deal with the complicating factor of what is commonly described as "population substructure"—that is, patterns of genetic similarity within a sample population that are interpreted in terms of shared descent from particular geographical regions at different scales and in terms of shared ethnic origins. In case-control studies in biomedical genomics, the genetics of a group of people with a disease are compared with the genetics of a group without the disease to identify possible distinctive genetic variations, or markers, that are more common among the disease group. However, genetic variations due to different ethnic or geographical origins can be mistaken for variations associated with the disease. The effort is often to find ways to avoid genetic similarity due to shared geographical ancestry among donors of genetic material thereby complicating attempts to find links between parts of the genome and common complex diseases in genome-wide association studies, often using the work of human population geneticists to selectively sample in constructing the "control" database or to devise analytical procedures to avoid this problem.[25] The project was funded by the Wellcome Trust to contribute to its large Case-Control Consortium project by producing a database of regional genetic variation in the United Kingdom so that comparisons between disease and nondisease groups can be made among those who share that regional genetic profile and therefore preventing genetic differences due to "geography" from being mistaken for those that might be linked to disease.[26] The dual aim is to explore geographies of genetic variation and to provide ways of seeing beyond these "differences."

Though the biomedical value of the project is often stressed, the public presentation of the project concentrates on the cultural and historical value of its mapping of regionally distinctive patterns of genetic variation as a means to confirm, revise, or refine historical accounts of the premodern settlement of Britain and Northern Ireland. This focus is not unique to the project. Since the late 1990s, studies of human genetic variation in

Britain and between Britain, Ireland, and continental Europe have sought to explore the history of early settlement in Britain and Ireland in relation to the broader pattern of prehistoric migration to and within Europe. Some work confirms the largely accepted east-to-west patterns of the prehistoric settlement of Europe; some has pursued theories of significant migrant routes from the Iberian Peninsula; other studies address genetic evidence of particular early medieval Anglo-Saxon or Viking settlement sometimes with a specific regional focus; others map and often name patterns of mtDNA and Y-chromosome haplogroup variation within Britain and Ireland.[27] Often this work is interpreted and presented in terms of popular and politically potent themes of collective origins—that is, identity within Britain and between Britain and Ireland—as in popular accounts such as geneticist Bryan Sykes's *Blood of the Isles: Exploring the Genetic Roots of Our Tribal History*, Stephen Oppenheimer's *The Origins of the British: A Genetic Detective Story*, the book and radio documentary *The Scots: A Genetic Journey* and incorporated into popular accounts of British early history based on archaeological and historical sources such as David Miles's *The Tribes of Britain: Who Are We? And Where Do We Come From?*[28]

The functional nomenclature of human population genetics is worked over imaginatively to make accounts of genetic variation also accounts of cultural variation.[29] Both Sykes and Oppenheimer name mtDNA and Y-chromosome haplogroups in terms of culturally resonant clan names such as, in the case of Sykes, giving the personal name Oisin (from Celtic mythology) to the R1b haplogroup found in high concentration, but not exclusively, in Ireland. Studies of the human population genetics of Britain commonly make use of historical narratives of ancient settlement in the formulation and interpretation of research projects and are increasingly being undertaken in cross-disciplinary genetic and historical projects and disseminated in popular forms. The Viking DNA Project studying evidence of Viking settlement in the Wirral Peninsula and in West Lancashire in northwest England is one notable example, involving collaboration between geneticists, historians, and a regional heritage enthusiast, and published in a report for nonexpert audiences as well as a specialist academic paper.[30]

This research is clearly located within the international field of human population genetics in terms of technologies of investigation, nomenclature, and interpretation. But there is also a distinctive flavor to some of this work not just in terms of its local objects of study but also in terms of its relationship to traditions of historical practice in Britain and, more specifically, to an English and especially East Midland tradition of local history and place-name studies. The Department of English Local History at the University of Leicester, founded in 1948, was at the heart of efforts to challenge the denigration of local over national studies as academic history professionalized over the nineteenth century and to provide a forum for engaging with, guiding, and fostering the growth of popular local history since the 1960s.[31] The practice of using geographical patterns of place-names as historical sources for reconstructing early settlement patterns, which had been previously associated with antiquarian studies, also has an East Midland home in the University of Nottingham. The use of place-name and surname expertise in the development of Y-chromosome surname studies in the Viking DNA Project reflects the work of geneticists Mark Jobling and Turi King in the University of Leicester whose Y-chromosome surname studies draw together the tradition of English local history at the University of Leicester and the place-name studies tradition of the Institute for Name-Studies in the nearby University of Nottingham. The genetic research being undertaken by Jobling, King, and others brings together high science of molecular genetics, the scholarly and popular empiricism of place-name studies (often linked to local and regional history), and the genealogical tradition of single-surname studies in this East Midlands nexus of scholarly traditions and new scientific practices.

Y-chromosome surname studies developed and applied by Jobling, King, and Bryan Sykes in the United Kingdom and Daniel Bradley in Ireland and now being applied in popular and often transnational genealogical projects make use of the ways in which the common, but by no means universal, pattern of surnames inherited patrilineally from father to children, and more specifically to sons, mirrors the pattern of sons inheriting their father's Y chromosome.[32] This means that surnames can stand as proxies for particular ancestral groups and thus be used to structure research projects in terms of sampling and that patterns of genetic variation within or between men sharing historically linked surnames or an individual surname can be explored. As the 2001 BBC Radio Four documentary series *Surnames, Genes and Genealogy* explained, Y-chromosome surname studies can be used in traditional genealogical projects but are especially appealing to those interested in single surname studies, a practice in which genealogical connections between individuals (most often men) sharing a surname are traditionally pursued and now genetically tested.[33] The first research paper to emerge from the People of the British Isles project presents its results in terms of a regional pattern of diversity discerned from a Y chromosome and a surname-based analysis of its data.[34] Old traditions of popular and scholarly history and historical geography and new geographical information systems are being brought together in Y-chromosome surname studies.[35]

The geographical particularity of this strand of human population genetics in Britain—a geographical particularity in terms of its British focus, practice, and framing—is exemplified by a project building on the work of Jobling and King in the University of Leicester. A large, multidisciplinary, Leverhulme Trust–funded, five-year project began in 2011, based primarily at the University of Leicester but also involving the Institute for Name-Studies at the University of Nottingham, titled "The Impact of Diasporas on the Making of Britain: Evidence, Memories, Inventions."[36] This has itself evolved from a collaborative research initiative between staff in the departments of genetics, archaeology and ancient history, historical studies, and English at the University of Leicester titled "Roots of the British, 1000 BC–AD 1000: Histories, Genetics and the Peopling of Britain," focusing on "the fundamental population history of Britain and the roots of the identities of the historical nations of the island (the Welsh, Scots and English)."[37] The aim of the subsequent project is to explore the "impact of ancient diasporas on the cultural and population history of Britain and how these events have shaped identities in the British Isles both in the past and in the present" through interdisciplinary work that will "create a fuller picture of the complex origins of the British people." One of the two genetic projects within the larger project continues the work of King in focusing on surnames and the Y chromosome in relation to the "Viking genetic legacy and its impact in different regions in Britain."

Though framed by the novel power of new technologies brought into new cross-disciplinary encounters with traditional historical research, these studies are also part of a longer tradition of tracing the characteristics, differences, and affinities of people—as races, cultures, or national types—within and across national borders in Europe that in the late nineteenth century preoccupied those devoted to the new science of race. The construction of distinctions between European and non-European people is the most well-known aspect of racial science. Yet, as Robert

Young points out, "much of the research on race, certainly from the 1840s onwards, was devoted to analyses of European ethnicity."[38] The new science of race being developed in zoology, anthropology, and comparative anatomy in the late nineteenth century took up the long-standing concern with race and nationality in history and philology since the late eighteenth century and turned to the human body as a source of evidence for debates about national origins and cultural identity. Ideas of culture, race, blood, lineage, stock, pedigree, and breeding—human and animal—overlapped in the making of ideas of similarity and commonality, difference and distinctions between and within European countries.[39]

Rather than being understood as the enlightened corrective to these earlier studies, as they sometimes tend to be, contemporary scientific interests in delineating patterns of genetic variation and interpreting them through accounts of the migration movements of the past are located within this tradition of interest in difference within Europe. Research on human genetic variation in Britain that is presented in terms of a national survey, like the People of the British Isles project or geneticist Brian Sykes's "Genetic Atlas of the UK," returns to the interest in embodied difference as evidence for differentiated ancestry and origins that fostered late nineteenth-century efforts to undertake an ethnographic survey of the British Isles including a focus on folklore, archaeology, and anthropometric measurements. Interests in tracing the successive invasions of different races in Britain continued as a strand of geography and in archaeology, but by the 1930s, ideas of culture replaced the increasingly politically suspect idea of race.[40] But research on variation in Britain continued within physical anthropology and in the genetic studies of the late 1960s and 1970s that preceded the development of contemporary molecular genetics.[41]

The reference to a "family tree of the UK" also evokes the wave of interest in personal family history, which is itself entangled with ideas of collective ancestry and categories of identity. Popular fascination with personal and celebrity genealogy, as evident in the success of programs such as the BBC series *Who Do You Think You Are?*, is paralleled by media interest in featuring new genetic technologies to locate the "ancestral homelands" of Black British people, as in the documentary *Motherland: A Genetic Journey*; to test the "truth" of people's national identities—or more specifically, their Englishness—as in the *100% English* documentary; or to explore the early settlement history of Britain in documentaries such as *Blood of the Vikings*.[42] The People of the British Isles project has similarly located itself within the popular science of collective and personal genetic narratives of origins and ancestry through the Channel 4 television series *Face of Britain*, first screened in April 2007, and the associated book *Face of Britain: How Our Genes Reveal the History of Britain*, which featured the project's pilot research.[43] The project's title, though inaccurate in terms of its actual focus on the United Kingdom, is undoubtedly chosen for its public appeal and in the spirit of Walter Bodmer's long-standing interest in promoting the public understanding of science.[44] This informs a publicity strategy that describes the degree of mixedness of the people of the British Isles as the project's focus of investigation.

A "Mixed Up" People

While the project's biomedical value lies in its potential to help gene–disease studies overcome the "noise" of regional genetic variation, it is this regional genetic variation that is central to the project's aim to uncover the "genetic heritage of our present day UK population." Given this focus on regional variation, the idea of "genetic heritage" does not imply genetic homogeneity or a singular national genome. While one media report on the project suggested in its headline that "scientists go in search of the true Brit," its aim is not to produce a collective national genetic profile or somehow identify genetic markers for Britishness[45]—nor is it to test for or establish genetic distinctions between the Scottish, Welsh, (Northern) Irish, and English. Instead, it is to construct and interpret a map of regional genetic variation that is the product of specific patterns of premodern settlement "starting with the Romans, continuing through the Anglo-Saxons, Vikings and ending with the Normans." This focus on the geographies of genetic variation within the United Kingdom is framed by an idea of mixedness. As the project's first newsletter stated under the subheading "Mixed Up Populations," "one of the exciting challenges we have is to investigate how mixed up the people of the British Isles really are."[46] Similarly, Robert McKie begins his account of recent genetic studies of the British Isles in the *Face of Britain* with the comment, "We are, after all, a complex, baffling, disparate bunch of individuals, a mongrel people . . . in cultural terms, we are a very odd mixture."[47] There are echoes of other discourses of mixedness here, old and new.

The project's emphasis on regional genetic diversity echoes the ways in which the new science of race in the late nineteenth century challenged ideas of the English as pure Saxons. From the late seventeenth century onward, Englishness had been defined not as a "mix of Celtics, Vikings, Angles, Saxons, Jutes and others" but in terms of an "ideology of Saxonist purity" coupled with Protestantism and defined in opposition to Catholic France and later Catholic and Celtic Ireland.[48] Robert Young argues that despite the ways in which the racial science of the late nineteenth century helped legitimate discourses of race (themselves a mix of ideas of culture, history, religion, and, through new anthropometric techniques, the body), the idea of "a singular racial identity for the English, derived loosely from history and philology" was "disproved by the emergence of 'proper' racial science which argued that the English were irreducibly mixed."[49] By the late nineteenth century, Britain as a whole was represented in science and in popular accounts in terms of "regional variations within a general account of racial heterogeneity."[50] While very different in terms of its measures of variation (genetic rather than morphological) from these earlier maps of "the races of Britain," the project's discourse of mixedness has well-established precedents in the science of the late nineteenth and early twentieth century.[51]

The project's language of diversity and mixedness are, at the same time, very much of the moment, bound up and reflecting the wider politics of national identity and belonging in the United Kingdom. At the time that the launch of the project was being publicized through ideas of diversity, Sykes's and Oppenheimer's popular accounts of the prehistoric and premodern settlement of Britain and Ireland were published.[52] One argument that ran through these books was that after the Neolithic period, the arrival of new groups of settlers had little effect on the genetic composition of Britain. Most people in Britain, it was argued, descend from very early inhabitants, not the groups who came after. This was widely reported in terms of the continuity and persistence of an ancient and native gene pool: as the *Sunday Times* headline put it, "British genes are invasion proof."[53] This account of genetically identified "native Britons" featured heavily in the far right British National Party's online magazine *Identity* to support their model of a natural and now scientifically proven white indigeneity under threat from immigration.[54] Arthur Kemp, former British National Party foreign affairs spokesperson and arch anti-immigrationist, has used this research as the basis for an argument for the existence and rights of indigenous Britons under the UN Declaration of the Rights of Indigenous People. For Kemp, "The genetic evidence fully supports the historical record and proves the liberal allegation that Britain is a 'nation of immigrants' to be a disgraceful lie . . . Mass immigration is subjecting the British people to the loss of their integrity as distinct peoples . . . The rights of indigenous people not to be subjected to forced assimilation and the destruction of their culture, heritage and territory, applies therefore equally to the native people of the British Isles as it does to any other people or nation on earth."[55] Though this case stands out for the explicitness of its racist appropriation of indigeneity as a political claim, it indicates the political potency of genetic accounts of the ancient and subsequent settlement of Britain.

The People of the British Isles project's focus on regional diversity is not incompatible with the theory of the dominance of "ancient" genes in Britain. For Bodmer, "mixture" is relative—"a matter of degree"—and Britain is "actually relatively more homogenous than many other countries."[56] Yet the project's emphasis on "mixed up populations" makes it less easily incorporated into far right English nationalist discourses of a natural white indigeneity. Instead, its focus on regional geographies of genetic variation resonates with accounts of Britishness that challenge an idea of a primordial people and homogenous collective identity by pointing to the waves of migration that have long shaped the country and to the regional diversities that fracture ideas of a single national culture. The project's use of the term "mixed up" and McKie's "mongrel people" echo wider appropriations of the term "mongrel" in descriptions of the United Kingdom as a "mongrel nation" in political discourse and public culture to undermine ideas of purity. These range from journalist and author Yasmin Alibhai-Brown's framing of interracial experiences and identities in Britain to former prime minister Gordon Brown's celebration of British multiculturalism and include the Discovery Channel's 2003 documentary series of the same name featuring Eddie Izzard discrediting myths of pure Englishness.[57] This also aligns it with the ways other studies of genetic variation in Britain are presented as resources that enrich and complicate understandings of British history and the meaning of Britishness itself.

In January 2007, it was widely reported that scientists had discovered that a rare form of the Y chromosome that had hitherto only been found in men in West Africa was shared by a group of men in Yorkshire. This finding had emerged within the project—Surnames, Genes and the History of Britain: Surnames and Genetic Structure: A Molecular Analysis Using Y-Chromosomal DNA Polymorphisms—undertaken by Turi

King, then a graduate student working under the leadership of Mark Jobling.[58] The project applied the recent use of surnames as indicators of shared patrilineal descent among men to explore the relationship between Y-chromosome types and traditional British surnames. It sought to consider the results in terms of what influences affect the expected correlation between the patrilineal inheritance of both and in terms of the wider history of Britain. The research paper featuring the discovery of an "Africa-specific" Y chromosome among the men sampled in the study (by King, Jobling, and colleagues) and its newspaper report presented it in terms of its contribution to a progressive vision of diversity, understandings of the long historical presence of Black Africans in Britain, and the complexities of migration in the past and in terms of the wider genetic challenge to ideas of race. In contrast to the interpretation of accounts of genetic continuity in Britain that had recently been published, it was reported that the research showed that "Britain's multiracial society dates back hundreds of years earlier than most people realise."[59] The research was also featured in a broader newspaper account of how new genetic technologies are revealing the many cases of white British people with slave ancestors as well as the white patrilineal ancestries of many black British people. The newspaper report includes the comment by geneticist Mark Thomas that "you need go back only ten generations (250 years) to find a 'non-English' ancestor for everyone in England."[60] Mark Jobling's sense of the significance of the result is similarly couched in terms of its meaning for understandings of Britishness as well as race: "'This study shows that what it means to be British is complicated and always has been,' Professor Jobling said. 'Human migration history is clearly very complex, particularly for an island nation such as ours, and this study further debunks the idea that there are simple and distinct populations or "races" . . . This chromosome has nothing to do with how you look or with who you are, beyond making you male. But it is a very reliable marker of African ancestry.'"[61] The research paper introduced the findings by posing the question of whether the long history of African presence in Britain has "left a genetic trace among people regarded as 'indigenous' British?"[62] The circumspect use of quotation marks around "indigenous" reflects Jobling's concerns about the political implications of studies of human genetic variation being interpreted in terms of either leading to a divisive and exclusionary politics of national belonging or leading to the geneticization of ethnicity and race.[63]

The research by Turi King and colleagues that featured here is being extended in the "Impact of Diasporas on the Making of Britain: Evidence, Memories, Inventions" project.[64] While the earlier University of Leicester Roots of the British project was framed by the idea of indigeneity, despite its focus on ancient migrations, the subsequent project takes up the academic and popular discourse of diasporas. However, the diasporas to be explored in this instance are not those modern and recent migrations that have shaped British "super diversity" and characterize contemporary global mobility. They are "ancient diasporas."[65] The aim is to explore the "impact of ancient diasporas on the cultural and population history of Britain and how these events have shaped identities in the British Isles both in the past and in the present" through interdisciplinary work that will "create a fuller picture of the complex origins of the British people." The focus is on the cultural, linguistic, and population history of Britain, and by including social psychological research on ideas of indigenism and immigration in popular historical discourses in relation to regional and national belonging in Britain, it also seeks to examine "the influence of ancient diasporas—remembered or suppressed, perhaps exaggerated or even invented—on the construction of British identities, past and present."[66] Its framing in terms of diasporas, immigration, and "complex origins" signals the project's location within the broader historical and cultural emphasis on the making of Britain through migration that resonates with wider discourses of complexity and diversity and so riles those opposed to this version of Britishness. Thus, as Mark Jobling, one of the project investigators, reports, when the project was announced to the public, it was denounced in a British National Party website commentary as "another government-funded (sic) justification for immigration which will say there is no such thing as indigenous British."[67]

More popular versions of the use of new genetic techniques to challenge ideas of national purity include the Channel 4 television documentary *100% English* (2006), which analyzed the genetic material of eight white English people. Its premise was set out in the opening narration:

Take eight people. All of them born in England. All of them white. All of them convinced they are 100% English. Convince them to provide a sample of their DNA. Then submit it to a series of state of the art DNA tests; and some of them will be in for a shock when they discover just how English they really are. "I was born in

England. I was born English, my parents were English, my grand-parents were English and their parents were English and it goes back and back, so I am English through and through," says comedian Danny Blue. A prime-minister's daughter, a peer of the realm, a tabloid journalist, a lawyer, a country lady, a trainee soldier, a stand-up comic and a woman who works in the fishing industry: all of them are convinced they come from solid Anglo-Saxon stock. With the help of cutting edge DNA analysis, 100% English reveals the secrets of their hidden origins which cover most of the globe.[68]

The eight included former conservative member of Parliament Norman Tebbit, journalist Garry Bushell, comedian Danny Blue, and Carol Thatcher, daughter of Margaret Thatcher. They also included noncelebrity participants: Carol Manly, described as a "country lady" in Kent; Jane Philips, an enthusiast for an Anglo-Saxon English heritage; Nicola Hale, from Grimsby's fishing industry; and eighteen-year-old army recruit Damen Barks in Leicestershire—all of whom were invited to reflect on what defines Englishness and were then told the results of the analysis of their genetic material in terms of the percentage components of different ancestries. The aim was to find participants who would articulate versions of Englishness based on ideas of pure English ancestry and to achieve a dramatic effect by using new genetic tests to suggest that their own genetic material indicates ancestral links to places beyond England. Norman Tebbit, for example, is described as "an arch opponent of multiculturalism." Participants were pressed on the implications of their definitions of Englishness for the politics of race and belonging in Britain and varied in their responses. Not all relied on or expressed a genealogical model of Englishness, but it was Danny Blue's criteria of Englishness as requiring twelve generations of family born and bred in England or Nicola Hale's criteria of a thousand years of pure English ancestry that was the genealogical model to be genetically tested.

The potency of this combination of personal accounts of genealogically rooted Englishness and scientific tests in a context of public debate about nationality was clear to the program makers. The documentary clearly sought to make compelling television by finding those who would articulate racist or xenophobic versions of exclusive white Englishness and debunk them through science for the sake of a progressive message about the genetic mixedness even of those "convinced they are 100% English."

This is clear in the way its plot summary was described: "With issues of ethnic and national identity foremost in Government policy and public thinking, *100% English* challenges the core beliefs of those who believe they are archetypal Englishmen and women with fascinating results."[69] None were found to be 100 percent "Northern European." Instead, they were invited to respond to the company scientist's interpretation of their results as likely evidence of Romany, Middle Eastern, Turkish, Russian, Ukrainian, or Mongolian ancestry. In contrast to more subtle efforts to progressively rework rather than simply critically deride Englishness, the documentary was premised on a liberal metropolitan assumption that identification with Englishness is necessarily exclusive, racist, and reactionary. Nevertheless, it clearly sought to suggest that ideas of national purity and pure descent can be genetically disproven. The final two reactions of the participants convey the message of the documentary as a whole. Damen Barks reflects on the antiracist implications of discovering mixed ancestry. For Danny Blue, his result "throws" his genealogical model of Englishness "out the window." The emphasis on mixedness in these accounts counters the idea of a pure and bounded national family—a genetic community of descent—to be protected from racial or cultural corruption. But the idea of mixedness needs further scrutiny.

A Mix of Distinctive Lineages

The project's maps of regional genetic variation do not correspond to internal national boundaries. The United Kingdom is figured neither as a homogenous genetic category nor as a collective of Scottish, Welsh, and English (and in a complex sense, Northern Irish) communities of descent. However, its regional geography of variation is based on naming patterns of genetic variation in people today in terms of old categories of ancient ancestry, such as Viking, Anglo-Saxon, or Celtic. This is a common practice within human population genetics. The People of the British Isles project is based on a considerable body of work by Bodmer and others studying genetic variation within Europe through sampling contemporary people in order to trace the nature and impact of patterns of settlement hitherto known only through historical narratives and archaeological evidence. The study of evidence of Viking settlement in patterns of genetic variation in the Scottish island of Orkney, featured in the *Face of Britain* book and documentary, exemplifies this practice. The project builds on

Bodmer's earlier genetic studies of the island population and subsequent work that focused on patterns of Y-chromosome variation and analyzed the occurrence of forms that were identified as indicative of Norse Viking ancestry in Orkney.[70] A Norse Viking Y chromosome is established by studying Y-chromosome variation in men in Norway who are presumed to have the same Y chromosome as their Viking ancestors and by identifying the form (or markers) most indicative of Viking descent. The presence of this form in men in Britain is then taken to be indicative of their Viking ancestry and Viking settlement. As Deborah Bolnick has argued, this relies on assuming genetic continuity over time so that, as in the case of Viking descent, the pattern of genetic variation in contemporary Norway is assumed to be largely the same as it was more than one thousand years ago in the Viking era, and any recent "incursions" are avoided by sampling only "native" Norwegians. Accounts of Viking markers give the impression that a named group bears unique markers rather than have them at high frequencies. "Viking" markers are not only found in groups assumed to descend from Vikings—nor would all Viking people in the past have had those "Viking" markers.[71]

The preliminary work by Bodmer and his researchers used the same rationale but studied an expanded range of markers in the genetic material of a sample of contemporary people on the island and similarly suggested a "picture of Vikings coming over and taking local women for their wives and mothers of their children" (an account whose models of sex, violence, and mobility I turn to in the next chapter).[72] The conclusion that the contemporary pattern of genetic variation on the island indicates that Viking men not only raided the island but also killed the local men and settled is an example of the sort of historical narrative that is being genetically explored in the People of the British Isles project. The construction of ideas of Viking ancestry that can be genetically ascertained may not seem particularly politically consequential in terms of understandings of collective identity and difference. But this is the same technique of associating a pattern of markers or a frequency of genetic variation for a named group that is used to genetically describe a wide range of historical and contemporary ethnic groups. It underpins commercially available tests for named ancestries such as Native American or specific tribal or ethnic ancestries in Africa. Bodmer is adamant that ancient categories that are genetically identified should not be confused with contemporary cultural or ethnic categories.[73] However, the language of "Celtic" or "Anglo-Saxon" genes suggests that cultural or ethnic groups are genetically distinctive in ways that obscure how geographies of genetic variation grade across space rather than correspond to bounded groups, and discounts the complex mobilities that complicate any assumption of the purity of groups in the past and in the present.

The project's emphasis on regional genetic diversity within Britain is, therefore, based on analytical and descriptive practices that suggest congruence between genetic and ethnic distinctiveness. Britain is figured as regionally and genetically diverse but through the idea of genetically identifiable "ancestries" that correspond to ancient settler groups such as the Celts, Anglo-Saxons, or Vikings. For geneticist Bryan Sykes's genetic ancestry tracing company, Oxford Ancestors, this is extended to suggest that an individual man "whose paternal roots are in Britain or Ireland" can discover via Y-chromosome analysis whether his ancestors were Celtic, Saxon, or Viking. Customers receive a "Tribes of Britain" certificate and "information about your ancient tribal ancestors and insights into their life and times."[74] In his account of the People of the British Isles project in the *Face of Britain* book, Robert McKie is, in contrast, careful to dissociate these categories from their popular associations while sensitive to their meaning for people. The "Celts," for example, is simply the term used to describe the inhabitants of the islands before Roman and Anglo-Saxon presence rather than refer to a heavily and romantically mythologized ancient people. He is also careful to highlight that having a "Norse Y-chromosome does not mean, on its own, that a person has a distinctive Viking make-up."[75] However, the idea that is it possible to genetically characterize these ancestries remains unproblematized.

Bodmer's survey of English counties in terms of the ratios of their "Celtic genes against their Anglo-Saxon genes"[76] is used to explore the probability of Anglo-Saxon and Celtic ancestry for some participants in the *Face of Britain* documentary. This relies on assuming from historical accounts of settlement that "Cornwall, Devon and Wales are the most Celtic parts of southern Britain and that East Anglia and Lincolnshire are the most Anglo-Saxon" and on studying the pattern of variation of a range of genetic markers in these regions and describing them as Celtic and Anglo-Saxon. These were then used in county-based genetic surveys to work out ratios of Anglo-Saxon and Celtic ancestry as indicators of historical patterns of settlement. In the *Face of Britain* documentary, these ancient regional ancestries were also linked to regional facial types in ways that evoked early twentieth-century anthropometry, but this was the initiative of the television producers rather than a reflection of the project. For Bodmer, the attempt to produce an "average" regional facial type was "nonsense" and was focused on at the expense of scientific depth.[77] The idea of regional facial types did, however, dominate the documentary. As Anne-Marie Fortier has argued in her incisive discussion of the series, the average regional facial types are shown to be technical fabrications, but at the same time, they naturalize the idea of faces as products of regional genetic variations and distinctive ancient ancestries: "This twenty-first century version of physiognomy is used in *Face of Britain* to mediate between the micro-scale of molecular genetics, and the macro-scale of the (pre)historical genealogy and changing demographics of the 'People of the British Isles.'"[78] Despite Bodmer's comments about the documentary, the project has since been extended in new work to "identify genes involved in facial features" by photographing those who had previously donated blood samples and then considering "how they vary throughout the UK."[79] This suggests a more systematic return to old ideas of regional types, but it is likely to be a complicated move rather than a simple revival of anthropometry.

The documentary's familiar gambit of individual tests and results was closer to the project, though participants in the broader study do not receive individual results. In the documentary, selected participants who had donated blood samples were invited to reflect on their sense of identity and offered an analysis of their genetic material that would describe their likely descent from Celtic or Anglo-Saxon people. This is not through the identification of mtDNA or Y-chromosome lineages alone, as in many commercial genetic ancestry tests, but through comparing an individual's markers with those frequencies identified as Celtic or Anglo-Saxon. The results were presented in terms of probabilities of being of Anglo-Saxon ancestry over being of Celtic ancestry. These degrees of probability suggest that the ancestral mixedness of individual genomes is the norm. It suggests that people in different regions differ in terms of having more or less probability of having Celtic or Anglo Saxon ancestry. Thus while the project echoes late nineteenth- and early twentieth-century ideas of the mixedness of Britain, mixedness is imagined in terms of the mixed within any one person rather than the idea of a population of permanent types—"a composite of the descendants of the country's ancient invaders, still individually visible and classifiable."[80]

Yet the varying probabilities suggest that some are closer to a true type than others and thus that it is possible to talk of genetically recognizable Anglo-Saxon or Celtic ancestry. So while people are not defined simply in terms of degrees of purity of one ancestry or another, the ancestral categories become geneticized. The implication is that while Britishness or Englishness is not a genetically identifiable category in the present, these ancestries and ancestral groups are genetically identifiable. The idea of the genetic distinctiveness of cultural, national, or ethnic groups is thus disrupted at one level and reinforced at another. Bodmer's earlier television documentary featuring his genetic research in Orkney, *Sir Walter's Journey*, similarly both evoked the idea of genetically defined ancestries and suggested the power of science to undermine them.[81]

This is also a feature of the *100% English* documentary. The tests that featured in this case are those developed by DNAPrint Genomics (based in Florida) and marketed online by AncestryByDNA, which claim to identify the proportions of an individual's ancestry that derive from different categories of race or geographical origin. They are based on those ancestry-informative markers (AIMs)—genetic markers that take different forms and whose forms have been identified as having substantial differences in frequency across "populations" defined in terms of continental distinctions (such as European, Asian, African, and Native American or subcontinental groups such as northern European or southern European). An individual's AIMs are analyzed, and these frequencies are used to produce an estimate of the percentage contribution of different ancestral origins to their genetic profile.[82] As I discussed in chapter 2, these results are deeply dependent on decisions about sampling regions, populations, donors, and the number of samples that shape the content of the genomic databases as well as the categories used to denote different geographical ancestries.

So though the results in *100% English* suggest that Englishness cannot be genetically defined or that a shared English identity does not necessarily map onto a shared ancestral origin, this depends on describing other ancestries as geographically and genetically bounded. Englishness is not a genetic category, we are encouraged to realize, but other ancestries are presented as if they correspond to genetically and geographically bounded groups—sub-Saharan African, Native American, northern European, or East Asian or at other scales of analysis, northern European, Middle Eastern, South Asian, or southeast European. One participant is told his genetic profile would be typical of someone who lives in Russia or Ukraine. But the corollary of this would be to describe a genetic profile as typical of someone who lives in England. Because the mechanisms of producing these genome geographies entail screening out the "mixed" or "nonnative," this would effectively be those defined as white and "indigenous." Englishness, or any other ethnic identity, is thus not simply undermined as a genetic category nor refigured as a community of mixed descent through these tests.

Their problematic nature is exposed in one participant's comments early in the documentary. At first, Danny Blue stands for an exclusive model of Englishness in arguing that even second-generation children born in Britain but of Caribbean ancestry cannot be English. It is an ancestry, he argues, that would, even centuries from now, be revealed by genetic tests. In the logic of genetic ancestry and origins testing, they would certainly be linked to Africa rather than England, thus offering weight to his position even if it is one under attack here via the same science he calls upon. He later changes his mind about his genealogical definition of Englishness in light of his own results, but the problem of producing ideas of genetically defined categories of origin, identity, and belonging remains. The science of genetic ancestry that is used here to undermine his definition of white Englishness could logically also be used to undermine the Englishness of those of Caribbean ancestry.

Similarly, the idea of genetic evidence of an early African presence in Britain relies on describing a Y chromosome as African, which suggests a simple congruence of genes, geography, and old continental races despite Jobling's intentions. For the men involved, the discovery of patrilineal descent probably from a black slave brought to Britain from the mid-sixteenth century produces a personal encounter with the wider histories of race in Britain that are also being explored by other white British families tracing black ancestry. But the surprise of the result—as implied in the paper's title, "Africans in Yorkshire?" and as expressed in one headline, "Genes Reveal West African Heritage of White Brits"—depends on evoking race and ideas of genetic difference between people occupying different places on a conventional racial epidermal schema in order for it to be disrupted in the service of antiracism.[83] The men with the "African" Y chromosome are variously described as "white," "Caucasian," or of "typical European appearance" by the researchers and some reporters. Naming a Y-chromosome type only hitherto found in men in Senegal and Guinea-Bissau as "African" produces an association between genetics and that old racial category "African" that does not reflect Jobling's own awareness of the methodological contingencies and interpretive simplifications that produce this particular "genome geography." These include the significance of the practices of sampling, existing data availability, the use of "African" as a shorthand for the actual locations of the men whose Y chromosomes match those found in the research in Britain, as well as the partiality of this model of ancestry. The public message of complexity, understandably but significantly, also does not convey the complex contingencies and simplifications that produce the idea of an "African" Y chromosome. The study thus "further debunks the idea that there are simple and distinct populations or 'races,'" but at the same time, the idea of an African Y chromosome suggests a more problematic simplification of the geography of human genetic variation. To name a bit of genomic material "African" does not convey the actual complexity of the geography of human genetic variation but instead suggests much neater and more distinctive genetic regions. At the continental scale, this returns us to the idea of continents as natural units of human difference—the old racial homelands. These are the contradictory and ambiguous implications of how genetics, ancestry, and identity are aligned in scientific and popular accounts—even those broadly characterized as espousing an antiracist celebration of multicultural diversity. Geneticists are often aware of these tensions.[84] But there is more to consider about how the practice of human population genetics enacts and reflects the politics of inclusion, difference, and diversity in Britain.

Old and New Diversities

The People of the British Isles project is concerned with the genetic evidence of a series of ancient arrivals rather than native purity. However, the project's strategies of investigation produce an implicit, yet crucial, distinction between different sorts of genetic diversity. This is the effect of the project's strict screening of potential donors. As *The Observer* report of the launch of the project explained,

> [It] is intended to provide a complete overview of the nation's genetic structure, though researchers say only those living in the countryside will be asked to take part. "Urban populations are

already far too mixed up for us to be able to tease out their genetic roots," said the project's leader, Sir Walter Bodmer. "However, in the country there has been much less genetic input from 'outsiders' over the past century. People there will give us a far better picture of ancient populations." To be included in the study, not only will a person have to have lived in one rural locality, but his or her parents and grandparents will also have been residents of that neighbourhood. "A century ago, public transport—mainly trains— had not had a major effect in shaking up the population," said Bodmer. "We want to find the descendants of such people."[85]

Those who donate blood samples to the project must be rural, rooted, and effectively white. This clearly discounts the majority of people whose families have been mobile within the country and all those whose family histories include migration to the country in recent and earlier generations. As Anne-Marie Fortier argues, this is another case of contemporary anxiety about the "vanishing indigene" as bearer of ancient DNA. As she argues, "Viewed as storehouses of the unique genetic history of Britain, sections of the rural population are indigenised against those whose presumably more admixed genetic signatures result from more recent internal and external migrations."[86] But this is not meant to imply an exclusionary model of belonging. Instead, it is a means to explore premodern settlement by investigating the genetic material of those who descend exclusively from these earlier populations. From the perspective of human population genetics, there is nothing problematic in this. Screening populations by selecting donors whose genetic material is thought to be inherited from ancient populations in order to study patterns of genetic variation before recent "mixing and migration" is standard practice. The purity of descent of ideal participants is not intended to imply a pure national community of descent.

Indeed, in this case at least, there is a self-consciousness about the potential implications of this selectivity in relation to wider discourses of cultural diversity in Britain. In his introduction to *Face of Britain*, Bodmer addresses this selectivity directly: "There is one obvious gap in our study, however. We have not taken account of recent waves of immigrants, including myself, a refugee from Nazi Germany. Though many have come, they still represent only a small proportion of the overall British population. In any case, their history relates to their country of origin, not to the

British Isles."[87] Early in the book, McKie similarly forestalls any concern over this selectivity with a celebration of contemporary ethnic diversity:

> I should also make it clear at this point that this book will not be concerned with an issue that is one of the most welcome and invigorating aspects of modern British life: the nation's increasing ethnic mix. When I look at the faces in my children's classroom photographs, I see British faces that clearly show their friends have genetic histories which lie in Africa, the Caribbean, the Indian subcontinent, China and South East Asia. These backgrounds are every bit as important as those outlined in this book but they are also recent and relatively easy to elucidate. Our prime concern in *The Face of Britain* is to show how scientists are teasing out a much more mysterious genetic inheritance that goes back to the beginnings of recorded history and into the depths of our prehistoric past.[88]

There seems to be the making of an idea of white lack or mystery here. Other people's ancestries are read off their visible difference, but whiteness is imbued with hidden but genetically accessible and differentiated "genetic inheritance." Nevertheless, the broad message is that the project's exclusiveness is not aligned with any malign idea of racial, cultural, or genetic purity. This methodological selectivity is based on the scientific meaninglessness of including people with recent immigrant backgrounds in a study of the ancient populations of the United Kingdom. Instead of their scientifically illogical inclusion, Bodmer argues that it would be more appropriate for studies similar to the People of the British Isles project to be conducted in the ancestral homelands of "ethnic minorities" (e.g., in India, China, or Pakistan).

Bodmer's comments reflect what is at stake in producing an account of the genetics of "modern Britons" that is based on only studying the genetics of those descended directly from premodern inhabitants in the context of pervasive public discourses of ethnic diversity and sensitivities about "minority ethnic groups" in Britain. This is a matter for both the way the project is constructed and presented and the practice of gathering blood samples themselves, since being rejected as a potential donor to a project presented as a study of the national population on the basis of ethnicity implies the rejection from this collective category. Different studies adopt different approaches to this. His concerns about these exclusionary effects have led geneticist Mark Jobling to adopt the strategy of accepting anyone who volunteers to donate genetic material as a donor but not including samples from those who have recent immigrant ancestry in the samples to be analyzed: "It would be wrong to turn them away" even if their material has no relevance to studies of genetic variation among those who are effectively viewed as "indigenous" British people.[89]

It is the overt framing of the People of the British Isles as a national survey that intensifies these sensitivities about inclusion and exclusion. The political implications of the project's selective sampling were recognized by those responding to initial funding applications. Reflecting on the project, Jobling, who was involved in early discussions about it, suggested that the failure of a Heritage Lottery Fund bid may have been due to reviewers' concerns that the project was "defining Britishness genetically in some sense."[90] Concerns about the project's approach to ethnic diversity were also raised by the Wellcome Trust. As Bodmer explained, the scientific illogicality of not confining the study to those descended from "the original populations that came to Britain" meant that nothing about "minority populations" was included in the initial funding application to the Wellcome Trust. However, the applicants were encouraged by Wellcome Trust officials to put something in for "political reasons" but told to cut it again by scientific reviewers who recognized its methodological irrelevance.[91]

These tensions between scientific sense and the politics of inclusion also occurred in debates taking place at the time about the inclusion of people from "ethnic minority" backgrounds in UK Biobank. National biobanking projects frequently draw on ideas of a collective national endeavor, heritage, and identity yet vary in the ways ethnic difference is conceptualized and "ethnic minority" groups are included in these projects. Though there have been similar concerns about the scientific usefulness of doing so, UK Biobank has been constructed to reflect the ethnic diversity of Britain as a whole.[92] The national population to be representatively sampled in the UK Biobank is the citizenry of the United Kingdom. Policy and consultation reports focused on the multicultural and thus genetic diversity of Britain in claims about its scientific value and inclusiveness.[93] More generally, those involved in the construction of biomedical genetic databases adopt different strategies of screening or ethnically labeling samples in order to reconcile ideals of ethnic inclusiveness and scientific utility.[94] Most genetic epidemiology studies in the United Kingdom do not include "ethnic minority" samples. Those that do often do not include them in the analysis, since the numbers involved are not statistically significant. Though many researchers are conscious of the tension between these practices and their support for social inclusiveness, and despite some researchers' ambiguities in defining whiteness, Richard Tutton argues that "this has the effect of reinforcing white Caucasians or white Europeans as a homogenous group relative to a collection of smaller, heterogeneous minorities grouped under the heading 'non-white.'"[95]

Unlike other biomedical or population genetics projects, the People of the British Isles project does not use self-assigned ethnic classification to produce a homogenous white population. Instead, it uses geographical ancestry—those four rural and rooted grandparents—to produce a white population whose relative heterogeneity is the focus of investigation. Unlike other projects, it does not strive to achieve a homogenous white database for case-control studies but addresses small but significant variations within the population, since large differences due to more distant geographical origins have already been screened out. White heterogeneity can be studied because other sources of heterogeneity have been avoided. The project's use of surnames in the analysis of the donated material is a means to further differentiate "local" and "nonlocal" ancestries in order to produce a clearer geography of population structure.[96] Mixedness or diversity thus stands for a premodern regional diversity rather than the diverse origins and cultural heritages of contemporary British people. The distinction that it makes is between what are presented as the foundational waves of settlement that shaped the British population—prehistoric arrivals that then become ancient Britons, then Romans, Anglo-Saxons, Vikings, and Normans—and more recent arrivals over the subsequent centuries and especially the last. The People of the British Isles project thus constructs a national population differentiated into "modern Britons" of ancient direct descent living in regionally distinctive patterns of variation, those of "mixed" but ancient descent, and those whose ancestral origins and "genetic heritage" are beyond the country.[97]

This matters in terms of the project's contribution to the ways ideas of difference and commonality and "genetic heritage" are imagined in the United Kingdom. But it also matters in terms of the project's other key claim to its value—that is, its biomedical usefulness. As a commentary on the project's first publication recognized, the project's "sampling choices mean that naïve use of PoBI samples as controls in case-control comparison, where the cases come from multi-ethnic cities, would lead to false positives due the different ascertainments."[98] The medical usefulness of the data is to allow comparisons between the "native" cases and the "native" controls and thus between those who belong to a particular version of the "national population."

Our History and Their History

There is a particular sort of "multicultural genomics" at work in the People of the British Isles project. When Bodmer states in the introduction to the *Face of Britain* book that for ethnic minorities "their history relates to their country of origin, not to the British Isles," he is referring to the history that shaped the patterns of genetic variation in their countries of origin. This is undoubtedly an attempt to acknowledge the contemporary ethnic diversity of Britain that cannot be encompassed in the project and is imbued with the multicultural principles of sensitivity toward the diverse ethnic origins of people in Britain and the validity of expressing these heritages. It is clearly not meant to delimit belonging through ancestry. Yet an ostensibly progressive and inclusive model of awareness of, and respect for, the varied ethnic origins of people within Britain can imply an "our history, their history" model of heritage, culture, and identity. Until recent attacks on multiculturalism, the principles of sensitivity toward the diverse ethnic origins of people in Britain and validity of expressing that heritage were firmly established within British public culture and conceptions of British society as inclusive, tolerant, and diverse, and they have not been simply displaced. However, discourses of respect for the culture and heritage of "ethnic minorities" can imply a model of identity, culture, and heritage based on ancestral inheritance—a heritage and identity defined by descent alone.[99] Thus well-intentioned efforts to foreground the significance of the history, culture, and heritage of British people with immigrant origins can imply that the history and heritage of Britain belongs to a certain portion of the British people of native descent and that other people have their own equally valid but different heritages. A sort of genetic or genealogical culturalism is the result in which the culture of groups is imagined as a biological inheritance that is the natural possession of that group; interests and identifications that blur those categories are anomalies. The idea that other people have their own histories suggests that the ancient and early history of Britain is naturally only of interest to those of native descent—that it is, understandably, a heritage that belongs to them genealogically. Ancient history, archaeology, and ultimately the landscape and land itself are the natural possessions of those whose ancestors were there before. Multicultural ideas of respect for difference, a genealogical model of identity and belonging, and the power of scientific knowledge together imply that the "our" of "our national history" is constituted as those of native descent.

Pushed to logic, this is a genetic model of the nation. It is genetic in the sense of heritage being passed on via biological descent, but it is also being constituted as such through the ways in which the genetic material of people in Britain is being explored through the distinction between genetic roots in Britain and roots elsewhere. The existence of different sorts of genetic ancestry tests for different sorts of people in Britain, between "native" British people and those of Caribbean ancestry as featured in the *Motherland* documentaries, follows the logic of genetic accounts of roots and ultimate belonging that depend on putting different temporal definitions of indigeneity to work. Though the People of the British Isles project, like much work on the human population genetics of Britain, is premised on an ancient history of arrivals that undermine an idea of primordial rootedness, in practice, these studies do not define all people in Britain as ultimately of immigrant origin. Having ancestors here before the late medieval period makes the descendants of ancient arrivals indigenous—a temporality that might have some elasticity to include some later arrivals but definitely not stretching into the twentieth century. Similarly, despite the rhetoric of universal human origins in Africa, human population genetics and their commercial by-products in genetic tests for ancestry are all about differentiated origins. In the British context, white British people are invited to consider themselves in light of research on genetic variation in Britain and explore their "Celtic" or "Viking" ancestry as in the "Tribes of Britain" test. Black British people are invited to use genetic tests to explore their roots in Africa. Counterposed in this way, these models of genetic ancestry and descent construct distinctions between people naturally adhering to different senses of heritage and identity by virtue of descent—a model of "genetic heritage" that effectively produces an exclusive model of national belonging. The national story of the peopling of Britain is one that stops short of the recent century and is a national story that is the natural heritage of "native Britons." Other people have their own stories and heritages that "we" respect. But there is naturally no sense of "them" being interested in or having a sense of ownership of that ancient heritage. This is not the intention of the People of the British Isles project in itself but reflects the entanglements of the science and politics of difference. These ideas of "genetic heritage" have to be understood as inescapably entangled too in the deeply emotive, contested, and politicized question of what sort of history—or, more specifically, national history—should be taught in schools in England.[100] The suggestion that an individual's sense of connection to, interest in, and imaginative shared ownership of the past of a place is naturally a function of his or her genetic and genealogic relation to that place divides up a national past into the portion that really belongs to the "indigenous"—largely the past before the twentieth century—and the recent past, despite efforts to figure the national past as a whole more inclusively in terms of a "mongrel nation" shaped by ancient and modern immigration.

Accounts of genetic variation in the United Kingdom are produced and presented by individuals who are themselves located in social as well as scientific networks and contexts, negotiating personal and wider models of identity and difference. As this case has shown, many of these studies are undertaken by geneticists who espouse antiracism, ideas of cultural plurality, and inclusive models of British society. Yet their rejection of ideas of cultural or genetic purity or oversimplified ideas of national, ethnic, or racial groups as genetic categories is paralleled by the production of other sorts of genetic categories and other sorts of distinctions. The idea that cultural categories such as Britishness or Englishness are genetically distinct is both disrupted and reinforced. Ideas of a genetically or ancestrally pure Englishness, for example, are challenged, while ancient groups such as the Vikings or other contemporary national populations are genetically described. Some scientific and popular accounts suggest that genetics can complicate ideas of British history or English identity but do so by implying that continental or regional ancestries—African or Ukrainian, for example—can be genetically identified and described as bounded natural categories. Race, ethnicity, and nation are thus simultaneously deconstructed and produced as genetic categories.

Ideas of indigeneity are also being remade genetically. While the ethics of genetically sampling indigenous people has been the subject of intense scrutiny, new discourses of indigeneity in Europe are also emerging in science and in public culture that deserve consideration. As Anne-Marie Fortier has argued, the People of the British Isles produces a geneticized national indigeneity, but it is a version of indigeneity that includes regional diversity and ancient ancestral connections to other parts of Europe.[101] And as I have argued here, it does not simply construct a pure indigenous population. A native homogenous population is not counterposed to new immigrant sources of genetic diversity. Instead, a pattern of indigenous regional diversity is set against the heterogeneity due to recent immigration. The project's accounts of regional genetic diversity are produced by distinguishing between people in Britain in the present on the basis of ancestral origins. Studying indigenous diversity relies on effectively purifying the sample by screening out "nonnative" donors. The "genetic map" of Britain is effectively and, for those involved, admittedly a map of genetic variation in a white indigenous but "mixed" population. "Genetic heritage" is defined and differentiated through a geography of ancient origins, within the United Kingdom or elsewhere.

Nikolas Rose is right in arguing that the ethical and political implications of new molecular accounts of human similarity and difference, especially in racialized biomedicine, should not be understood in terms of an old biopolitics of race that is overtly "negative, exclusionary and malign."[102] Yet the social illegitimacy of overt racism and the decline of a biopolitics of national racial fitness does not mean, as Rose would agree, that the political implications of accounts of genetic relatedness for old categories of difference, including the nation, do not deserve scrutiny. It is the foregrounding of biological or genetic similarity based on shared ancient geographical ancestry as the basis of identity, belonging, and relatedness that needs critical attention, in terms of the figuring of difference within and between states and in contrast to ideas of solidarity and care across geographical distance and categories of difference.

This involves, as this case has shown, attending to the ways ideas of genetic relatedness are mediated by, rather than at odds with, the politics of multiculturalism and antiracism and the effects of scale on these mediations. Accounts of human genetic diversity on the global scale are often framed by ideas of genetic unity and shared origins, despite the focus on variation. In contrast, the idea of diversity at the national scale counters ideas of national purity of blood. But multiculturally inflected accounts of human genetic variation are clearly not unambiguously progressive. The nature and implications of these mediations are also locally specific. This chapter has traced the genome geographies and particular molecular multiculturalisms that are condensed in that knowingly provocative question of the scientific meaning of being British.

4

Finding the "Truths" of Sex in Geographies of Genetic Variation

Human population genetics is as much about sex as it is about race, ethnicity, or nation. It is about multiple instances of who has sex with whom or, to put it more scientifically, how their specific and cumulative reproductive outcomes shape individual ancestries and patterns of genetic variation. Human sexual reproduction is fundamental to human evolution as a species and to genetic diversity within the human species. Genetic reconstructions of the geography of human origins and global, continental, and regional patterns of early human migration long relied on studying reproductive lineages—maternal and paternal direct line ancestry—as proxies for wider patterns of relatedness and patterns of migration. Studies of a much wider range of markers have proliferated as the field has developed, but accounts of genetic variation between populations and their relationships still are concerned with tracing the history and genetic outcomes of "gene flow" or "intermarriage" between groups. At this level of generality, human population genetics simply works with the "natural facts" of life: sexual difference and the production of genetic uniqueness and genetic similarity and the evolution of humanity itself through sexual reproduction—fundamental, eternal, unchanging, and universal and far from the complexities of desire and power.

But recent developments in human population genetics suggest a less straightforward distinction between what is taken to be scientifically fundamental in terms of human reproduction and what might have been hitherto viewed by human population genetics as the incidentals of social relations. Some human population geneticists argue that their work is not simply premised on the natural facts of life—the fundamentals of human reproduction—but is also able to address questions of sex and power both in terms of historically specific contexts and in terms of long-established social and cultural practices. When prominent human population geneticists claim that their research offers more than the potential to reconstruct human evolutionary origins and prehistoric and premodern human migrations, they do so primarily on the basis that it can also elucidate fundamental dimensions about human culture and social life with regard to sex, sexual difference, and reproduction. Evolutionary genetics can "tell us who we are" "and who is related to whom" through accounts of ancestral origins, migration, and settlement but, it is argued, also throw light on what is geographically and historically variable and what is universal in terms of the reproductive natures of, and the nature of sex between, women and men.

Human population geneticists' accounts of the social organization of human reproduction and the roles, positions, and different mobilities of women and men, or accounts of human migration histories that claim to have identified particularly gendered patterns of settlement, are increasingly prominent in scientific journals and in popular science. They feature accounts of patterns of "interbreeding" and sex-specific mobility at different scales, from those concerned with the interactions of farming and hunter-gatherer groups in the European Neolithic transition to accounts of sexually differentiated patterns of in-migration (e.g., Viking migration to the British Isles, or to specific islands off the northern coast of Scotland, and to Iceland).[1] Geneticists claim to have identified male-dominated migration in some instances and family migration including women in others or social constraints on "interethnic marriage/unions" in early medieval England.[2] Others model the genetic impact of "sex-biased short-range migrations" related to different postmarital residence rules such as patrilocality—that is, when women move to their husband's birthplace after marriage.[3] These claims and accounts are based on the production and analysis of gendered geographies of human genetic variation.

This chapter extends my engagement with the making of ideas of difference and relatedness within avowedly antiracist science by turning to these gendered geographies. This includes considering the making of accounts of human genetic diversity and migration that are differentiated in terms of female and male patterns of variation and lineage and in terms of interpretations of patterns of human genetic variation that are based on particular assumptions about the differences between women's and men's mobilities and reproductive strategies or that use patterns of genetic variation to scientifically prove what were assumed to be these differences. Here I explore the gendered and sexualized imaginative geographies of human population genetics through a focus on the ways in which particular ideas of gendered mobility and particular models of the organization of human reproduction are simultaneously drawn on and naturalized in explanations of geographical patterns of human genetic variation.

In exploring the nature and implications of this extension of the explanatory reach and influence of human population genetics, I address a strand of human population genetics that has largely escaped critical scrutiny in contrast to the well-established and considerable body of work addressing questions of ethnicity and race. But turning to sex and gender is not to turn away from questions of ethnicity or race, or indeed nation, because of the ways in which race and sex are enmeshed in the practice and objects of bioscience. At the same time, the ways in which ideas of sexual difference are produced and deployed within human population genetics reflect the different political freight attached to sex in comparison to race and different degrees of self-consciousness about the politics of sex among human population geneticists. Sex and sexual difference remain relatively unproblematized concepts within the field itself in comparison to the deeply politicized question of race, and this matters in terms of the making of sexual difference through interpretations of geographies of genetic variation.

Sex in an Expansive Science

In the practice and presentation of gendered geographies of human genetic variation, human population genetics is at its most expansive—at ease, reaching out, extending its scope, and open to cross-disciplinary exchanges. Accounts of the power of human population genetics both to reveal the deeply established cultural practices of human societies, especially regarding reproduction and marriage, and to deepen understanding of gendered migration patterns and reproductive interrelationships between human groups in specific historical and geographical contexts suggest a widening scope and purchase for the discipline. There is a sense in these accounts of a relaxed release from the political controversies about race that dog the subject. The pleasures of risqué science replace the risk and threat of race. Pronouncements of its expanded explanatory reach are also often made in terms of openness to or announcements of new cross-disciplinary developments, especially in relation to anthropology. This is an expansive science also in terms of the purposeful extension of human population genetics into the world of commerce and culture through gendered (as well as ancestral) products and ideas and in the traffic of ideas of sex and sexual difference across the porous boundaries of science, popular culture, and social life.

In his argument about the potential of human population genetics to address questions of human culture, including gender roles and marriage patterns, Spencer Wells suggested that this potency is the product and promise of the subfield of "anthropological genetics."[4] For some geneticists, this term names a new field in which geneticists address anthropological themes and draw on anthropological knowledge. For others, it is part of a longer history of the use of genetic methods and data in anthropological studies of human evolution and human biological variation.[5] Arguments about the value of bringing together human population genetics and anthropology thus come from geneticists turning to anthropological concerns about kinship, migration, and marriage in past human societies to explain patterns of human genetic variation. They come also from anthropologists bringing together archaeology, ethnography, and human genetics to offer better interpretations of patterns of genetic variation and to challenge models of the migration and interaction of human groups that either work on the basis of "asexual individuals" or are insensitive to the varied historical and geographical permutations of the intermarriage between colonizing and indigenous groups.[6] Geneticists are drawing on historical expertise; historians are incorporating genetic accounts of a gendered past.[7] With advocates on each side but with a range of styles and degrees of cross-disciplinary collaboration and exchange, these new fusions and borrowings have different results in terms of the figuring of gender, kinship, and reproduction in human population genetics.

Engaging with these gendered geographies in this expansive science is also a matter of considering how human population genetics, as a science, is conventionally situated not only as above the messiness of human social life but also as the arbitrator of social truth. This is by both accident and design. Human population geneticists may stress the pure nature of their research and argue for its social value. Some insist that the implications of their research are not in their control or fundamentally not their concern and argue that their work is always open to being taken up by interest groups with particular agendas. But they design research projects and present outcomes with public audiences and potential publicity in mind. This is clear in cases in which new techniques of addressing relatedness on a group level are put to work to directly address deeply political questions of parentage. Human population genetics is premised on analyzing the cumulative outcomes of instances of human reproduction in patterns of genetic variation. But when the techniques used to address questions of humanity's evolutionary origins and ancient histories of human migration are applied to address questions of who is related to whom and how, in the recent or personal past, human population genetics is positioned as a source of truth about the reproductive outcomes of race, sex, and power, and the resulting "truth" has been used to demonstrate the power of genetic lineage analysis.

The ability to establish genetic relatedness through mtDNA or Y-chromosome analysis was, indeed, brought to the public's attention in the late 1990s through one deeply political case of alleged fatherhood. As developments in human population genetics and claims about its power to address questions of humanity's past and solve more specific historical or personal puzzles of relatedness began to be widely publicized, one of the "success stories" that was often pointed to—and that has since become an established reference point in popular science exhibitions and textbooks—was profoundly a matter of the politics of sex and race. In 1998, human population geneticists published their efforts to resolve the long-standing dispute about whether Thomas Jefferson was the father of any of the children of his slave Sally Hemings through Y-chromosome comparisons between men of recognized and claimed Jeffersonian descent.[8] Deeply racialized and sexual imaginations of purity, miscegenation, cross-racial union, illicit sex, and sexual power run through the long-standing controversy about this dispute, interests in the case, and the resistance to the claim—which the genetic research verified—that Thomas Jefferson was the father of the last son of Sally Hemings.[9] Questions of sexual and racialized power surface also in genetic genealogy when many African American men who have undertaken these tests are informed that though they have African mtDNA lineages, their Y chromosomes suggest patrilineal descent from the slave-owning men of European ancestry. These cases are profoundly significant in terms of the ways in which questions of racial and sexual power are interwoven within national and family histories.

Addressing the figuring of sex, sexual difference, and reproduction in human population genetics, this chapter takes up established concerns about deeply embedded assumptions about gender and mobility and the powerful naturalization of particular models of sexuality, gender, reproduction, and race in the tradition of critical feminist cultural analysis. Here I explore the way in which accounts of the diversity of specific Y-chromosome and mitochondrial lineages in differently defined human groups are interpreted through ideas of the different roles and positions of women and men and the social organization of marriage and gendered patterns of migration. In following these ideas across science scholarship, popular science, media reports, and popular culture, some prominent voices reappear—authors of popular science such as geneticists Spencer Wells and Bryan Sykes and *New York Times* journalist Nicolas Wade—but their perspectives are situated within academic science and public culture more widely.

Tracking the production of gendered geographies of genetic variation across these domains means considering the scientific claims themselves, attending to the ways their potential popular appeal shapes the science itself, and exploring the deeper entanglements and intersections of science and popular culture. This again includes the application of the data and methods of human population genetics in the commercial sector of personal ancestry testing. Running through these accounts of sex, reproduction, and kinship in human population genetics in their scholarly and popular forms are different ways of figuring women and men and different versions of an anthropologically informed and informative anthropological genetics. And running through this exploration of these accounts is the crucial question of what is presented as fundamental and what is figured as historically, culturally, and geographically variable in new genetic accounts of kinship, reproduction, sex, and gender. Does "human culture," as in Spencer Wells's question, mean something as fixed as the "natural facts" of life or, in contrast, variable and thus to be investigated in new ways via studies of genetic variation? The geography of human genetic variation is a fundamental focus of human population genetics. This concern with geography is also central to questions I pursue here: What models of masculinity, femininity, heterosexuality, reproduction, and gendered mobility are drawn on, naturalized, and allegedly scientifically proven in interpretations of the geographies of human genetic variation? How is a gendered geography of genetic variation naturalized as a model for imagining and understanding human mobility as a whole and differentiated migration histories?

"Systematic Differences": Women, Men, and Geographies of Genetic Variation

The new turn to questions of gender, reproduction, and kinship in human population genetics is, in part, a reflection of the technoscientific centrality of mitochondrial DNA (mtDNA) and the Y chromosome in this field. However, as Amade M'charek has demonstrated, this centrality is produced, enacted, and naturalized through the practices, technologies, and materialities of human population genetics. It stems from the ways in which this form of genetic material is passed on in human reproduction, but the utility of this is the product of a range of other biosocial artifacts and particular models of lineage. Textbooks on human population and evolutionary genetics often start with an explanation of the production of human gametes through the process of meiosis that produces ova and sperm with half the usual chromosomal constitution of human cells. They combine at fertilization to produce a diploid zygote with forty-six chromosomes. One copy of each of chromosomes 1–22 comes from each parent. Women have two X chromosomes, one from each parent. Men have one X chromosome that comes from the mother and a Y chromosome from the father.[10] These explanations of the basic genetics of human reproduction also often include an explanation of the inheritance of the nonnuclear genetic material, mtDNA, which is contained in energy-supplying mitochondria of the cytoplasm rather than the nucleus of the cell and is passed on unchanged from a woman's ova to her offspring in human reproduction. Similarly, the noncombining region of the Y chromosome (NRY) is directly inherited by male children from their father. The inheritance of other maternal and paternal genetic material is, in contrast, both random and mixed. Over time, mutations in mtDNA and the Y chromosome lead to small but identifiable differences that are then passed on in this way and can be used to identify shared maternal or paternal descent. Those who have similar forms of this genetic material are thought to share direct maternal or paternal lineages. Following the relatively recent turn to Y-chromosome population studies in the early 1990s in comparison with the use of mtDNA in human population genetics that began in the 1970s, both extended maternal and paternal lineages have been widely used as proxies for general patterns of human genetic diversity and as sources for reconstructing the geography of prehistoric and premodern human migration. The genomes that are the product of cell division, recombination, and conception at the cellular scale are then the focus of molecular analysis; the accounts of patterns of similarity and difference that result are interpreted in terms of the global, continental, and regional scales of human evolutionary history.

Here I concentrate on the figuring and interpretation of gendered geographies of genetic variation. But, as M'charek argues, the production of these geographies depends on naturalized technologies of comparison. Genetic sequences, like genetic ancestry test results, are meaningless in themselves. As we have already seen (in chapter 2), they only accrue meaning comparatively. In the case of research using mtDNA lineages as proxies for wider patterns of ancestry, mtDNA haplotypes are described in terms of their differences and similarities to an internationally recognized reference mtDNA genome known as the Anderson or Cambridge Reference Sequence (CRS). As M'charek elucidates, the making of this itself was a technical and social process that reflected different cultural, political, and biomedical geographies of the accessibility of human bodily material and international networks of exchange. This reference sequence was originally produced by analyzing mtDNA from placentas that could be accessed through British hospitals by the Cambridge scientists as research material and mtDNA from the HeLa cell line derived from the cancerous cervical tissue of Henrietta Lacks, a terminally ill African American patient in 1951.[11] The original Cambridge Reference Sequence, as a composite of British placental mtDNA and the Henrietta Lacks cell line, is entangled both with the "long history of the medicalization of the female body, of birth giving in Western medical practice and of reproductive technologies" and with the politics of "race, class, gender and sexual reproduction" in the United States.[12] As Hannah Landecker shows in tracing the metaphors of sexual and racial contamination that frame the HeLa cell line, themes of race and sex are enmeshed in the practice and objects of bioscience.[13] The specificity and local making of the Anderson sequence are largely erased in order to make it a globally recognized tool for studying genetic variation—or what M'charek describes as a "difference producing technology."[14]

The parallels between the nature of mtDNA and Y-chromosome inheritance mean that both forms are often presented as symmetrical, complementary, comparable, and compatible.[15] This involves eliding their differences. Though mtDNA is found in the cells of both men and women, it is figured as a specifically maternal resource for specifically maternal lineages.[16] Unlike the Y chromosome, which is only passed on from fathers to sons and indeed determines maleness in a genetic sense, mtDNA does not confer femininity. Yet as M'charek has argued in relation to the laboratory practice of human population genetics, the sexual specificity of these lineages in the interpretations of mtDNA and Y-chromosome lineages is produced through practices and technologies and can be either relevant or irrelevant depending on the nature and focus of specific projects and at different stages of analysis and interpretation. Mitochondrial DNA (mtDNA), for example, being found in men and women but passed on maternally might be treated as a proxy for human genetic lineages in general. But in studies comparing mtDNA and Y-chromosome variation, mtDNA is interpreted in terms of women's histories as distinct from and in relation to men's.

In some genetic accounts of human population history, the sex-linked specificity of the Y chromosome and the differentiated focus on direct paternal or maternal descent is underplayed. Reconstructions of migration pathways based on either one of these lineages are taken to be representative of humanity as a whole. The reconstruction of migration flows from patterns of Y-chromosome diversity—for example, as in the Genographic Project—sometimes stands for the collective migration pathways of all humanity, not just those of men. Similarly, in the famous case of Mitochondrial Eve (the name popularized to personify the mtDNA type identified as the form from which all others evident in people today derive), the analysis of mtDNA variation resulted in an account of the genetic similarity and collective African origins for all humanity, though this account of dispersal from Africa was based on examining mtDNA diversity.[17] In both cases, the geography of paternal or maternal lineages stands for collective human origins and migrations.

While the specificity of the use of mtDNA in accounts of shared African origins now usually goes unremarked, early responses to the work suggested the masculinism that dominates accounts of human evolution.[18] Rebecca Cann recounts the ways in which the use of the term "Eve" or "African Eve" by her coauthor Allan Wilson as a shorthand name for the woman from whom all modern mtDNA lineages derive became the focus of critical backlash in which the idea of foregrounding a maternal founding ancestor was even more outrageous to some commentators than a recent collective African origin. For Cann, the focus on mtDNA is a corrective to the unreflective ways in which most accounts of human evolution are exclusively male, but the critical "gang-thrashing" of "mitochondrial Eve" suggests the persistence of a misogynist refusal to accept an account of human evolution based on maternally inherited genes. For her, it was a deep but veiled misogyny that underlay critiques of the biblical connotation of the name, which were used to trivialize the research and undermine the seriousness of its message about the biological similarity of humanity.[19] However, the results of this research using mtDNA are widely held to refer to humanity as a whole rather than to a human maternal ancestry and origin.

In other strands of work, the sexual specificity of these lineages is central. Until Y-chromosome genetic lineages began to be the focus of research in addition to the more well-established mtDNA studies, the sexual specificity of mtDNA was irrelevant. However, over the last decade, the identification of distinct mtDNA and Y-chromosome haplogroups and the analysis of the geography of their variation to explore the nature and timing of divergence between lineages are producing new cartographies of human origins and migration that are differentiated by gender. These global maps locate the points of origin of the oldest lineages in east Africa, and the lines extending outward from this region, which are labeled according to haplogroup codes, suggest migration pathways and locations at which lineages branched through mutation into more recent lineages. These are lines of mtDNA and Y-chromosome lineages, not of individuals or groups.

Yet, inadvertently, they produce an imaginative geography of human migration that seems to suggest that women and men bearing those maternal and paternal lineages somehow migrated in female-only and male-only bands and, furthermore, that humans traveling in groups are characterized by these haplogroups. This is inadvertent, since geneticists do not suggest that at the level of human evolutionary and early migratory history that human groups migrated in all-female or all-male groups—nor do they suggest that any population is homogenous in terms of a single mtDNA or Y-chromosome haplogroup. This illusion may derive from the mode of representation, but it is also shaped by the ways these maps are framed by the idea of "tracking the sexes by their genes," as the 2001 report in *Science* on developments in the field suggested.[20] This gendered geography of human origins and migration has since become commonplace, normalizing and naturalizing what is a very particular way of thinking about demographic histories and geographies in terms of differentiated maternal and paternal lineages.

They also help naturalize what is also a very particular version of genealogy. Human population geneticists present the genealogical and "genetic history of the sexes" as independent and distinct. As the authors of an account of the pattern of Scandinavian settlement in Shetland and Orkney through an analysis of mtDNA and Y-chromosome variation put it, "Although patrilineal (Y-chromosome) and matrilineal (mtDNA) genealogical pathways only represent a fraction of all genealogical pathways between a given set of individuals, these genealogies are entirely nonoverlapping and discrepancies between them thus have a clear interpretation, that is differences in the genetic history of the sexes."[21] While ideas of ethnic or geographic origins are undoubtedly central to attempts to construct these genetic ancestry tests and the knowledges they produce as desirable and even necessarily fundamental to selfhood and identity, the idea that descent and identity can be traced through direct maternal lines if you are a woman or through direct maternal lines and paternal lines if you are a man still has to be made obvious, natural, and ordinary. Despite the development of "biogeographical ancestry" tests, genetic genealogy remains dominated by mtDNA and Y-chromosome tests, and central to these services is a simply gendered differentiation. Men can undertake the two sorts. Women can only undertake one sort. And central to the marketing of these tests is the effort to make a genealogical tree composed of a single direct maternal line for a woman and two direct lines—maternal and paternal—for a man appear to be a taken-for-granted model of ancestry and descent in contrast to the conventional thicket of lineage in ordinary documented, partially documented or imagined, and endless ramifying family trees. These maps of mtDNA and Y-chromosome haplogroups are key devices in the work of making commercial genetic ancestry tests meaningful commodities for collective and individual explorations of ancient origins in genetic genealogy.

Furthermore, comparative work on both lineages comes with an increasing emphasis on the paternal or maternal specificity of these lineages. As the author of one review of the field put it, "The NRY which is passed from father to son, reflects the demographic history of males, whereas the maternally inherited mtDNA reflects that of females. In principle, comparisons of the patterns of diversity found on these two chromosomes can reveal systematic differences between male and female patterns of reproduction and migration."[22] There are two distinct but entangled strands in this work. One focuses specifically on patterns of Y-chromosome variation in accounts of the relationships between social status and the reproductive "success" of specific named men (and for men, in general) in relatively recent human history in the distant as well as recent human past. Another is concerned with exploring and explaining comparisons between patterns of mtDNA and Y-chromosome variation in terms of accounts of differentiated mobilities as well as reproductive roles of women and men. In what follows, I first consider research focusing on Y-chromosome variation alone and then turn to these comparative studies.

Founding Fathers: Men, Power, and Sexual Success

The strand of work on patterns of Y-chromosome variation alone—such as the predominance of particular Y-chromosome haplotypes within and between groups—is one that increasingly features named historical men and a universalized model of male reproductive practice. The thirteenth-century Mongolian warrior leader Genghis Khan, in particular, has become a popular and scholarly exemplar of a particular version of masculinity that is supposedly confirmed by and used to explain patterns of Y-chromosome variation. Genghis Khan's rise to contemporary prominence began in February 2003 when a series of features appeared in newspapers and online news pages reporting on a research paper that had just been published in the *American Journal of Human Genetics*.[23] The paper presented the results of research led by Chris Tyler-Smith, then of the University of Oxford, that entailed examining Y-chromosome patterns within genetic material sampled from men living in what was once the Mongol empire in central Asia. The authors found a higher than expected dominance of one Y-chromosome haplotype and argued that the relatively high proportion of men with this particular haplotype indicated their shared descent from a single powerful and sexually successful man, who, its authors speculated, could have been Genghis Khan, whose descendants, they suggest, now total sixteen million men. The authors supported their interpretation by reference to "historically documented accounts of events accompanying the establishment of the Mongol empire," the "largest land empire in history," including the large numbers of children fathered by Khan and his close male relatives and the practice of slaughtering conquered populations.[24]

Unsurprisingly, the media was much more explicit and much less circumspect in reporting this claim that a contemporary pattern of Y-chromosome diversity reflected the sexual success of a medieval ruler. *The New York Times* reported, "A Prolific Genghis Khan, It Seems, Helped People the World." The UK broadsheet *The Observer*'s headline suggested that "we owe it all to superstud Genghis." The UK *Sunday Times* picked up the story later via geneticist Bryan Sykes's account in his book *Adam's Curse* under the headline "Genghis Super-Y: The Genes for a True Alpha Male."[25] Accounts of the research in newspapers and online are full of references to rape, sexual appetite, well-stocked harems, and the availability of women—beautiful women especially or sometimes, more specifically, virgins—as the benefits of power for Khan, his male relatives, and his "super-virile" male descendants. The online *National Geographic News* report titled "Genghis Khan a Prolific Lover, DNA Data Implies," for example, explained that the genetic results verify historical records: "Documents written during or just after Khan's reign say that after a conquest, looting, pillaging, and rape were the spoils of war for all soldiers, but that Khan got first pick of the beautiful women. His grandson, Kubilia Khan, who established the Yuan Dynasty in China, had 22 legitimate sons, and was reported to have added 30 virgins to his harem each year."[26] Others later report that the genetic results correspond to historical accounts of how Genghis Khan "labored assiduously in his large harems" when not at war or to his "penchant for raping his enemies' daughters."[27] These accounts conjure up images of a harsher and simpler world of unlimited and often violent sex enjoyed by powerful men. They convey a fascination, wonderment, and, in some cases, frisson of identification with a time when the supposedly natural links between sex, male power, and reproductive success were unhindered by what are viewed as the contemporary artificial constraints of modern civilized societies at least nominally based on ideals of sexual equality.

In contrast to the internationally agreed alphanumeric nomenclature of Y-chromosome haplotypes whose codes alone have no cultural or historical resonance, other than the authority of Western scientific modes of knowledge production, linking a haplotype to named, documented, and often mythologized heroes animates human population genetics and imbues specific Y-chromosome lineages with historical significance. Genghis Khan is not alone even if he remains preeminent among what one journalist calls the "giants of the gene pool."[28] Population geneticists involved in similar, subsequent studies have clearly recognized the effectiveness of this strategy of suggesting an association between a predominate lineage and a historic and ideally heroic figure in the public dissemination of their work and the potential for it to be seen to be more carefully informed by historical or anthropological work and thus more valuable in contributing to understandings of the past and the cultural and social organization of human life. The Genghis Khan paper was followed by another in 2006 that argued that a similar dominance of a particular Y-chromosome haplotype could be linked to a fifth-century Irish high king, Niall of the Nine Hostages, and that conjured up an ancient or medieval world of patriarchal power, combat, and honor in which powerful men enjoyed unlimited and uncomplicated sex with women.[29] Newspapers report on efforts to find similar links between particularly infamous male rulers and Y-chromosome patterns in other parts of the world in subsequent research by Chris Tyler-Smith and others.[30]

This romance of powerful and sometimes heroic masculinity is played upon in the conversion of the research results into commodities in genetic genealogy. This involves investing the Y chromosome with particular masculine attributes and simultaneously presenting Y-chromosome genetics as potentially conferring distinguished or special ancestry and evoking an ordinary but profound model of male paternal relatedness. In the influential popular science of geneticist Bryan Sykes, the Y chromosome not only produces maleness in a genetic sense in human reproduction but also is a molecular entity that is itself characterized in terms of masculine ambition and heroic struggle to be passed on in a specifically gendered version of the selfish gene. In *Adam's Curse: A Future without Men,* Sykes's account of his work and wider research on Y-chromosome genetics framed by a concern with the evolutionary fate of the Y chromosome, men and women come to be figured in terms of anthropomorphic chromosomes in a sexual struggle.[31] As Venla Oikkonen has argued, this production of micronarratives focused on molecular entities provides a way of making the process of evolution by natural selection into a story that is otherwise difficult to narrate, since the process lacks entities with any evolutionary agency. Neither individuals nor species drive evolution. These gendered micronarratives of anthropomorphized chromosomes bridge the gulf between evolution at the level of the species and the lives of individual men and women by rendering social and cultural versions of femininity and masculinity as properties of and not just the products of these molecules. Deeply conservative and polarized versions of femininity and masculinity are thus further naturalized.[32]

In popular accounts like Sykes's, the masculinity of the Y chromosome is both entwined with masculinity of the famous or infamous historic or semimythological men and charged with memorializing what are figured as the deep bonds between ordinary fathers and sons. The appeal of named founding father figures is clearly put to work in the domain of genetic ancestry tests. Soon after the publication of the Genghis Khan paper, Oxford Ancestors, Bryan Sykes's genetic genealogy company, began to offer their male customers the service of exploring their possible genetic descent from Genghis Khan. In 2006, in a publicity stunt that in the end went awry, Brian Sykes checked through his database of previous male customers to see if any genetically matched the profile associated with Genghis Khan. One match was found, and the US and British press widely reported that an accountancy professor in Florida with British ancestry was contacted by Sykes and informed of his descent from Genghis Khan. In the end, the scientific validity of the claim was queried and refuted.[33] Nevertheless, Oxford Ancestors still offer this service and similarly offer to identify descent from Niall of the Nine Hostages and Somerled, a twelfth-century hero of Gaelic resistance to Norse invasion in the Hebrides and Western Scotland. Family Tree DNA also offers to test male customers' closeness to Niall of the Nine Hostages. The idea of a famous genetic father figure spins out from the commerce and culture of genetic genealogy too. The launch of the test was followed by one London restaurant specializing in Middle Eastern and Central Asian food offering the tests free to male customers to honor the decision of the government of Mongolia to reintroduce surnames after their banning under Communist government.[34]

But the power of Y-chromosome genetics and Y-chromosome tests also play upon another version of masculinity—quietly heroic rather than self-proclaiming and more democratic than distinguished. All men inherit their father's Y chromosome; most, at least within dominant Anglo-American contexts, also inherit their surname. This is a fortuitous coincidence of the biological and the social for human population geneticists and for commercial genetic ancestry companies. Men are thus encouraged to think of their Y chromosome as a biological entity traveling through time along paternal lineages linking men to fathers and grandfathers and beyond and linking men who share unknown paternal ancestry beyond the limits of their genealogical knowledge. Surnames are presented as "the basic unit of genetic analysis."[35] The marketing of

Y-chromosome tests for knowledge of "deep ancestry" emphasizes the link between genetic patrilineage and patrilineal surnames and figures genetic patrilineage as naturally and profoundly significant. The popular presentation of the potential of Y-chromosome tests in genetic surname studies admits of no sense that they depend upon a masculinist model of family naming that reflects a social model of male power, women's subordination, and the historical exchange of women through marriage and property through patrilineage.

Instead, explanations of the symmetry between Y-chromosome inheritance and patrilineal names from father to sons through the biblical story of who begat who are imbued with the cultural resonance of what Carol Delaney identifies as the origin story of the West. This is an origin story based on an entirely male lineage, in which women are passive vehicles for the transmission of life between fathers and sons and in which relationships between fathers and sons, and paternity itself, are paramount.[36] Daughters are irrelevant. In genetic genealogy, when surnames are not passed on at all because no sons are born in a marriage, the surname is said to have "daughtered out." There have been some efforts to invest mtDNA lineages with a similar naturalized significance, mainly through deeply romanticized accounts of mother-child and especially mother-daughter bonds, and to fabricate names for mtDNA haplotypes—names such as Helena, Velda, and Jasmine in Bryan Sykes's account of European mtDNA haplotypes, or what he dubbed "matrilines"—so as to invest them with a similarly appealing cultural specificity.[37] But this requires much more cultural work in contrast to the ways in which Y-chromosome tests and Y-chromosome surname projects offer scientifically verified significance to ordinary surnames and potential links to named historical figures sometimes beyond the time span of ordinary genealogy and back before the development of patrilineal surnames themselves.

Apart from those references to rape in media reporting of the Genghis Khan case, this popular science of gendered descent might simply be seen as playful, imaginative, and inconsequential. Indeed, FamilyTreeDNA has one test that is not based on genetic lineage or a "warrior gene" on the X chromosome but is instead marketed with the following proviso: "Among the many advances and discoveries of modern DNA and genetics are 'scientific' oddities. These genetic wonders make it into popular culture and develop a life there that far outpaces their academic worth. These factoids are best used as 'cocktail conversation' starters. We present them to our customers as just that."[38] This is an unusually openly playful and knowing version of "recreational genetics" that absolves them of any responsibility for their production of these commodities and popularizations of these "factoids." But this focus on particular founding fathers and named male lineages is deeply underpinned by significant claims about masculinity, power, and reproduction. While these named patrilineages are meant to bring accounts of Y-chromosome descent to life, work on broader patterns of Y-chromosome variation also appeals to a historical imagination of millennia of human history whose patterns of social organization can, it is claimed, be generalized and verified through interpretations of contemporary human genetic variation. Genghis Kahn and Niall of the Nine Hostages animate a much broader history of reproduction and descent but one in which their sexual success is a model for masculinity and male reproductive strategies much more generally.

There are particular versions of heterosexual masculinity at work here. The authors of the Genghis Khan paper claim to have identified the genetic results of "reproductive fitness" through which the social position of some men leads to the "increase in frequency of their Y lineage."[39] "Reproductive fitness" stands for a model of reproduction in which male social, economic, or political power affords sexual power and results in more children who inherit their father's genes—or, more specifically, more male offspring who inherit their father's Y chromosome. For Spencer Wells, one of the coauthors of the paper, as reported in the *National Geographic News*, "This is a clear example that culture plays a very big role in patterns of genetic variation and diversity in human populations." For Wells, "It is the first documented case when human culture has caused a single genetic lineage to increase to such an enormous extent in just a few hundred years."[40]

In his longer discussion of this work, Wells is at pains to make clear that he is not arguing that culture is genetically determined and thus to distance himself from "old fashioned eugenicists."[41] Instead, his point is that cultural patterns of behavior can have genetic effects—that these cultural or social patterns leave signals in patterns of genetic diversity and that once understood, these genetic patterns can be used to infer the cultures of human groups in the past. While "human culture" might refer here to specific contexts—and in the cases of both Genghis Khan and Niall of the Nine Hostages, the authors refer to historical sources in offering explanations of the results—the emphasis on historical specificity slips easily away in more general accounts. Instead, references to the particular social and cultural conventions of specific medieval societies are taken as evidence for a universal human history of male struggle for power and sexual dominance that is presented as fundamental, foundational, and universal.

"Reproductive Fitness" and Genetic Puzzles

This naturalization is evident in the ways the idea of the "reproductive fitness" of certain men in particular contexts is extended to explain the predominance of not just particular Y-chromosome haplotypes in historical and geographical cases but also common patterns of Y-chromosome variation much more widely, indeed, universally. The idea of a gendered geography of genetic variation is key here. Central to much recent work using mtDNA and the Y chromosome is the finding that the range of variation of Y-chromosome haplotypes in human groups is generally smaller than the range of variation of mtDNA within those groups. Y-chromosome patterns tend to be very geographically specific with a limited number of haplotypes in particular localities. In contrast, mtDNA haplotypes tend to be less regionally specific and more varied within any one locality. Y-chromosome variation is described as geographically clustered.

There are two dimensions to explanations of these patterns. One involves ideas of gendered mobilities, which I will turn to in the next section. The other involves ideas of "reproductive fitness" and what population geneticists call "effective population size," and these concepts have become central to these accounts of the organization of human reproduction. They are explained by Spencer Wells through a recent genetic puzzle that he solves in his book *The Journey of Man* under the subheading "Sexual Politics." In 2000, it was reported that a study of human Y-chromosome variation had estimated that the most recent common male ancestor of all humanity had lived 59,000 years ago. The fact that this was about 84,000 years after the estimated presence of Mitochondrial Eve (143,000 years ago) led to headlines posing the puzzle that "Genetic Adam Never Met Eve."[42] Despite the biblical terminology, these dates do not refer to some original man or women existing in isolation but, as Wells makes clear, to an individual who had the Y chromosome or mtDNA genome from which all other forms derive and beyond which no earlier human genetic variation can be discerned from studies of contemporary populations.

As Wells explains in *The Journey of Man*, "The coalescence time—the time elapsed since our common recent ancestors, Adam and Eve—is much more recent for the Y-chromosome than it is for mtDNA."[43] In theory, this should be the same, as the rate at which lineages would be lost would be the same if there are equal numbers of men and women in a population. Smaller numbers within a population would mean a faster rate of genetic drift—the process by which certain lineages are lost and some come to dominate. Yet, as he points out, female to male birth ratios are usually 50:50. The explanation, he suggests, lies not in the absolute numbers of men relative to women but in what he describes as the "effective population size." "In a genetic sense," he writes, "those who don't reproduce don't count, and should be excluded from the equation. What we are interested in, then, is what is known as the effective population size—the number of breeding men and women."[44] While this might also be assumed to be roughly the same size for men and women, a profound assumption about prehistoric and historic sexual patterns is lightly evoked to explain the discrepancy. Wells writes,

> The likely explanation for why there is greater rate of lineage loss for the Y-chromosome is that a few men tend to do most of the mating. Furthermore, their sons—who inherit their wealth and social standing—also tend to do most of the mating in the next generation. Carried through a few generations, this social quirk will produce exactly the sort of pattern we see for the Y-chromosome: a few lineages within populations, and different lineages in neighbouring populations. It will also produce a very recent coalescence time for the Y, since the lineages that would have allowed us to trace back to Adam living some 150,000 years ago were lost while our ancestors were still living in Africa. The definitive proof of this hypothesis will come only from careful studies of traditional societies, where the same social patterns have been practised for hundreds or thousands of years, but my prediction is that it will be confirmed by the data.[45]

The "social quirk" Wells takes as a fact—"that a few men tend to do most of the mating" and that the "effective population size" of men is smaller than that of women and thus more subject to genetic drift (the loss of lineages) and linked to wealth and status—rests upon a whole set of claims about the evolutionary role of sexual competition among men and the nature of women's and men's investments in reproduction. Wells's reference to questions of social status evokes a sociological or anthropological perspective attuned to the dynamics of social structures and relationships, but underpinning this is an idea of male competition for status and sexual dominance that echoes evolutionary psychology with its accounts of fundamental differences in the reproductive strategies of women and men and the nature of masculinity and femininity that have their origins in human prehistory.[46] This is a version of human nature in which women and men have fundamentally different and biologically determined approaches to reproduction and in which men are driven to sexual promiscuity to guarantee the reproduction of their genes.

For evolutionary psychologists and their devotees, human life, like all biological life, is driven by the evolutionary drive to pass on one's genes. But, they suggest, women and men have different strategies to maximize their reproductive success that developed in the early human evolutionary context. Because women have longer investments in reproduction than men, women, they argue, work to secure resources from men, while men try to achieve reproductive success by accessing as many fertile women as possible and only investing resources in children they know are genetically theirs by violently policing the sexuality of spouses. In this account, human nature is genetically determined by inherited mental structures derived from early human existence and culture, and cultural differences are irrelevant to this "genetic and gender calculus."[47] As Susan McKinnon and others have argued, this is a deeply reactionary and reductive account of human nature based on a neoliberal model of individual competitive self-interest and specifically Euro-American models of gender and sexual morality, which completely misreads the shared but differentiated labor of women and men in securing resources. It is disconnected from and discounts the hugely diverse meanings and practices of sex, marriage, and reproduction in human societies.

Yet, however strongly argued these explanations of contemporary gendered social life are, accounts of that distant human past and the specific reproductive strategies supposedly embedded in the psyches of women and men today can only remain suppositions, since there is no way of directly accessing that past. In contrast, it is being argued that recent work on mtDNA and Y-chromosome variation can provide new sources of evidence for reconstructing the gendered dynamics of sex, kinship, and reproduction in recent and distant human history. But human population geneticists are *not* trying to find the specific material within the genome that determines the inherited dispositions "within all of us" that evolutionary psychologists claim determine human sexual and all social behavior. Instead, those involved are exploring the ways cultural practices surrounding reproduction have shaped patterns of genetic variation at the level of the "population." However, their claims to use patterns of genetic variation to prove or reconstruct accounts of kinship and reproduction supply sources of genetic evidence that can supposedly prove what were hitherto thinly supported accounts of human nature and the human past. This is because their accounts of "culture" rely on assumptions about women's and men's natures, which are then reinforced by the new genetic "evidence." The danger here is that ideas of the innate drives of men to have as much sex with as many women as possible and to intensely compete between men to achieve this and for the strongest and most violent men to have the greatest success, which is central to evolutionary psychology, are gaining new credibility through human population genetics. Stories of sexually successful men are not limited to Genghis Khan. In 2003, one *New Scientist* feature announced, "A Few Prehistoric Men Had All the Children." In 2000, British audiences were informed in one BBC news report that more than 95 percent of European men descend from ten paternal lineages—"Europe's 10 Founding 'Fathers.'"[48] More recently a headline reporting on further research in this vein announced that "More Women Than Men Have Added Their DNA to the Human Gene Pool." This might suggest some sort of recognition of a biohistorical contribution from women, but again the suggestion is that "relatively few men got to mate with multiple women."[49] Underpinning the concept of the reduced "effective population size" of men is a set of ideas about the genetic survival of the fittest, sexual selection based on competition between men, and a universal "male sexual mind" obsessively in pursuit of sex.[50]

Wells, at least, is conscious of what appears to be the distance between contemporary values of sexual equality and the supposed social organization of sexual relationships and reproduction in the human past. His dedication of his book *The Journey of Man* to his wife and daughters includes in brackets the comment, "Y-chromosomes are overrated anyway."[51] He is keen to assert the scientific logic of the focus on the Y chromosome but to distance this from any assumption of women's inferiority. But others are much more unreservedly enthusiastic for what seems to be new proof of what have hitherto been strongly postulated but unproven accounts of the fundamental basis of human relationships established in the prehistoric past. For *New York Times* science correspondent Nicholas Wade, the research is fuel for his persistent argument that society should recover from the temporary foolishness of denying the fundamental truths of sex and race. For him, "The finding seems to be the first proof, on a genetic level, of the occurrence in humans of sexual selection, a form of sex based natural selection in which a male or female has an unusual number of offspring."[52]

But if this seems a matter of equal opportunities for men and women, it is clear that for Wade, and for many others commenting in more or less scientific terms on the study, sexual selection is deeply tied to a version of humanity in which men compete for sexual opportunity to maximize reproductive success and in which those strongest are most successful. There is nothing in most of these reports to acknowledge that many men would rather dissociate themselves from, rather than identify with, the sexual violence that is purported to lie behind these patterns of genetic variation. Sometimes these accounts of the apparent genetic evidence for this model of the supposedly fundamental but now tempered drives of human society are presented with a sort of matter-of-fact satisfaction with this image of a more raw and brutal world of sex and power. Sometimes they are framed by a liberal distancing and disapproval yet presented in ways that nevertheless reinforce these ideas of the fundamental relationships between male sexual success and violence.

Bryan Sykes, in an article in *The New York Times*, for example, takes the case of Genghis Khan as evidence of "some very unpleasant behaviour":

Take Genghis Khan's Y chromosome, which is now found in 16 million men in Central Asia. It started as a single copy from the man himself in the 12th century. What drove this? Well, when he conquered a territory, he killed the men and systematically inseminated the most attractive women. A thousand years later, his Y chromosome has survived and proliferated, which is sexual selection in a very grand scale. In fact whenever geneticists look at evolutionary diagrams, they see some frequently occurring Y chromosomes, not closely related to others. These genetic "explosions" are the legacy of a relatively few successful men who have supplanted the Y chromosomes of their contemporaries, as Genghis

Khan did. My guess is that the Y chromosome of every living man has spent at least one generation in the testis of a warlord.[53]

The genetic "proof" of Genghis Khan's sexual success is now routinely reproduced as evidence of the link between male power and reproductive success. Nicolas Wade, who has long expounded his views of the masked but deep male drives for unlimited sex that motivate political leaders to compete for power, now turns to genetic evidence to strengthen his case.[54] Wade finds support in Bryan Sykes, who he features in his account of the case of the (later refuted) match to the Genghis profile:

"Mini-Genghises were probably all over the place in medieval times," Sykes said. "Under a patriarchal inheritance pattern," he added "sons will inherit wealth and empire and the same attitude to women." The same instincts have not necessarily vanished from contemporary rulers, despite societal disapproval of straying from the marriage bed. "I'm sure that's one of the reasons they try to get to the top," Sykes said, referring to leaders' desire to spread their genes. "The constraints on people holding public office must be very frustrating, but they manage it somehow," he said.[55]

In Wade's popular account of historical reconstructions of the human past through human population genetics, *Before the Dawn*, he uses the case of Genghis Khan and subsequent work by Chris Tyler-Smith on the "Manchu chromosome" to argue that they "bear witness to the power of male sexual selection in reshaping the genetic structure of populations," and Wade "raises the question of whether grandiose procreation wasn't just a perk of Genghis Khan's power but a motivation for it."[56] He encourages us to believe so.

The version of human sexual relations and reproduction featured in these accounts is not in itself very surprising; its terms and core concepts of evolutionary psychology—like the alpha male or the supposed likeness of newborn infants to their fathers that allays their suspicions about paternity—have become embedded within public culture. What is new and more troubling is that the truth of evolutionary psychology's sexual and gendered imaginaries of the prehistoric human past is "proven" in contemporary patterns of genetic variation. Assumptions of fundamental differences in women's and men's relationships to reproduction are used to explain what would otherwise be inexplicable discrepancies between Y-chromosome and mtDNA patterns, and gendered patterns of genetic variation are, in turn, used to prove those assumptions. In genetic accounts of the "correlation between culture and genetics," culture names social patterns that are presented through historically and geographical specific cases—of medieval Ireland or Mongolia—*and* naturalized as timeless and universal "facts of life."

But if ideas of men's natural promiscuousness and the sexual benefits of social power are satisfyingly being "proven" by human population genetics, for some, issues of sexual disorder haunt other strands of the science and culture of identity via genetic descent. In Y-chromosome surname studies, it is very common for a small proportion of men, 5 percent or so, who have the particular surname being investigated not to have the Y-chromosome haplotype that has been established for that name. Genetic research papers and popular guides explain that this lack of correspondence between the surname and an expected Y chromosome can include stepsons adopting their stepfather's surname, men taking the surnames of their wives to secure inheritance or the surnames of former owners on buying significant estates, or the simplification of an immigrant's name, or a simple misspelling that persists.[57] But the "nonpaternity events" most commonly used to explain this discrepancy are illegitimacy (where a male child is given the mother's surname) and women's infidelity in marriage, which means that a son would get the surname of her husband but the Y chromosome of the adulterous woman's partner. "Nonpaternity" thus effectively means paternity outside the patriarchal order of marriage. The "natural" double standard beloved of evolutionary psychologists—in which men are driven to reproduce their genes but anxiously police the behavior of the women they support to avoid investing resources in children that are not theirs—lurks behind these apparently benign statements of satisfaction when the genetic results of particular studies suggest low rates of "nonpaternity events" and thus that women have been reliable conduits for men's names and genes.[58] In 2013, the esteemed British science journal *The Proceedings of the Royal Society* featured research on the Y-chromosome analysis of patrilineal genealogies that reported on what was described as "low historical rates of cuckoldry" in western European populations.[59] The culturally anachronistic but scientifically rehabilitated term "cuckoldry" is indicative of the evolutionary psychology framework at work here, with all its associations with that evolutionary "logical" double standard of male sexual license and the enforced fidelity of women.

Yet alongside this concern about regulating women's sexuality is an anxiety about the ability of men to violently disorder as well as order the regulation of sex and inheritance. Births that result from the rape of women are the other reason given for "nonpaternity events." Male sexual violence has also been juxtaposed to more benign versions of paternity and genetic fraternity in accounts of the potential usefulness of national databases of Y-chromosome haplotypes linked to surnames in identifying the surnames of rapists from semen at the scene of the attack.[60] So while ideas of the drive for male sexual dominance and reproductively strategic promiscuity run through this strand of human population genetics, the results of that drive are also the cause of concerns that genes and surnames may not always flow down well-regulated and legitimate paternal lines of descent.

Patrilocality, Mobility, and "Women's Ways"

The second sort of explanation of contrasting geographies of mtDNA and Y-chromosome variation rests on accounts of gendered differences in migration and has a different pattern of slippage between the historically and regionally specific and the timeless and universal as well as a different configuration of kinship, culture, and gender. The occurrence of greater mtDNA diversity and a greater local concentration of a limited number of Y-chromosome haplotypes within a locality is also frequently explained not only in terms of the "reproductive fitness" of some men but also through claims that it is the genetic result of patrilocal kinship arrangements in which women move to live with their husband's family in a new lineage group.

For Wells, and most other geneticists exploring the relationships between genetic variation and kinship, patrilocality is taken to be the global norm and characteristic of 70 percent of the world's societies, a figure drawn from one anthropological source that is frequently cited in these studies.[61] The tradition of women moving from their group for marriage and of men staying put explains, he suggests, the greater diversity of mtDNA patterns and the more local and more limited range of Y-chromosome haplogroups: women joining a group from other groups bring their mtDNA with them, whereas the men and their Y chromosomes stay put and develop locally dominant distinctive patterns. For Wells, this is supported by research on mtDNA and Y-chromosome variation in matrilocal tribes in northern Thailand published in 2001, which found the opposite pattern thus, he argues, proving the case.[62] In contrast to patrilocal groups, Y-chromosome variation was found to be greater than mtDNA variation in these matrilocal tribes: "Simple, local decisions about marriage and property, summed over hundreds of generations," he writes, "had produced profound differences in the pattern of genetic variation on the male and female sides."[63] Here the exception proves the rule. Widely observed differences in patterns of mtDNA and Y-chromosome variation are thus taken to be the result of what must be dominant and persistent patterns of gender mobility in marriage. This is a case not of finding evidence of genetically driven social patterns but, as the authors of the 2001 report concluded, of finding "evidence for the importance of social structure in influencing human genetic diversity."[64] The widely occurring contrast with patterns of mtDNA and Y-chromosome variation are taken to reflect a global pattern of patrilocality.

Wells's account of the explanation of the generally observed geographical localization of Y-chromosome haplotypes and the relative lack of geographical concentration of mtDNA lineages also drew on the earlier work of Mark Seielstad, Eric Minch, and Luca Cavailli-Sforza, which had proffered a similar explanation.[65] Newspaper reporting of the first airing of this research made much of the revolution it suggested in thinking about gender and mobility.[66] In contrast to the conventional association of men and masculinity with mobility, this research was reported to have produced a challenging counterdiscourse of feminine mobility: "Forget Genghis Khan, Bluebeard, Casanova, Steve Norris and all the other notorious rakes and serial fornicators who have left their sticky genetic footprint on future generations. It is women, not men, who are best at spreading their genes around the world," wrote Robin McKie in *The Observer*. "The stereotype of pillaging armies of men fathering swathes of illegitimate offspring throughout history is simply wrong, according to a new study. Moving genes into new terrains is actually women's work."[67] The report included the explanation offered by Eric Minch:

"Certainly men travel farther, but it seems they usually come home to father their kids—and we can see that in the spread of their Y-chromosome variations," added Dr. Minch. "By contrast, women move very little until they suddenly up and go—usually to other tribes—to have their kids. We can see that in the pattern of their mitochondrial DNA." Anthropologists have always suspected such behaviour. The surprise has come from seeing its effects so clearly etched in people's genes today. There is nothing new about the women's movement, in other words.[68]

The idea of the male adventurer's mobility remains intact in this account. Men, it appears, are more adventurous over their lifetime; women "up and go" only once. Yet for some, at least, this account of women's prehistoric mobility offered an alternative reading of assumptions about men's mobility and women's stasis. Until this work, genetic studies of human migration history had been based on the assumption that demographic change is driven by the arrival of bands of men who variously rape, marry, or mix with local women and kill off or disempower local men. Many accounts blithely evoke an image of male sexual conquest as they describe prehistoric population movements between Scandinavia, Iceland, and Britain, for example.

For Mark Stoneking, the work of Seielstad and colleagues was a welcome corrective to the masculinist nature of the evolutionary anthropology he encountered as a student. For him, "The underlying message of Seielstad's study" is "if we really want to understand human migrations, we must pay more attention to women's ways."[69] However, "women's ways" are the product of a patrilocal system that, as described by Stoneking, is determined by men's ways: "That is, when males seek a mate, they frequently venture beyond their village, obtain one or more women (by arrangement, trade or force), and bring them back to reside in the male's village."[70] Wells is similarly cautious of interpreting this research as a progressive account of women's mobility. Enthusiasm for this evidence of women's prehistoric and historic mobility as a corrective to assumptions of male mobility is misplaced, he argues, since it fails to take into account the relative insignificance of maternal descent in patrilocal societies.[71]

In contrast, most accounts of genetic variation as the product of patrilocality figure the mobilities that result from traffic in women as social systems whose universality is proven through genetics rather than dominant social systems to be denaturalized.[72] Again, this is not in terms of the identification of genes for inherited proclivities but through the patterns of genetic variation that suggest their universality and naturalness.

Just as the ova itself is rendered as a passive entity in conventional bio-logical accounts of reproduction, there is no space for women's agency here.[73] Instead, women's mobility is determined by this kinship system. Some enthusiasts for scientific support for "common sense" about gen-der, sex, and race celebrate genetic accounts of the universality of these "sex gender systems." Genetic evidence of women's subordination is the source of masculinist satisfaction for commentators like Nicolas Wade, for whom that account of women moving "very little until they suddenly up and go" is framed not by ideas of women's volition but by the assumption that women's movement is the result of forced trade between men or the capture of women by men. For Wade, "Differences notwithstanding, chimp and human societies serve the same purpose, that of providing males and females appropriate ways of securing their individual repro-ductive advantage."[74] In *Before the Dawn*, he makes much of Napoleon Chagnon's controversial account of the Yanomami, especially accounts of practices of warfare and its roots in the male struggle for "repro-ductive advantage." Women may be captured in raids, and as Wade describes, "Capture of women is seldom the prime reason for a raid but is an expected side benefit. A captured woman is raped by all members of the raiding party, then by everyone else back home who wishes to do so, and then is given to one of the men as a wife." But it is killing an enemy that gives men prestige, and this leads to more wives and more children: "Raiders will be rewarded and have sons of a similar charac-ter. That is the logic of patrilocality."[75] A very particular account of male sexual violence and the reproductive rewards of male violence in one society is used to assert the fundamental basis of all human society. In this model of human society, ideas of women's mobility and men fighting it out for reproductive success are not incompatible.

Yet not all attempts to explore gendered differences in human migra-tion through patterns of Y-chromosome and mtDNA variation work with accounts of social structure or culture that effectively naturalize the social and cultural as universal patterns of human life. In accounts by those who call for a "continued dialogue between molecular genetics and the social sciences, whose observations can inform more sophisti-cated analyses of human genetic data," culture and human demographical processes, more specifically, are figured as a much more fluid and hetero-geneous set of practices—geographically variable, complex, and subject to rapid change.[76] Patterns of Y-chromosome and mtDNA variation are interpreted through "known historical events" rather than in terms of ahistorical assumptions of either men's migration in conquering bands or the universality of women's limited local mobility under patrilocality. This is notable in the approach of anthropologists interested in combining historical, ethnographic, and archaeological expertise to explore the relationships between patterns of genetic variation and gendered patterns of migration in relation to a key problem in studies of how human populations grow and disperse. That is the "key problem [of] determining the extent to which colonizing populations (e.g., modern humans, Neolithic farmers, European colonists) overwhelmed or 'replace' native populations (e.g., Neanderthals, hunter-gatherers, non-European indigenous societies), as opposed to having integrated into or intermarried with them." This is all about sex and power, about how patterns of intermarriage (or gene flow) are shaped by the relative power of colonizing and native groups and men and women within these groups. But anthropologists interpreting patterns of mtDNA and Y-chromosome variation are alert to the "situation-specific" nature of these interactions.[77]

In some cases, these less-universalizing accounts are inflected by contemporary perspectives on the injustices and violence of European colonization. The term "asymmetrical gene flow" is used to describe the "introgression" of the Y chromosomes from one locality into another that follows male-dominated patterns of migration and can be traced through the existence of high frequencies of "European" Y chromosomes but not mtDNA in South America or among the Inuit of Greenland.[78] This has led some geneticists to confer a sort of commemorative function on contemporary mtDNA in places whose indigenous populations were largely destroyed through Spanish colonization in the fifteenth and sixteenth centuries. In one recent study of mtDNA and Y-chromosome patterns in Colombia and Gran Canaria, the continued presence of indigenous mtDNA lineages reflects the results of native women's impregnation by European men. The survival of preconquest mtDNA lineages but destruction of Y-chromosome lineages reflects the killing of men but rape of women. In this account, mtDNA is figured as "witness mtDNA" that "indicates a unique possibility of rescuing part of the lost history of the extinct aboriginal group."[79] Genetically distinct fragments of minute cell organelles are figured as molecular memorials to the victims and survivors of the sexual dynamics of colonization and as traces of formerly distinctive and now extinct indigenous groups. Indigenous men and

European women are erased from this gendered and genetic account of colonization. Here anthropological genetics offers the possibility not only of reconstructing gendered migration histories but also of bearing witness to those subject to colonial violence. Framing human population genetics with these potent ideas of recovery or reclamation following the violence of European colonization is strongly paralleled by the heavy emphasis on the purported ability of genetic tests to provide senses of origin and belonging in specific regions of Africa for those whose ancestors were enslaved.[80]

In these cases, as in the wider claim that genetic research has undermined ideas of race, human population genetics is presented as a progressive science overturning social misunderstanding and ameliorating the trauma of historical injustice. The complex entanglements of these claims in the politics of race and human difference need addressing in themselves, but the progressive framing of these claims also can shore up the authority of these less self-conscious but deeply problematic accounts of sex and gender. Even in accounts that argue for attention to the complexities of culture and kinship and emphasize geographical and historical variability, specificity, and change, the idea of the reduced "effective reproductive population" of men due to the dominance of those who win out in the battle for power and women remains a given of nature.

But sex, sexual difference, and reproduction are not simply naturalized in particular ways in human population genetics. The politics of sex is also genetically commodified. In the case of the arguments about "witness mtDNA," a fragment of genetic material that is found in women and men, but figured as a maternal DNA, is made to commemorate indigenous men who died in the violence of European colonization. Making mtDNA "a witness" implies a critical awareness of the injustice of the colonial past, an idea of collective loss, and a sensitivity to the dynamics of power and subordination within the early modern patterns of migration being addressed through studies of human genetic variation. In this case, colonial violence and the sexually differentiated fates of indigenous men and women are evidenced in patterns of Y-chromosome and mtDNA variation. In other cases, claims to redress the historical equities of patriarchy are used in the making of gendered genetic commodities. Bryan Sykes's book *The Seven Daughters of Eve* is an account of his research on mtDNA variation and his effort to produce and ultimately sell maternal direct-line ancestral lineages, through a deeply romanticized account of motherhood and by associating mtDNA lineages in Europe with named, located, and imagina-tively made up ancient mothers.[81] Through his Oxford Ancestors website, "Customers can discover the identity of their 'ancestral mother' through MatriLine™ which determines which one of seven female mtDNA groups for 'indigenous' European populations is yours, order a map of the cur-rent distribution of any surname in Britain (MyMap™)." As a MatriLine customer, you receive a read out, chart, explanation, certificate, and "infor-mation about your ancestor and her life and times." *The Seven Daughters of Eve* is concerned with European mtDNA ancestry, but Sykes dreams of a "complete maternal genealogy for the whole of humanity" whose lin-eages he would also name.[82] Maternal genetic origins are not sold on the basis of romanticized motherhood alone. They are, he suggests, also a corrective to the injustice of women's historical subordination. This matri-lineal genealogy, he argues, counters the emphasis on the surname and patrilineal family trees—the "male monopoly of the past," a monopoly that he is, nevertheless, equally willing to promote through genetic sur-name studies. In *The Seven Daughters of Eve*, he presents the traditional emphasis on male descent (that he has done much to promote elsewhere through ideas of Y-chromosome genetic relatedness and surname stud-ies) as a problem of inequity. It is a problem that serves his efforts to generate interest and a market for mtDNA tests. Sykes espouses a liberal postfeminist celebration of motherhood and deploys images of ancient earth mothers to strengthen his case for a "woman-centred" geneticized genealogy. Women are encouraged to read MatriLines in terms of deep and deeply significant ancestral connections to primordial earth mothers, who stand against male dominance of women and nature, and in terms of redressing the traditional social and historical marginalization of women. Sex, gender, and human population genetics are thus not only entangled in the making of reactionary models of sexual difference but in purport-edly progressive correctives to gender inequality. There is naturalization at work here too, but this is also a case of enlisting sexual politics in savvy product development.

This strand of human population genetics devoted to exploring gen-dered geographies of human genetic variation is, I argue, increasingly the illiberal *and* liberal complement to the neoliberal genetics of evolutionary psychology. Susan McKinnon identifies how evolutionary psychology is wedded to and reinforces a natural neoliberalism of individual competi-tiveness and struggle for advantage.[83] The accounts of the nature and causes of sexually specific patterns of genetic variation which I have explored here in the mutually implicated domains of science, popular culture, and social life make use of these models of women's and men's reproductive natures and strategies to produce decidedly illiberal accounts of sex, sexual difference, reproduction, and kinship. But while it is clear that this field bears the imprint of evolutionary psychology, my point is not simply to have identified another case of the influence of its models of human nature—nor is it to suggest that human population geneticists are aligning themselves with evolutionary psychology; the influence of evolutionary psychology is much more implicit and largely unreflective. The vision of scientists pursuing this work is instead of a potent and potentially more influential synthesis of genetics and anthropology. My point is that human population genetics may now be seen to provide new scientific evidence for what are its assumed and asserted but hitherto unprovable models of sex, gender, and reproduction. Now armed with the central tenets of evolutionary psychology, human population geneticists are interpreting the gendered geographies of genetic variation that they construct as evidence for, and outcomes of, what are taken to be fundamentals of human society.

Rapidly published and converted in some cases into commodities for genetic genealogy, these accounts of a naturally brutal or, at best, ordered world of male dominance, sexual competition, and women's and men's profoundly different "reproductive strategies" dangerously legitimate and naturalize a whole range of reactionary "truths" about the "universals" of sex, gender, and reproduction. The ostensible aim of this work in human population genetics is to explain patterns of genetic variation through accounts of the social organization of reproduction and, conversely, to use patterns of genetic variation to reconstruct the organization of reproduction and gendered migration patterns in the human past in general and in specific geographical and historical contexts. Yet at a fundamental level, the cultural and the social are also renaturalized and universalized. In these gendered geographies of genetic variation, "culture"—the new object of genetic investigation—turns out to be closer to "nature."

Yet this expansive science of gendered genetic variation is at the same time an overtly liberal science. Perspectives on what counts as "universal" vary from those who find support for regressive and reactionary accounts of sex and gender in human society, or take it as a matter of fact of nature, to those who recognize their problematic nature. The human population genetics of gendered variation is not a monolithic field, and its liberal side is itself diverse. Some challenge universal claims and models and call for more sensitivity to historical and geographical specificity. Accounts of male sexual aggression and competitiveness and male dominance are, on the one hand, "proven" in patterns of genetic variation and, on the other, enrolled as a negative past to be redressed as compensatory genetic maternal tests and knowledges are commodified. A liberal critical stance on sexual inequality serves the work of making genetic products and services but does little to challenge the wider dominance of accounts of "sexual fitness," and the violence at the heart of this model of sex and kinship, as fundamental to human evolutionary history and human societies. These are the geographical and sexual imaginaries of genetic variation and descent in this antiracist science of difference.

Degrees of Relatedness

"Natural" Geographies of Affinity and Belonging

Writing about a set of practices, technologies, and knowledges that are embedded within or closely aligned to the competitive forward rush of human genomics means there will always be a time lag between new research on human genetic variation, new applications, and new popular accounts of that work and the emergence of critical academic discussion of these developments. As I bring this book to a conclusion, new material springs up. Empirical examples multiply and more will follow as the time scales of writing and book production are outpaced by the science and culture of human population genetics. The results of research projects will get published in the academic science journals, publicized by press officers, reported on, often incorporated into genetic genealogy, and put to use in a range of personal and collective deliberations about origins and ancestry, identity and identification. The pace of scientific development is matched by the proliferation of new accounts of ancestry results or projects in the public culture, often orchestrated by commercial genetic ancestry testing companies seeking publicity and profit and organized in new alignments of heritage promotion and human population genetics or produced as liberal antiracist genetic family history television, following the new but already repetitive format of revelatory personal genetic ancestry tests and travel to ancestral origins and newfound "relatives." Cases of individuals whose ancestry is genetically tested and revealed, especially public figures whose results make good "public interest" stories, will continue to be pursued by population geneticists with strong commercial interests and taken up in the media.

There is no sense then that, at this point, the public and scientific interest in ancestry and origins has run its course. Instead, the power and popularity of genetic accounts of origin and relatedness that I have been considering this book are becoming more firmly entrenched.

Notwithstanding the effects of some criticisms of late, especially by some population geneticists themselves, this is not likely to quickly nor radically change. Instead, technologies for the making of collective and individual origins and ancestry are likely to permeate more widely with different sorts of permutations, in terms of claims about rights, justice, recompense, or group membership and in terms of practices of governance, policing, and immigration control.

The question of the history and geography of human origins and evolution is also in no way finally answered. Despite the now well-established place of the idea of humanity's collective African origins and the weight this carries in antiracist arguments in public culture, this is not a stable nor uncontested scientific position but subject to further scrutiny and debate as new technologies are applied to old questions and new archaeological evidence. The recent publicity afforded to research that suggests a degree of interbreeding between modern humans as they encountered archaic humans, rather than simple replacement of the archaic with the modern, returns to long-standing debates about human unity and difference, including the decades long debate between those who espouse a single African origin for anatomically modern humans and those that envisage multiple "out of Africa" migrations and multiregional evolutionary histories.[1] It is not clear how evidence of some Neanderthal or Denisovan ancestry in contemporary non-African people will shape ideas of human difference. It does not simply undermine ideas of African origins, since Africa is understood to be the original site for both archaic and later humans[2]—nor is the conventional image of the Neanderthal a ready focus of identification. But it might suggest more blurred categories of the hominin within human evolution or a more profound reimagining of the human as an "interspecies," fracturing a single story of evolutionary origins.[3] However, the scientific and commercial investment in sustaining public interest in ancestry leads the Genographic Project in its second phase—Geno 2.0—to offer participants tests that might detect this well in advance of any sense of the meaning or value of this new ancestral knowledge.[4] There is a future to follow here.

The broad dimensions of the science and culture of human genetic variation that I have identified and the arguments about the making of difference and relatedness within and beyond the scientific domain that I have been pursuing provide a foundation for addressing future developments. Of the projects and research strands that I have considered, it is the research that treats patterns of genetic variation as a means to know the human past in terms of differentiated women's and men's mobilities and reproductive natures that has most recently emerged as an extension of anthropological genetics and been incorporated into product development in the genetic genealogy sector. In comparison to work on human genetic variation more widely, this is at an early stage, and there is likely more to come as population geneticists pursue novel research avenues. As I have argued here, this work is becoming a new scientific source for wider claims about the fundamental nature of human social organization and natural sexual difference. Like the field of human population genetics more widely, scientists vary in their approach to what is at stake in this. But despite the liberal, proequality tone of some accounts and discussions, this strand of research is predominantly one of matter-of-fact assumptions about the human past, informed by conservative and essentialist models of gender, sex, kinship, and reproduction. These models are assumed to be universal (with some exceptions) and then purportedly proven by the research itself and avidly publicized by those commentators who are gratified to have their masculinist perspectives genetically endorsed.

However, the issue here is not of an overt, or even covert, intention in the work of human population genetics to naturalize women's subordination. But like the making of race in antiracist genomics where there is a failure to fully consider how genetic accounts of difference contribute to the problem of the making of race despite antiracist commitments of those involved, there is a failure to recognize how the genetic making of sexual difference contributes to the reactionary ideologies of sex and gender that at least most population geneticists would not explicitly or even implicitly endorse. Extending Jenny Reardon's diagnosis of the problem of liberalism in antiracist genomics, human population genetics can also be described in terms of the liberal commitment to gender equality that is coupled with a predominant failure to address the assumptions that underlie and are reinforced by its interpretation of gendered geographies of genetic variation. But in contrast to the question of race, there is much less anxiety about the making of sexual difference in what could be described as liberal antiracist *and* antisexist genomics.

These recent but increasingly prominent accounts and claims need to be challenged as part of a wider critical engagement with the genetic making of difference. This means tracing the ways questions of gender and sex are implicated in the making of race, ethnicity, nation, and family through accounts of ancestry and genetic relatedness but also specifically addressing the making of sex and sexual difference through accounts of genetic variation itself. The focus on the making of difference in this book has thus been one that is concerned not only with the making of race, ethnicity, and nation but also with the making of sexual difference through gendered geographies of genetic variation.

This has been one strand of an effort to address the science and culture of genetic ancestry and relatedness in an expanded sense not only by bringing questions of sexual difference to the fore but also by situating the question of the making of race in the wider context of the making of other categories of identity and difference. This is not to underplay the crucial significance of critiques of the making of race in the sense of naturalized continental geographies and categories of genetic distinctiveness. It has, however, involved arguing that the problems of the making of boundaries within gradients of genetic variation at the continental scale not only exist at that scale but also persist in the making of other categories as genetic populations at national, regional, and local scales. The idea that a sequence of DNA has a geographical origin in turn implies that places—localities, regions, countries, and continents—have a particular genetic character and that the people who live in that place share that character and differ genetically to varying degrees from people in other places. In this line of thinking, those who are in a specific place but are genetically different from the "indigenous" inhabitants have other natural genetic ancestral places and, therefore, at some fundamental level, naturally belong elsewhere. The implications of this for the politics of belonging are contingent upon the specific configurations of categories of the "indigenous," "settler," or "immigrant." Like the formal reckoning of genealogical closeness and distance, genetic accounts of ancestry are as much about making distinctions and differentiating degrees of relatedness as they are about making connections and emphasizing commonalities, despite the stated emphasis on human unity and shared ancestry.

This issue, I suggest, cannot just be collapsed into familiar critiques of the genetic making of race. Instead, a focus on relatedness foregrounds the ways in which accounts of the geography of genetic variation are about groups being not only categorized or differentiated genetically but also twinned with a model of natural genetic relatedness. The problem is not just about how sociocultural racial or ethnic groups are figured as genetic units but also that genetic difference and similarity are figured as the basis for relatedness and the foundation for social relations. In exploring the making of geographies of genetic relatedness, in this book, I have been reflecting on the relationships between two different sorts of messages that are not usually set side by side. One is this celebration of the ancestral relatedness—whether proven or found—that is most strongly propagated in the genetic genealogy business and in popular accounts of anthropological genetics: that sense of connection and commonality with genetic "matches" or with people figured as distant but definite relatives in the hybrid travel-science-family history television documentaries that now constitute a particular media genre. The other is the account of human genetic difference being "geographically structured" with genetic similarity decreasing with geographical distance, whose model of gradients is frequently used to challenge the existence of races and genetically identifiable bounded groups. It is a point that continues to need to be made, but with care. For if this "geographical structure" of human genetic variation is combined with the idea of natural genetic relatedness, it produces a world in which patterns of affinity and antipathy are also understood as naturally "geographically structured." Proximity and distance would be imagined as correlating with natural senses of affinity and difference. It suggests that people living near each other are more similar genetically and thus more bound to each other than they are to people far away. This seems to conform to a commonsense notion of geographies of identity, belonging, and care extrapolated from the intimate scale of the family to the family of nations, confirming a naturalized geographical distribution of care, empathy, and interest based on geographic proximity rather than pursuing the possibilities of care, commonality, or solidarity across distance and across cultural difference.

This, of course, is to read the science and culture of human genetic variation against the grain of its prevailing antiracist message of human unity. But it emerges from pursuing the logic of the idea of shared ancestry and genetic similarity as the basis of valuable, meaningful, and rewarding senses of commonality, affinity, and connection. Simply put, pursuing this logic implies that genetic similarity through shared ancestry is the natural foundation for solidarity, care, and collective identity, and a sense of social or cultural difference, antipathy or alienation naturally correlate with genetic dissimilarity. This idea of increasing affinity with increasing genetic similarity and increasing antipathy with increasing genetic difference does not rely on race, and accounts of special bonds through shared descent are comfortably accommodated into liberal antiracist genomics. But ideas of gradients and gradations coexist with more bounded categorizations in anthropological genetics. When the correlation between affinity and genetic similarity is coupled with the suggestion that culturally and geographically defined human groups are genetically distinctive or that places—localities, regions, nations, or continental regions—have an "indigenous" genetic character that can be discerned through those practices of selective sampling and differentiation among contemporary inhabitants, a deeply troubling image of natural geographies of amity and enmity emanates from the science and culture of anthropological genetics despite its antiracist and multicultural inflections, especially where that idea of the fundamental geographical structuring of human genetic variation has been complicated by immigration.

Notwithstanding their specific historical and contemporary geographies of immigration, the UK and U.S. contexts, which I have addressed here, are ones deeply shaped by immigration itself and how immigration has been imagined in terms of a national origin story. In different ways, ideas of cultural pluralism have profoundly shaped their national imaginaries. In the U.S. case, immigration is a founding narrative even if not necessarily matched by contemporary proimmigration attitudes. In the United Kingdom, postwar immigration deeply challenged a national mythology of homogeneity, and while principles of cultural pluralism continue to inform education and public culture, they are currently awkwardly combined with the political capital invested in and public support for anti-immigration rhetoric and policy. But the continued significance of the particular brands of cultural pluralism in both contexts means that it is not only issues of race and antiracism that frame contemporary accounts of human genetic diversity but also multiculturalism.

Much of what I have been exploring here can thus be understood in terms of the tension between geneticists' desire to reconstruct and interpret an old geography of genetic variation while holding true to a multicultural sensitivity to, or celebration of, cultural diversity as the product of migration. This imaginative historical geography, as I have traced here, is of a world whose genetic and cultural mosaic was the product of the original ancient settlement of the world and then relatively fixity in a "patchwork" geography of "populations" until the advent of modernity. It is now only knowable through its indigenous "remnants" or by devising genetic sampling strategies to screen out the "nonindigenous." As we have seen in the

British context, this is not about pitting national genetic "purity" against genetic "incursions" but, in this form of "molecular multiculturalism," setting an indigenous diversity against new immigrant diversity.[5]

This is accompanied by the assumption, which pervades the science and culture of human genetic variation more widely, that interests in or identification with a particular national or ethnic history, culture, or heritage flow naturally from one's genetic and genealogical ancestry, just as senses of commonality or affinity with others derive from genetic similarity. This genetic model of belonging and relatedness—a natural symmetry of genes, geography, culture, and identity—that coexists in tension with the multicultural commitments of many human population geneticists should, I argue, be the focus of a critical geographical engagement with ideas of genetic identity, difference, and relatedness rather than a concern with race alone. It may have racializing effects, but it does not depend on ideas of race and can indeed be articulated through antiracist genetics.

The different inflections of studies of human genetic variation reflect not only their specific context of production but also the scale of the analysis. As I have argued in relation to the Genographic Project, the stress on a fundamental genetic unity on the global scale frames the study of human genetic difference with an apparently progressive message that offsets potential concerns about its emphasis on delimiting geographies of genetic difference. However, accounts of genetic unity or sameness at the scale of the nation-state raise the specter of ethno-nationalist models of original genetic purity and primordial presence under threat from invasive difference, hence the emphasis on diversity instead. Accounts of human genetic similarity and difference are held in tension, juxtaposed, or reconciled in different ways at different geographical scales in relation to the antiracist discourse of human unity and the multicultural discourse of diversity.

The effect of scale on accounts of human genetic variation is entangled also with the question of the different imaginative geographies and temporalities of indigeneity, diaspora, and mobility in human population genetics and genetic genealogy. The development of fundamentally different distributions of power and authority between anthropogeneticists and indigenous people remains a pressing issue. At the same time, it is worth considering the political implications of the different configurations of indigeneity that run through the science and culture of human genetic variation. That imaginative historical geography of ancient genetic homelands is a geography of global indigeneity. All of humanity is figured as indigenous in this premodern geography of genetic variation shaped by thousands of years of human movement and mixing now being "distorted" by modern and contemporary migration. The view of global human migration in human population genetics is two broad sorts: the prehistoric original migrations and the migrations that followed the thousands of years of stability in those ancient patterns in genetic accounts of the human past. This global past in which all were indigenous is set against a new present in which some still are but in ways that fix them in that precontact, premodern past as "living ancestors."

At the same time, however, genetic studies of people and places not conventionally described as indigenous are producing new discourses of indigeneity. As I have argued in relation to the People of the British Isles project, this is especially apparent in the European context, in which genetic accounts of the indigenous furnish both evidence and an idiom for asserting the rights of "indigenous" Europeans to the protection of their national cultures from immigrants. So while that imaginative historical geography of a world of natural homelands in which all people were once indigenous is tied to a discourse of indigenous groups as the last surviving "relics" of that pattern, with all the archaic assumptions that implies, indigeneity is also being produced as a feature of white Europeans who are genetic sources for reconstructing a Europe before modern migration. Similarly, while the genetic genealogy sector encourages an understanding of all people, with the exception of the contemporary indigenous, as diasporic and thus in need of knowledge of origins, studies of human genetic variation in national contexts distinguish between old and new diasporas, old and new sources of diversity.

While Europeans are selectively being figured as indigenous, discourses of diasporic mobility and displacement are being applied in both universal and differentiated ways. The narrative of humanity's African origins suggests a diasporic condition for all except Africans and thus for all those whose ancestors were migrants from Africa but who became indigenous in the settled geography of premodern homelands. But those with "nonnative" ancestry in the New World are figured as diasporic—ultimately, from somewhere else. As I have argued in relation to the development of the genetic genealogy sector in the United States, a specific African American sense of loss and lack is amplified and extended to suggest a generalized sense of the troubling absence of knowledge for anyone who is "nonnative." The appeal of being indigenous (of not being from somewhere else) and the appeal of ethnic distinctiveness (of being from somewhere else) are both harnessed to produce a market for genetic ancestry tests. But those who are genetically "nonnative" in the "Old World" of European countries like the United Kingdom are effectively deemed to be genetic erratics—out of place—at best included in a vision of a culturally plural society but with "naturally" different genetic and cultural heritages.

This book has been about the making of sexual as well as racial, ethnic, or national difference through geographies of genetic variation and thus has sought to further understand and critically engage with the dimensions of antisexist and multicultural, as well as antiracist, genomics. Both sexual and ancestral categories of difference are, as I have explored, being produced within studies of the spatial pattern of human genetic variation. While I have largely considered them separately to give a depth of focus to each in turn, the theme of reproduction runs across them: patterns of genetic variation and individual ancestries are the outcome of sexual reproduction (sexual combination and biological recombination), which produces genetic uniqueness and produces genetic genealogies, and patterns of genetic variation are being used as evidence for the nature of reproduction (in accounts of "reproductive fitness," for example) and specific reproductive histories (such as colonial genetic "incursions").

But just as the theme of reproduction, as the process that produces genetic variation and produces genealogies, unifies what might seem like different strands of the field, is it also fruitful to think about how the theme of relatedness links together issues of ancestry, origins, and reproduction. They are linked through the ways in which the significance of relatedness via ancestry, and relatedness via reproductive relations, are both entangled and mutually intensified. The idea of the profound and natural significance of knowledge of biological parentage and the idea of the profound and natural significance of knowledge of ancestry inform each other. Prominent stories of ancestral knowledge unknown and recovered resonate with accounts of biological parents being searched for and found. Both sorts of discoveries are not unambiguous in their effects, but they are underpinned by the wider sense of identity and subjectivity as ideally constituted not just by ancestry and parentage itself but also by knowledge of that ancestry and parentage. This is emphasized in the genetic genealogy sector and underpins accounts of collective "genetic heritage" in the science and culture of human population genetics and is manifested in the contemporary emphasis on the right of individuals to know their biological parentage as adoptees or as children born through new reproductive technologies.[6] The search for distant ancestors and the search for recent biological parents (and increasingly, donor-assisted siblings) are based on both the significance of biological relatedness and the knowledge of a familial and ancestral past that is deemed to be profoundly formative and necessary for a fully realized sense of self.[7]

Cultural and scientific imaginaries of stretched-out diasporic geographies of ancestry and origins shaped by human migration in the distant and recent past have implications for the contemporary politics of identity, difference, and belonging. But they are not just about the past in the present. They also have implications for understandings of future geographies of ancestry, origins, and relatedness. While this book has been about the geographies of relatedness premised on shared and distinctive ancestries and ancestral origins—"biohistories" with their orientation to the past— this furnishes a basis for also thinking about what might be called "future geographies of relatedness."[8] By this I mean the understandings and practices of relatedness shaped by new global geographies in which places of ancestral origin and places of birth, upbringing, and residence do not coincide, shaped in particular by the increasingly transnational and globalized nature of assisted reproduction. My focus on the making of sexual difference, especially concerning sex and reproduction in accounts of human genetic variation, can be joined to a focus on the meanings of ancestry, origins, and relatedness in new geographies of assisted reproduction that are increasingly global in their reach, involving the mobility of human gametes (i.e., ova and sperm), embryos, donors, surrogates, and those who hope to become parents, across national borders and between places where assisted reproduction is expensive or restricted or where particular techniques, especially involving donor eggs and sperm or surrogacy, are illegal, to where reproductive technologies are cheaper and less regulated.

As genetic ancestry testing and accounts of human origins intensify the significance of knowledge of ancestry as fundamental and foundational to senses of self, families are increasingly being formed through extended geographies of transnational adoption and transnational assisted reproduction. And as genetic ancestries stretched across space are the subject of scientific and popular investigation, new family histories are being created through globalized configurations of recent ancestry and origins for families shaped by the extended geographies of new reproductive technologies. Transnational families are, of course, not new given the long histories of migration and given the scale and volume of global migration over the last century. What distinguishes these families is the sense that knowledge of the place of origin does not travel with migrants (i.e., babies, children, or in the case of assisted reproduction, embryos, ova, or sperm). But in the case of transnational adoption, this knowledge is increasingly being cultivated by parents for the sake of their adopted children and in order to respect what are described as the heritage rights of transnational adoptees. This includes taking part in geographically and ethnically themed adoptee summer "culture camps" where children and adoptive parents can learn about their child's country and culture of origin or includes family travel to their place of birth.[9]

Given the cultural and scientific emphasis on genetic relatedness, how will families constituted through transnational geographies of reproduction experience or reconfigure ideas of relatedness, origins, and ancestry in a context in which the desire for knowledge of ancestry and origins is so strongly naturalized, fostered and fed by such energetic scientific, commercial, and media sectors? How will those born from these new spatialities of reproduction negotiate these discourses of origins and relatedness in terms of their sense of themselves and senses of connection and belonging? Recent developments in a globalized geography of assisted reproduction raise pressing questions about the understandings and practice of relatedness that these geographies entail and will involve as babies born as a result of these transnational technologies of reproduction grow up. My point here is that these familial geographies of belonging and identity, as well as the wider politics of multiculturalism, will be negotiated in contexts in which discourses of the significance of genetic ancestry and origins to personal identity and the significance of genetic relatedness are accorded so much significance.

It is this concern with the implications of genetic accounts of ancestry, origins, and relatedness for intimate and extended understandings of who is related to whom and how—in families, countries, and within humanity itself—and with the personal and political, symbolic and material effects of genetic accounts of similarity and difference, unity and differentiation on geographies of belonging that has driven this work. The implications are complex, contextual, and ambiguous rather than crudely obvious, and tracing these implications requires a matching dogged, painstaking persistence. This is not only because these collective accounts of ancestry and origins and individualized genetic genealogical tests get put to use in different ways and in different domains but also because of the multiple and contradictory ways in which ideas of ancestry, origins, indigeneity, and diaspora are produced within anthropological genetics. I am less willing than others, however, to suspend judgment and defer to ethnographies of consumption in order to assess the political effects of ideas of genetic ancestry and relatedness. In part this is because it mirrors the moves in liberal antiracist genomics to delegate to participants or consumers the interpretation and use of genetic knowledges in relation to questions of collective identity, which Jenny Reardon has challenged.[10] As Sarah Franklin has argued in relation to new reproductive and genetic technologies, "Greater precision about shared genetic substance exists in inverse relation to the plasticity of kinship thinking."[11] Ideas of genetic relatedness do not simply displace the flexible plasticity of practices and understandings of kinship. Nevertheless, there is clearly an imperative to engage with the science, culture, and commerce of genetic ancestry itself in order to challenge the ideas that seem hardest to dispute both because of their appeal to the positive associations of the family and because of their status as science. Despite the ambiguities and contradictions of genetic historical geographies in their scientific and popular forms, there still remains the problematic implication that shared ancestry and genetic similarity are the basis of the most significant sorts of human relationships.

My broadest intention in this book has been to challenge the acceptance and often celebration of ideas of shared ancestry and ancestral interconnection as the progressive message of the science and culture of origins, diversity, and relatedness. This is a challenge to their embeddedness both in critical social science and in wider public culture. Ideas of shared ancient ancestry and genealogical interconnectedness in a global human family tree clearly do counter ideas of race imagined in terms of human groups with distinct evolutionary origins, evolutionary histories, and genetic character. But ideas of ancient shared origins are not incompatible with ideas of subsequent separation, isolation, and genetic distinctiveness whether these groups are deemed races, ethnic groups, or nations. Discourses of shared origins and genealogical connectedness can be put to work in specific contexts to challenge ideas of ethnic, national, or racial difference and antipathy. But ancient shared ancestry does not necessarily undermine ideas of subsequent genealogical and genetic difference. Discourses of shared ancestry can suggest genealogical and historical interconnectedness between groups at certain scales and resolutions but suggest genealogical and, by implication, cultural difference at others—linking countries in Europe, for example, but differentiating between Europe and its continental neighbors.

Furthermore, despite the political investment in ideas of genetic interconnectedness, the model of genealogical relatedness is not simply one of generalized and undifferentiated interconnectedness at a global scale but necessarily a geography of degrees and sorts of genealogical relationships—some close, some distant, within and between places imagined both in terms of ancient patterns of genetic distinctiveness and multicultural modernity. Within the logic of the global family tree, we are all related but not in the same ways or to the same degrees. While studies of human genetic variation point to shared ancient ancestry and ancestral interconnectedness, the focus is on ascertaining and interpreting degrees of genetic relatedness. So if ancestral relatedness is celebrated as the basis of human unity, empathy, and harmony, it implies quite differently and unevenly distributed senses of care and solidarity that are closer to rather than progressive alternatives to conventional geographies of identity, belonging, and difference. Given that humans vary genetically—but not by very much and not in bounded ways—and given that the genetic variation is both broadly geographical and profoundly complicated by migration in the past and present, it is better not to look to shared ancestry and genetic interconnectedness—that is, to ancestry at all—for progressive models of how humans might think about and treat each other. Ideas of relatedness and ancestry are always ready tools for differentiation, and ideas of genetic and geographical propinquity—natural symmetries of place, ancestry, people, and culture—can easily be put to work to support exclusive models of belonging.

The global human family is a genetic unity understood in terms of genetic difference as well as sameness. It is increasingly differentiated through reactionary accounts of sexuality, power, and violence into different genetic histories and geographies of the "sexes." The genetic human family tree stands as a metaphor for global unity beyond racial difference and thus is central to this antiracial science of difference. It is also a model of relatedness and belonging that is easily compatible with—and indeed can reinforce—old, persistent, and problematic imaginative geographies of natural difference, natural affinities, and natural homelands.

Notes

Introduction

1. Sir Walter Bodmer and Peter Donnelly, "Genetic Maps: Inherited Differences Reveal Our Ancestry," Science Live 2012, Royal Society Summer Science Exhibition, London, July 3–8, 2012, http://sse.royalsociety.org/2012/exhibits/genetic-maps. I address this project and related work on the human population genetics of Britain and ideas of national "genetic heritage" in chapter 3.

2. I use the terms "human population genetics" and "anthropological genetics" in this book since both are used to describe this research that falls under the broader heading of human genomics. When I use this term, I do so to refer to the work of geneticists addressing "anthropological" themes of origins and relatedness rather than anthropologists using genetic methods and data. See Denis O'Rourke, "Anthropological Genetics in the Genomic Era: A Look Back and Ahead," *American Anthropologist* 105, no. 1 (2003): 101–9; Jonathan Marks, "The Origins of Anthropological Genetics," *Current Anthropology* 53, no. S5 (April 2012): 161–72; and Jonathan Marks, "Lessons from History," *International Journal of Cultural Property* 16, no. 2 (2009): 199–204. However, the making of ideas of human collective and differentiated origins and ancestry is not confined to anthropological genetics, given the overlapping sets of interests, technologies, and epistemologies between evolutionary genetics, anthropological genetics, biological anthropology, and biomedicine.

3. Jon F. Wilkins, "Unravelling Male and Female Histories from Human Genetic Data," *Current Opinion in Genetics and Development* 16, no. 6 (2006): 611–17, especially 611.

4. Genographic Project, Public Participation Kit leaflet (Washington, D.C.: National Geographic Society, 2005), 18–19.

5. These themes are the subject of a significant and growing body of critical work addressing the making of ideas of race and human difference in genomic science and their ramifying uses and effects. See, for example, the edited collections that exemplify key strands and concerns in this work: Barbara A. Koenig, Sandra Soo-Jin Lee, and Sarah S. Richardson, eds., *Revisiting Race in a Genomic Age* (New

Brunswick, N.J.: Rutgers University Press, 2008); Ian Whitmarsh I and David S. Jones, eds., *What's the Use of Race? Modern Governance and the Biology of Difference* (Cambridge, Mass.: MIT Press, 2010); Katharina Schramm, David Skinner, and Richard Rottenburg, eds., *Identity Politics and the New Genetics: Re/Creating Categories of Difference and Belonging* (New York: Berghahn Books, 2012); Keith Wailoo, Alondra Nelson, and Catherine Lee, eds., *Genetics and the Unsettled Past: The Collision of DNA, Race, and History* (New Brunswick, N.J.: Rutgers University Press, 2012); Gísli Pálsson, *Anthropology and the New Genetics* (Cambridge: Cambridge University Press, 2007); Peter Wade, ed., *Race, Ethnicity and Nation: Perspectives from Kinship and Genetics* (New York: Berghahn Books, 2008).

6. In January 2001, *U.S. News and World Report* featured the use of genetics in genealogy (Nancy Shute, "Where We Come From: Recent Advances in Genetics Are Starting to Illuminate the Wanderings of Early Humans," *U.S. News and World Report*, January 29, 2001, 34–41). This was followed in March 2001 by a similarly high-profile themed issue featuring genetic research on human population history, titled "Human Evolution: Migrations," *Science* 291, no. 5509 (2001). The first companies selling genetic tests for genealogical research were founded in 2000 with reports in the popular science press, newspapers, and genealogical magazines heralding a new "double helix genealogy" (Mark Howells, "Double Helix Genealogy," *Ancestry* 18, no. 1 [2000]: 52–55) and "genealogical genetics" (Candace L. Doriott, "Genetic Codes Unravelled: New Clues to Human History," *Ancestry* 18, no. 1 [2000]: 14–21); family history, it was announced, could now be teased from a "few drops of blood" (H. Wolfson, "Teasing Family History from a Few Drops of Blood," *SF Gate News*, March 3, 2001). The science and culture of human population genetics and genetic genealogy rapidly proliferated in the decade that followed.

7. Marianne Sommer, "DNA and Cultures of Remembrance: Anthropological Genetics, Biohistories and Biosocialities," *BioSocieties* 5, no. 3 (2010): 366–90, especially 369.

8. Nadia Abu El-Haj, *The Genealogical Science: The Search for Jewish Origins and the Politics of Epistemology* (Chicago: University of Chicago Press, 2012).

9. Luigi Luca Cavalli-Sforza, Paolo Menozzi, and Alberto Piazza, *The History and Geography of Human Genes* (Princeton: Princeton University Press, 1994). See also Dennis O'Rourke and Jake Enk, "Genetics, Geography, and Human Variation," in *Human Biology: An Evolutionary and Biocultural Approach*, ed. Sara Stinson, Barry Bogin, and Dennis O'Rourke (New York: John Wiley & Sons, 2012), 99–142.

10. Much of this is the product of the National Geographic Society's Genographic Project, which I address in chapter 3. But see also Dominic J. Allocco, Qing Song, Gary H. Gibbons, Marco F. Ramoni, and Isaac S. Kohane, "Geography and Genography: Prediction of Continental Origin Using Randomly Selected Single Nucleotide Polymorphisms," *BMC Genomics* 8, no. 68 (March 2007); Lauren Cahoon, "'Genography' Puts European Ancestry on the Map," *ScienceNOW*,

September 2, 2008, http://news.sciencemag.org/europe/2008/09/genography-puts
-european-ancestry-map.

11. John C. Avise, *Phylogeography: The History and Formation of Species* (Cambridge, Mass.: Harvard University Press, 2000), 3.

12. John Novembre, Toby Johnson, Kararzyna Bryc, Zoltán Kutalik, Adam R. Boyko, Adam Auton, Amit Indap, Karen S. King, Sven Bergmann, Matthew R. Nelson, Matthew Stephens, and Carlos D. Bustamante, "Genes Mirror Geography within Europe," *Nature* 456, no. 7218 (November 2008): 98–101.

13. I bring this interpretative lens to bear on my engagement with specific cases in the science and culture of genetic origins, ancestry, and descent in scientific papers, in popular science, and in popular culture in print, online, and on-screen in the United States and United Kingdom. My methodology is one of close qualitative analysis of these sources and selective interviews with human population geneticists. Working within a tradition of feminist cultural geography and drawing on feminist cultural studies of science, I follow the making of geographies of difference and relatedness across the blurred boundary between scholarship, popular science, media reports, and popular culture. See Nina Lykke, "Feminist Cultural Studies of Technoscience," in *Bits of Life: Feminism at the Intersections of Media, Bioscience, and Technology*, ed. Anneke Smelik and Nina Lykke (Seattle: University of Washington Press, 2008), 3–15; and Maureen McNeil, "Roots and Routes: The Making of Feminist Cultural Studies of Technoscience," in *Bits of Life: Feminism at the Intersections of Media, Bioscience, and Technology*, ed. Anneke Smelik and Nina Lykke (Seattle: University of Washington Press, 2008), 16–31.

14. My intention here is not to underplay the existing attentiveness to the spatialities of relatedness within anthropological work but to foreground this dimension and demonstrate what it offers to engagements with the political geographies of identity and belonging. In their description of the analytical focus and substantive concerns of new kinship studies, for example, Sarah Franklin and Susan McKinnon have already pointed to the challenge of tracing "the connections and conceptual cross-overs between phenomena at these vastly different scales of embodiment . . . from the gene, to the body, to the family or species, to the nation, to the commodity form and cyberspace." (Sarah Franklin and Susan McKinnon, "Introduction: Relative Values: Reconfiguring Kinship Studies," in *Relative Values: Reconfiguring Kinship Studies*, ed. Sarah Franklin and Susan McKinnon [Durham, N.C.: Duke University Press, 2001], 1–44, 10). Attention to the geographical rhetorics and imaginations of human population genetics and arguments about the value of attending to sites and contexts are also evident in the works of social science and humanities scholars on this strand of genomics. See, for example, Priscilla Wald, "Future Perfect: Genes Grammar and Geography," *New Literary History* 31, no. 4 (2000): 681–708; and Alondra Nelson, who argues for attention to "site, scale and subjectification" in

188 · NOTES TO INTRODUCTION

"Bio Science: Genetic Genealogy Testing and the Pursuit of African Ancestry," *Social Studies of Science* 38, no. 5 (2008): 759–83.

15. See Audrey Kobayashi, "The Construction of Geographical Knowledge: Racialization, Spatialization," in *The Handbook of Cultural Geography*, ed. Kay Anderson, Mona Domosh, Steve Pile, and Nigel Thrift (London: Sage, 2003), 544–56; David. N. Livingstone, "The Moral Discourse of Climate: Historical Considerations on Race, Place, and Virtue," *Journal of Historical Geography* 17, no. 4 (1991): 413–34; David N. Livingstone, *The Geographical Tradition: Episodes in a Contested Enterprise* (Oxford: Blackwell, 1992); David N. Livingstone, "Race, Space and Moral Climatology: Notes towards a Genealogy," *Journal of Historical Geography* 28, no. 2 (2001): 159–80; David N. Livingstone, *Adam's Ancestors: Race, Religion and the Politics of Human Origins* (Baltimore: John Hopkins University Press, 2008); David N. Livingstone, "Cultural Politics and the Racial Cartographics of Human Origins," *Transactions of the Institute of British Geographers* 35, no. 2 (2010): 204–21; Heather Winlow, "Anthropometric Cartography: Constructing Scottish Racial Identity in the Early Twentieth Century," *Journal of Historical Geography* 17, no. 4 (2001): 507–28; Heather Winlow, "Mapping Moral Geographies: W. Z. Ripley's Races of Europe and the United States," *Annals of the Association of American Geographers* 96, no. 1 (2006): 119–41; Heather Winlow, "Mapping, Race and Ethnicity," in *International Encyclopaedia of Human Geography*, ed. Rob Kitchin and Nigel Thrift (Oxford: Elsevier, 2009), 398–404.

16. Jonathan Marks, "What Is Molecular Anthropology? What Can It Be?" *Evolutionary Anthropology* 11, no. 4 (2002): 131–35.

17. This is evident in the careers and approaches of figures such as Franz Boas and Carl Sauer in the United States and Estyn E. Evans and H. J. Fluere in the United Kingdom. See William A. Koelsch, "Franz Boas, Geographer, and the Problem of Disciplinary Identity," *Journal of the History of the Behavioural Sciences* 40, no. 1 (2004): 1–22; William W. Speth, "On the Discrimination of Anthropo-Geographies," *The Canadian Geographer / Le Géographe canadien* 31, no. 1 (1987): 72–74; William W. Speth, *How It Came to Be: Carl O. Sauer, Franz Boas, and the Meaning of Anthropogeography* (Ellenberg, Wash.: Ephemera Press, 1999).

18. This combination of geographical and anthropological approaches also follows a history of strong interdisciplinary cross-fertilization around questions of culture, representation, and power as both disciplines have been shaped by reflexive engagements with their colonial histories. It is also not the first argument for geographical attention to anthropological work on relatedness. Writing in 1991, Martin W. Lewis set out an anthropogeographic project that combined anthropological approaches to culture, identity, and politics and regional geographical approaches to detailed empirical mapping of sociocultural patterns to "specify the multiscalar territorial underpinnings of group formation and identity." Martin W. Lewis, "Elusive Societies: A Regional-Cartographic Approach to the Study of

Human Relatedness," *Annals of the Association of American Geographers* 81, no. 4 (1991): 605–26, especially 615.

19. Rachel Caspari, "'Out of Africa' Hypothesis," in *Encyclopedia of Race and Racism*, ed. John H. Moore (Detroit: Macmillan Reference, 2007), 391–97.

20. Mary Bouquet has traced the historical relationships between biblical trees of Christ's earthy ancestry, family trees, diagrams of human evolution, and anthropological kinship charts that inform the figurative and semantic affinities between family trees and phylogenetic diagrams. The scientific appropriation of the family tree in evolutionary biology and anthropological diagrams of kinship was, she shows, preceded by the historical tradition of secular family trees, which drew on the earlier model of sacred biblical pedigrees. See Mary Bouquet, "Family Trees and Their Affinities: The Visual Imperative of the Genealogical Diagram," *Journal of the Royal Anthropological Institute* 2, no. 1 (1994): 43–66. These borrowings were not only figurative. As Marilyn Strathern has shown, Darwin drew on genealogical understandings of human and animal pedigrees to visualize patterns of biological relatedness and descent and thereby explain his theory of evolution, natural selection, and biological unity and diversity. See Marilyn Strathern, *After Nature: English Kinship in the Late Twentieth Century* (Cambridge: Cambridge University Press, 1992).

21. Jenny Reardon, *Race to the Finish: Identity and Governance in an Age of Genomics* (Princeton: Princeton University Press, 2005).

22. Abu El-Haj, *The Genealogical Science.*

23. David Skinner, "Racialised Futures: Biologism and the Changing Politics of Identity," *Social Studies of Science* 36, no. 3 (2006): 459–88; David Skinner, "Groundhog Day? The Strange Case of Sociology, Race and 'Science,'" *Sociology* 41, no. 5 (2007): 931–43.

24. Ramya Rajagopalan and Joan H. Fujimura, "Making History via DNA, Making DNA from History: Deconstructing the Race-Disease Connection in Admixture Mapping," in *Genetics and the Unsettled Past: The Collision of DNA, Race, and History*, ed. Keith Wailoo, Alondra Nelson, and Catherine Lee (New Brunswick, N.J.: Rutgers University Press, 2012), 143–63.

25. Jenny Reardon, "The Democratic, Anti-racist Genome? Technoscience at the Limits of Liberalism," *Science as Culture* 21, no. 1 (2012): 25–47.

26. In their discussion of whiteness, property, and human genomics, and drawing on David Theo Goldberg, Jenny Reardon and Kim TallBear have used the term "antiracialist" to describe approaches by white dominant groups that seek to dissolve racial categories without any fundamental change to the structures of racial dominance, in contrast to "antiracism," which does so. This is a helpful distinction. However, I use the term "antiracist" here to reflect the way in which human population genetics is commonly figured while drawing out the limits of this description. See Jenny Reardon and Kim TallBear, "'Your DNA Is *Our* History':

Genomics, Anthropology, and the Construction of Whiteness as Property," *Current Anthropology* 53, no. S5 (April 2012): 233–45, especially 234.

27. Peter Wade, "Race, Ethnicity and Nation: Perspectives from Kinship and Genetics," in *Race, Ethnicity and Nation: Perspectives from Kinship and Genetics*, ed. Peter Wade (New York: Berghahn Books, 2007), 1–31.

28. Eviatar Zerubavel, *Ancestors and Relatives: Genealogy, Identity, and Community* (Oxford: Oxford University Press, 2012).

29. Abu El-Haj, *The Genealogical Science*, 22–23.

30. My work on genetic genealogy builds on my previous focus on the making of genealogical identities through the practice of genealogy and the politics of origin stories and belonging through descent in conventional genealogy, especially that shaped by diasporic desires and encounters. See Catherine Nash, "Genealogical Identities," *Environment and Planning D: Society and Space* 20, no. 1 (2002): 1–33; and Catherine Nash, *Of Irish Descent: Origin Stories, Genealogy, and the Politics of Belonging* (Syracuse: Syracuse University Press, 2008).

31. Spencer Wells, *Deep Ancestry: Inside the Genographic Project* (Washington, D.C.: National Geographic Society, 2006).

32. Marilyn Strathern, *Kinship, Law and the Unexpected: Relatives Are Always a Surprise* (Cambridge: Cambridge University Press, 2005).

33. Despite the very different intent of recent accounts of networks of radical relationality, they, too, Strathern argues, reflect the cultural value placed on connections. Marilyn Strathern, "Cutting the Network," *Journal of the Royal Anthropological Institute* 2, no. 3 (1996): 517–35.

34. Marilyn Strathern, "Nostalgia and the New Genetics," in *Rhetorics of Self-Making*, ed. Debbora Battaglia (Berkeley: University of California Press, 1995), 97–120.

35. Jeanette Edwards, *Born and Bred: Idioms of Kinship and New Reproductive Technologies in England* (Oxford: Oxford University Press, 2000); Sarah Franklin and Susan McKinnon, eds., *Relative Values: Reconfiguring Kinship Studies* (Durham, N.C.: Duke University Press, 2001).

36. Edwards, *Born and Bred*, 28.

37. Jeanette Edwards and Marilyn Strathern, "Including Our Own," in *Cultures of Relatedness: New Approaches to the Study of Kinship*, ed. Janet Carsten (Cambridge: Cambridge University Press, 2000), 149–66, especially 160.

38. Jonathan Marks, *What It Means to Be 98% Chimpanzee: Apes, People and Their Genes* (Berkeley: University of California Press, 2002), 251.

39. Genetic investigations into questions of genealogical relatedness to royal families are clearly efforts to demonstrate the utility of new techniques and benefit from the resulting publicity. This is especially the case in companies set up by population geneticists to offer genetic genealogy testing services. Many high-profile claims can be traced back to commercial enterprises including those that

are figured as contributions to national historical understanding. This includes the widely reported claim that genetic testing shows that Prince William, the future British king, has Indian ancestry, timed to capitalize on the public interest in the birth of the royal couple's first child. See Michael White, "Monarchs, Murdochs and Middletons: The DNA of Dynasties," *The Guardian*, June 14, 2013.

40. See Rogers Brubaker, "Ethnicity, Race and Nationalism," *Annual Review of Sociology* 35 (2009): 21–42.

41. Anne McClintock, "Family Feuds: Gender, Nationalism and the Family," *Feminist Review* 44, no. 1 (1993): 61–80, especially 66–67.

42. European colonial genealogical, ethnic, and racial categorizations, and the preexisting categories of inclusion and exclusion based on descent as forms of "political genealogy" in colonial and postcolonial east Africa, are the subject of a special issue of *Social Identities* published in 2006. See James R. Brennan and Cedric Barnes, "Political Genealogy, Race and Territory in Eastern Africa," *Social Identities* 12, no. 4 (2006): 401–4.

43. Catherine Lee, "The Unspoken Significance of Gender in Constructing Kinship, Race and Nation," in *Genetics and the Unsettled Past: The Collision of DNA, Race, and History*, ed. Keith Wailoo, Alondra Nelson, and Catherine Lee (New Brunswick, N.J.: Rutgers University Press, 2012), 32–40.

44. Franklin and McKinnon, "Relative Values."

45. Ruth Hubbard, *The Politics of Women's Biology* (New Brunswick, N.J.: Rutgers University Press, 1990); Anne Fausto-Sterling, *Myths of Gender: Biological Theories about Women and Men* (New York: Basic Books, 1985); Sandra Harding, *The Science Question in Feminism* (Milton Keynes: Open University Press, 1986); Evelyn Fox Keller, *Reflections on Gender and Science* (New Haven: Yale University Press, 1985); Evelyn Fox Keller, *Secrets of Life, Secrets of Death: Essays on Language, Gender and Science* (New York: Routledge, 1992); Donna J. Haraway, *Simians, Cyborgs and Women: The Reinvention of Nature* (London: Free Association Books, 1991); Donna J. Haraway, *Primate Visions: Gender, Race, and Nature in the World of Modern Science* (London: Verso, 1992); Donna J. Haraway, *Modest_Witness@ Second_Millennium.FemaleMan_Meets_OncoMouse: Feminism and Technoscience* (London: Routledge, 1997); Bonnie B. Spanier, *Im/Partial Science: Gender Ideology in Molecular Biology* (Bloomington: Indiana University Press, 1995); Myra J. Hird, *Sex, Gender, Science* (Basingstoke: Palgrave Macmillan, 2004).

46. Amade M'charek, *The Human Genome Diversity Project: An Ethnography of Scientific Practice* (Cambridge: Cambridge University Press, 2005).

47. Roger N. Lancaster, *The Trouble with Nature: Sex in Science and Popular Culture* (Berkeley: University of California Press, 2003).

48. Lancaster, *The Trouble with Nature*.

49. Livingstone, "Cultural Politics and the Racial Cartographics"; Winlow, "Mapping, Race and Ethnicity."

50. Karen-Sue Taussig, *Ordinary Genomes: Science, Citizenship, and Genetic Identities* (Durham, N.C.: Duke University Press, 2009). This is central to recent work on the geographies of science. See, for example, David Livingstone, *Putting Science in Its Place: Geographies of Scientific Knowledge* (Chicago: University of Chicago Press, 2003); Peter Muesberger, David Livingstone, and Heike Jöns, eds., *Geographies of Science* (New York: Springer, 2010); Richard Powell, "Geographies of Science: Histories, Localities, Practices, Futures," *Progress in Human Geography* 31, no. 3 (2007): 309–29.

51. Paul Gilroy, "Diaspora and the Detours of Identity," in *Identity and Difference*, ed. Kath Woodward (London: Sage, in association with the Open University, 1997), 299–346.

52. Amy Hinterberger, "Categorization, Census and Multiculturalism: Molecular Politics and the Material of Nation," in *Genetics and the Unsettled Past: The Collision of DNA, Race, and History*, ed. Keith Wailoo, Alondra Nelson, and Catherine Lee (New Brunswick, N.J.: Rutgers University Press, 2012), 204–24.

53. This focus on the ways in which ideas of indigeneity are reworked and called into use in human population genetics in relation to groups conventionally not described as indigenous—and taken up by groups in different ways in relation to the politics of belonging, sometimes using genetic accounts of ancestry in doing so—offers another strand to recent geographical work on indigeneity. See E. Cameron, S. de Leeuw, and M. Greenwood, "Indigeneity," in *International Encyclopedia of Human Geography*, ed. Rob Kitchin and Nigel Thrift (Oxford: Elsevier Science, 2009), 352–57; R. Howitt, S. Muller, and S. Suchet-Pearson, "Indigenous Geographies," in *International Encyclopedia of Human Geography*, ed. Rob Kitchin and Nigel Thrift (Oxford: Elsevier Science, 2009), 358–64; Wendy Shaw, R. D. K. Herman, and G. Rebecca Dobbs, "Encountering Indigeneity: Re-Imagining and Decolonizing Geography," *Geografiska Annaler B* 88, no. 3 (2006): 267–76; Jay T. Johnson, Garth Cant, Richard Howitt, and Evelyn Peters, "Guest Editorial: Creating Anti-colonial Geographies: Embracing Indigenous People's Knowledges and Rights," *Geographical Research* 45, no. 2 (2007): 117–20; Ruth Panelli, "Social Geographies: Encounters with Indigenous and More-Than-White/Anglo Geographies," *Progress in Human Geography* 32, no. 6 (2008): 801–11.

54. Nash, *Of Irish Descent*, 10–21.

55. See, for example, Corrine Hayden, "A Biodiversity Sampler for the Millennium," in *Reproducing Reproduction: Kinship, Power, and Technological Innovation*, ed. Sarah Franklin and Helen Ragoné (Philadelphia: University of Pennsylvania Press, 1998), 173–203; Jonathan Marks, "We're Going to Tell These People Who They Really Are: Science and Relatedness," in *Relative Values: Reconfiguring Kinship Studies*, ed. Sarah Franklin and Susan McKinnon (Berkeley: Duke University Press, 2001), 355–83; Reardon, *Race to the Finish*.

56. Bambi Ceuppens and Peter Geschiere, "Autochthony: Local or Global?

New Modes in the Struggle over Citizenship and Belonging in Africa and Europe," *Annual Review of Anthropology* 34 (2005): 385–407; Peter Geschiere, *The Perils of Belonging: Autochthony, Citizenship, and Exclusion in Africa and Europe* (Chicago: University of Chicago Press, 2009).

1. Genome Geographies

1. Joan H. Fujimura and Ramya Rajagopalan, "Different Differences: The Use of 'Genetic Ancestry' versus Race in Biomedical Human Genetic Research," *Social Studies of Science* 41, no. 1 (2011): 5–30, especially 7 and 17.

2. Jonathan Marks, "Genetic Marker," in *Encyclopedia of Race and Racism*, vol. 2, ed. John H. Moore (Detroit: Macmillan Reference, 2007), 28–29.

3. Mark A. Jobling, Matthew E. Hurles, and Chris Tyler-Smith, *Human Evolutionary Genetics: Origins, People and Disease* (New York: Garland Science, 2004).

4. Reardon, *Race to the Finish*; Lisa Gannett, "Racism and Human Genome Diversity Research: The Ethical Limits of 'Population Thinking,'" *Philosophy of Science* 63, no. 3 (2001): 1–8.

5. M'charek, *The Human Genome Diversity Project*.

6. M'charek, *The Human Genome Diversity Project*, 15.

7. Margaret Lock, "The Human Genome Diversity Project: A Perspective from Cultural Anthropology," in *Human DNA: Law and Policy, International and Comparative Perspectives*, ed. Bartha Maria Knoppers, Claude M. Laberge, and Marie Hirtle (The Hague: Brill, 1997), 228–37; Hayden, "A Biodiversity Sampler," 173–203; Marks, "We're Going to Tell These People," 355–83; Jonathan Marks, "Your Body, My Property: The Problem of Colonial Genetics in a Postcolonial World," in *Embedding Ethics*, ed. Lynn Meskell and Peter Pels (New York: Berg, 2005), 29–45; Reardon, *Race to the Finish*.

8. Eric T. Juengst, "Group Identity and Human Diversity: Keeping Biology Straight from Culture," *American Journal of Human Genetics* 63, no. 3 (1998): 673–77.

9. Morris W. Foster and William L. Freeman, "Naming Names in Human Genetic Variation Research," *Genome Research* 8, no. 8 (1998): 755–57; Morris W. Foster and Richard R. Sharp, "Race, Ethnicity, and Genomics: Social Classifications as Proxies of Biological Heterogeneity," *Genome Research* 12, no. 6 (2002): 844–50.

10. Reardon, *Race to the Finish*, 77; Marks, *What It Means to Be*, 202–3.

11. Duana Fullwiley, "The Biologistic Construction of Race: 'Admixture' Technology and the New Genetic Medicine," *Social Studies of Science* 38, no. 5 (October 2008): 695–735.

12. Rajagopalan and Fujimura, "Making History via DNA," 143–63.

13. Rajagopalan and Fujimura, "Making History via DNA," 155.

14. Fujimura and Rajagopalan, "Different Differences," 7.

15. Catherine Bliss, "Genome Sampling and the Biopolitics of Race," in *A Foucault for the 21st Century: Governmentality, Biopolitics and Discipline in the New Millennium*, ed. S. Bickley and J. Capetillo (Boston: Cambridge Scholars, 2010), 320–37.

16. Steven Epstein, "Bodily Differences and Collective Identities: The Politics of Gender and Race in Biomedical Research in the United States," *Body and Society* 10, no. 2–3 (2004): 183–203, especially 198; Jonathan Kahn, "Genes, Race and Population: Avoiding a Collision of Categories," *American Journal of Public Health* 96, no. 11 (2006): 1965–70. The case of the ways in which the greater incidence of hypertension and the difficulty of its pharmaceutical treatment in African Americans has been interpreted and addressed through the development of the first "ethnic" or "racial" drug, BiDil, demonstrates the entanglements of arguments that range from calls for social justice in medicine to spurious but widely accepted historical and evolutionary explanations of racial differences in health, to visions and justifications of a future of racialized bioscience. See Jay S. Kauffman, "The Anatomy of a Medical Myth," Is Race "Real"? web forum by the Social Science Research Council, June 7, 2006, http://raceandgenomics.ssrc.org/Kaufman.

17. Troy Duster, "Race and Reification in Science," *Science* 307, no. 5712 (2005): 1050–51; Troy Duster, *Backdoor to Eugenics* (London: Routledge, 2003); Alan H. Goodman, "Why Genes Don't Count (for Racial Differences in Health)," *American Journal of Public Health* 90, no. 11 (2000): 1699–1702; Nancy Krieger, "If 'Race' Is the Answer, What Is the Question?—on 'Race,' Racism, and Health: A Social Epidemiologist's Perspective," Is Race "Real"? web forum by the Social Science Research Council, June 7, 2006, http://raceandgenomics.ssrc.org/Krieger.

18. John H. Relethford, "Genetic Variation among Populations," in *Encyclopedia of Race and Racism*, ed. John H. Moore (Detroit: Macmillan Reference, 2007), 29–34.

19. Deborah A. Bolnick, "Individual Ancestry Inference and the Reification of Race as a Biological Phenomenon," in *Revisiting Race in a Genomic Age*, ed. Barbara A. Koenig, Sandra Soo-Jin Lee, and Sarah S. Richardson (New Brunswick, N.J.: Rutgers University Press, 2008), 70–85, especially 72.

20. For an account of the controversies surrounding attempts to study the relationships between race, ancestry, and genetic variation from within the field of human genetics, see Michael Bamshad, Stephen Wooding, Benjamin A. Salisbury, and J. Claiborne Stephens, "Deconstructing the Relationships between Genetics and Race," *Nature Reviews Genetics* 5, no. 8 (2004): 589–609.

21. This is evident in the different perspectives of contributors to a special issue of *Nature Genetics* in 2004. See Lynn B. Jorde and Stephen P. Wooding, "Genetic Variation, Classification and 'Race,'" *Nature Genetics* 36, no. 11S (2004): 28–33;

S. O. Y. Keita, R. A. Kittles, C. D. M. Royal, G. E. Bonney, P. Furbert-Harris, G. M. Dunston, and C. N. Rotimi, "Conceptualising Human Variation," *Nature Genetics* 36, no. 11S (2004): 17–20; Charmaine D. M. Royal and Georgia M. Dunston, "Changing the Paradigm from 'Race' to Human Genome," *Nature Genetics* 36, no. 11S (2004): 5–7.

22. One example is the article by Armand Marie Leroi, "A Family Tree in Every Gene," *New York Times*, March 14, 2005, which was the focus of a series of critical responses published in an online forum titled "Is Race 'Real'?" organized by the U.S. Social Science Research Council, available at http://raceandgenomics.ssrc.org.

23. Nicholas Wade, *Before the Dawn: Recovering the Lost History of Our Ancestors* (New York: Penguin Press, 2006).

24. Marks, *What It Means to Be*.

25. Bolnick, "Individual Ancestry Inference." See also Jonathan Marks, "Anthropology, Race and the Genome: The Profound Relevance and Irrelevance of Biology," *General Anthropology* 11, no. 2 (2005): 1 and 5–7, especially 5; Marks, "Your Body, My Property," 29–45, especially 39.

26. Bolnick, "Individual Ancestry Inference," 81.

27. Abu El-Haj, *The Genealogical Science*.

28. Jenny Reardon, "Democratic Mis-Haps: The Problem of Democratization in a Time of Biopolitics," *BioSocieties* 2, no. 2 (2007): 239–56.

29. Reardon, "Democratic Mis-Haps," 241.

30. Ibid., 244.

31. Bolnick, "Individual Ancestry Inference," 80.

32. Pamela Sankar and Mildred K. Cho, "Towards a New Vocabulary of Human Genetic Variation," *Science* 298, no. 5597 (2002): 1337–38; Duana Fullwiley, "Race and Genetics: Attempts to Define the Relationship," *BioSciences* 2, no. 2 (2007): 221–37.

33. Reardon, "Democratic Mis-Haps," 250.

34. The apt phrase is from Jonathan Marks, "Grand Anthropological Themes," *American Ethnologist* 34, no. 2 (2007): 233–35, especially 233. There is a growing social science scholarship addressing genetic genealogy. See, for example, Paul Brodwin, "Genetics, Identity, and the Anthropology of Essentialism," *Anthropological Quarterly* 75, no. 2 (2002): 323–30; Carl Elliott and Paul Brodwin, "Identity and Genetic Ancestry Tracing," *British Medical Journal* 325, no. 7378 (2002): 1469–71; Marianne Sommer, "'Do You Have Celtic, Jewish or Germanic Roots?' Applied Swiss History before and after DNA," in *Identity Politics and the New Genetics: Re/Creating Categories of Difference and Belonging*, ed. Katharina Schramm, David Skinner, and Richard Rottenburg (New York: Berghahn Books, 2012), 116–40; Stephen Palmié, "Biotechnological Cults of Affliction? Race, Rationality and Enchantment in Personal Genomic Histories," in *Identity Politics and the*

New Genetics: Re/Creating Categories of Difference and Belonging, ed. Katharina Schramm, David Skinner, and Richard Rottenburg (New York: Berghahn Books, 2012), 193–211; James D. Faubion and Jennifer A. Hamilton, "Sumptury Kinship," *Anthropological Quarterly* 80, no. 3 (2007): 553–59.

35. Since 2000, genetic ancestry testing providers have proliferated, sometimes as subsidiaries of others, while mergers and takeovers resort the relationships between the increasing number of competitor companies involved. For recent surveys of the range of companies and services, see Charmaine D. Royal, John November, Stephanie M. Fullerton, David B. Goldstein, Jeffrey C. Long, Michael J. Bamshad, and Andrew G. Clark, "Inferring Genetic Ancestry: Opportunities, Challenges, and Implications," *American Journal of Human Genetics* 86, no. 5 (May 2010): 661–73; and Henry T. Greely, "Genetic Genealogy: Genetics Meets the Marketplace," in *Revisiting Race in a Genomic Age*, ed. Barbara A. Koenig, Sandra Soo-Jin Lee, and Sarah S. Richardson (New Brunswick, N.J.: Rutgers University Press, 2008), 215–34.

36. Haraway, *Modest_Witness*, 255.

37. "DNA Genealogy," GeoGene: Tracing Your Genetic Roots home page, http://www.geogene.com.

38. "About the Sorenson Molecular Genealogy Foundation," Sorenson Molecular Genealogy Foundation, http://www.smgf.org/pages/overview.jspx.

39. I argued this in an earlier engagement with these developments: Catherine Nash, "Mapping Origins: Race and Relatedness in Population Genetics and Genetic Genealogy," in *New Genetics, New Identities*, ed. Paul Atkinson and Peter Glasner (London: Routledge, 2007), 77–100.

40. For full, rich, and critical discussions of the genetic accounts of Jewish and Native American ancestries and ancestral histories and their wider implications, see Kimberly TallBear, "Native-American-DNA.com: In Search of Native American Race and Tribe," in *Revisiting Race in a Genomic Age*, ed. Barbara A. Koenig, Sandra Soo-Jin Lee, and Sarah S. Richardson (New Brunswick, N.J.: Rutgers University Press, 2008), 235–53; and Abu El-Haj, *The Genealogical Science*.

41. See, for example, Charles N. Rotimi, "Are Medical and Non-Medical Uses of Large-Scale Genomic Markers Conflating Genetics and 'Race'?" *Nature Genetics* 36, no. 11S (2004): 43–47.

42. Scott MacEachern, "Genes, Tribes and African History," *Current Anthropology* 41, no. 3 (2000): 357–84; Lundy Braun and Evelyn Hammonds, "The Dilemma of Classification," in *Genetics and the Unsettled Past: The Collision of DNA, Race, and History*, ed. Keith Wailoo, Alondra Nelson, and Catherine Lee (New Brunswick, N.J.: Rutgers University Press, 2012), 67–80.

43. Katharina Schramm, "Genomics en Route: Ancestry, Heritage and the Politics of Identity across the Black Atlantic," in *Identity Politics and the New*

Genetics: Re/Creating Categories of Difference and Belonging, ed. Katharina Schramm, David Skinner, and Richard Rottenburg (New York: Berghahn Books, 2012), 167–92.

44. Hans-Jürgen Bandelt, Yong-Gang Yao, Martin B. Richards, and Antonio Salas, "The Brave New Era of Human Genetic Testing," *BioEssays* 30, no. 11–12 (2008): 1246–51, especially 1247.

45. Alan R. Templeton, "Human Races in the Context of Recent Human Evolution: A Molecular Genetic Perspective," in *Genetic Nature/Culture: Anthropology and Science Beyond the Two Culture Divide,* ed. Alan H. Goodman, Deborah Heath, and M. Susan Lindee (Berkeley: University of California Press, 2003), 234–57.

46. Schramm, "Genomics en Route," 187.

47. Royal et al., "Inferring Genetic Ancestry," 666.

48. Mark D. Shriver and Rick A. Kittles, "Genetic Ancestry and the Search for Personalised Genetic Histories," *Nature Reviews Genetics* 5, no. 8 (August 2004): 611–18, especially 612.

49. Shriver and Kittles, "Genetic Ancestry and the Search," 616.

50. The earlier version appeared in explanatory material that accompanied a test result I received in 2006. The later versions appear on the AncestryByDNA website: http://www.ancestrybydna.com/ancestry-by-dna-faq.php.

51. Sandra Soo-Jin Lee, Deborah A. Bolnick, Troy Duster, Pilar Ossorio, and Kimberly TallBear, "The Illusive Gold Standard in Genetic Ancestry Testing," *Science* 325, no. 5936 (July 2009): 38–39, especially 39. See also Keith Wailoo, "Who Am I? Genes and the Problem of Historical Identity," in *Genetics and the Unsettled Past: The Collision of DNA, Race, and History,* ed. Keith Wailoo, Alondra Nelson, and Catherine Lee (New Brunswick, N.J.: Rutgers University Press, 2012), 13–19.

52. Jobling, Hurles, and Tyler-Smith, *Human Evolutionary Genetics,* 9–10.

53. This dynamism and diversity of stakeholders with different interests makes the development of regulation and agreement on best practice in the sector difficult, as argued in Soo-Jin Lee et al., "The Illusive Gold Standard," 38–39.

54. Ysearch.org home page, http://www.ysearch.org; Mitosearch.org home page, http://www.mitosearch.org.

55. Debbie Kennett, *DNA and Social Networking: A Guide to Genealogy in the Twenty-First Century* (Stroud: History Press, 2011).

56. "Surname & Geographical Projects: Family Tree DNA Surname, Lineage and Geographical Projects," Family Tree DNA, http://www.familytreedna.com/projects.aspx.

57. One of the main popular guidebooks on the use of genetic tests in genealogy suggests that surname projects are the most common application of these tests. See Megan Smolenyak Smolenyak and Ann Turner, *Trace Your Roots with*

DNA: Using Genetic Tests to Explore Your Family Tree (New York: Rodale Press, 2004), 57.

58. I discuss the case of Irish Gaelic surname projects in Catherine Nash, "Irish DNA: Making Connections and Making Distinctions in Y-Chromosome Surname Studies," in *Identity Politics and the New Genetics: Re/Creating Categories of Difference and Belonging*, ed. Katharina Schramm, David Skinner, and Richard Rottenburg (New York: Berghahn Books, 2012), 141–66. Or see Nash, *Of Irish Descent*, 219–63, for a longer discussion. Marianne Sommer also considers these group projects in "DNA and Cultures of Remembrance," 366–90.

59. Alondra Nelson, "Bio Science," 759–83, especially 771. See also Alondra Nelson, "The Factness of Diaspora: The Social Sources of Genetic Genealogy," in *Revisiting Race in a Genomic Age*, ed. Barbara A. Koenig, Sandra Soo-Jin Lee, and Sarah S. Richardson (New Brunswick, N.J.: Rutgers University Press, 2008), 253–68.

60. Nash, *Of Irish Descent*, 10–19.

61. Abu El-Haj, *The Genealogical Science*.

62. Reardon, "The Democratic, Anti-racist Genome?," 25–47, especially 26.

63. Reardon, "The Democratic, Anti-racist Genome?," 39–40.

64. *Blood of the Irish: Who Are the Irish and Where Do They Come From?*, documentary, Crossing the Line Films, RTÉ 2009, see http://www.rte.ie/tv/bloodoftheirish.

65. I discuss this case more fully in Catherine Nash, "Blood of the Irish: Knowing 'Ourselves' Genetically," *Irish Review* 48 (Summer 2014): 1–16.

66. See Jennifer A. Hamilton, "The Case of the Genetic Ancestor," in *Genetics and the Unsettled Past: The Collision of DNA, Race, and History*, ed. Keith Wailoo, Alondra Nelson, and Catherine Lee (New Brunswick, N.J.: Rutgers University Press, 2012), 226–78; Alondra Nelson, "Reconciliation Projects: From Kinship to Justice," in *Genetics and the Unsettled Past: The Collision of DNA, Race, and History*, ed. Keith Wailoo, Alondra Nelson, and Catherine Lee (New Brunswick, N.J.: Rutgers University Press, 2012), 20–31.

2. Mapping the Global Human Family

1. National Geographic, Genographic Project website, https://genographic.nationalgeographic.com. This excerpt comes from an earlier iteration of the website as first accessed in 2006.

2. National Geographic, *The Human Family Tree*, television documentary, 2009. Documentary description available at http://channel.nationalgeographic.com/channel/episodes/the-human-family-tree1/. The original description that I quote here is as it appeared on the website in 2009. It has been edited since.

3. Sommer, "DNA and Cultures of Remembrance," 366–90.

4. This is recognized by other human population geneticists who are concerned about the degree to which "big science" projects of this sort undermine funding for other research in the field and often lag behind the latest developments. Bandelt et al., "The Brave New Era," 1246–51.

5. See the Genographic Project Classroom Companion, http://www.ngsednet .org/community/resources_view.cfm?community_id=278&resource_id=6477, and the Genographic Project lesson plans, http://www.nationalgeographic.com/ xpeditions/lessons/09/g912/genographic1.html.

6. Áine Ryan, "Enda Kenny May Be Related to Niall of the Nine Hostages," *The Irish Times*, June 24, 2013.

7. The kits were originally priced at $99.95. The new kit—Geno 2.0, released in 2012—costs $199.95.

8. National Geographic, "Genographic Legacy Fund Charter Document," May 2006, https://www3.nationalgeographic.com/geneographic/legacy_fund .html.

9. Lock, "The Human Genome Diversity Project," 228–37; Hayden, "A Biodiversity Sampler," 173–203; Marks, "We're Going to Tell These People," 355–83; Marks, "Your Body, My Property," 29–45; Reardon, *Race to the Finish*.

10. Haraway, *Modest_Witness*, 248–53.

11. Spencer Wells, "How Much We Have to Learn," *Cultural Survival Quarterly* 29, no. 4 (2005): 34.

12. Epstein, "Bodily Differences and Collective Identities," 183–203.

13. Hinterberger, "Categorization, Census and Multiculturalism," 204–24.

14. Walter Benn Michaels, *The Trouble with Diversity: How We Learned to Love Identity and Ignore Inequality* (New York: Metropolitan Books, 2006), 12.

15. Katharyn Mitchell, "Geographies of Identity: Multiculturalism Unplugged," *Progress in Human Geography* 28, no. 5 (2004): 641–51.

16. Anne Phillips, "From Inequality to Difference: A Severe Case of Displacement?" *New Left Review* 224 (July–August 1997): 143–53; Michaels, *The Trouble with Diversity*; Katharyn Mitchell, "Educating the National Citizen in Neoliberal Times: From the Multicultural Self to the Strategic Cosmopolitan," *Transactions of the Institute of British Geographers* 28, no. 4 (2003): 387–403.

17. Nancy Fraser, "Rethinking Recognition," *New Left Review* 3 (May–June 2000): 107–12.

18. Ghassan Hage, *White Nation: Fantasies of White Supremacy in a Multicultural Society* (Annandale, New South Wales: Pluto Press, 1998); Joyce M. Bell and Douglas Hartmann, "Diversity in Everyday Discourses: The Cultural Ambiguities of 'Happy Talk,'" *American Sociological Review* 72, no. 6 (2007): 895–914.

19. Ien Ang and Jon Stratton, "Multicultural Imagined Communities: Cultural Difference and National Identity in Australia and the USA," *Continuum: Australian Journal of Media and Culture* 8, no. 2 (1994): 124–58.

20. Wendy Brown, *Regulating Aversion: Tolerance in the Age of Identity and Empire* (Princeton: Princeton University Press, 2006).

21. Spencer Wells, *The Journey of Man: A Genetic Odyssey* (London: Penguin, 2003), xiii.

22. This text appeared on the Waitt Foundation website in 2005 but no longer does. Visitors are now directed toward general information about the Genographic Project at http://waittfoundation.org/?s=genographic.

23. National Geographic Society, *Journey of Man*, television documentary, 2004.

24. Wells, *The Journey of Man*, 8–13.

25. Ibid., 17; Richard Lewontin, "The Apportionment of Human Diversity," *Journal of Evolutionary Biology* 6 (1972): 381–98.

26. Rebecca Cann, Mark Stoneking, and Allan Wilson, "Mitochondrial DNA and Human Evolution," *Nature* 325 (January 1987): 31–36.

27. Alan R. Templeton, "Out of Africa Again and Again," *Nature* 416 (March 2002): 45–51; Alan R. Templeton, "Revolutionizing the 'Out of Africa' Story," *GEN: Genetic Engineering and Biotechnology News* 33, no. 7 (2013), http://www.genengnews.com/gen-articles/revolutionizing-the-quot-out-of-africa-quot-story/4804/?kwrd=Insight%20Genetics.

28. Genographic Project, Public Participation Kit leaflet, 19.

29. Catherine A. Lutz and Jane L. Collins, *Reading National Geographic* (Chicago: University of Chicago Press, 1993).

30. Celia Lury, "The United Colours of Diversity: Essential and Inessential Culture," in *Global Nature, Global Culture*, ed. Sarah Franklin, Celia Lury, and Jackie Stacey (London: Sage, 2000), 146–87.

31. Genographic Project, Public Participation Kit leaflet.

32. Novembre et al., "Genes Mirror Geography," 98–103.

33. Genographic Project, Public Participation Kit map (Washington, D.C.: National Geographic Society, 2005).

34. Livingstone, "Cultural Politics and the Racial Cartographics," 204–21. See also Winlow, "Mapping, Race and Ethnicity," 398–404.

35. Templeton, "Human Races in the Context," 234–57; S. O. Y. Keita and Rick A. Kittles, "The Persistence of Racial Thinking and the Myth of Racial Divergence," *American Anthropologist* 99, no. 3 (1997): 543–44, especially 540.

36. Marks, *What It Means to Be*, 202–3.

37. Juengst, "Group Identity and Human Diversity," 673–77.

38. See also Priscilla Wald's analysis of the *Journey of Man* documentary and her argument about the stories, languages, and images through which human population genomics is presented and interpreted by scientists, journals, and the public. Priscilla Wald, "Blood and Stories: How Genomics Is Rewriting Race, Medicine and Human History," *Patterns of Prejudice* 40, no. 4–5 (2006): 303–33.

39. Michael Shnayerson, "The Map of Us All," *National Geographic Adventure* 7 (2005): 78–83 and 89, especially 81. See also the account of Wells's work in Chad that uses similar terms and especially emphasizes the risk Wells encountered "given the unstable political situation in Chad": Gunjan Sinha, "Footsteps in the Sand," *New Scientist* 189, no. 2544 (2006): 48–49.

40. Quoted in Shnayerson, "The Map of Us All," 84.

41. Wells, *The Journey of Man*, 39.

42. Ibid., 48.

43. Ibid.

44. See John Edward Terrell and Pamela J. Stewart, "The Paradox of Human Population Genetics at the End of the Twentieth Century," *Reviews in Anthropology* 25, no. 1 (1996): 13–33.

45. Eric Wolf, *Europe and the People without History* (Berkeley: University of California Press, 1982).

46. Tim Ingold, "Ancestry, Generation, Substance, Memory, Land," in *The Perception of the Environment: Essays on Livelihood, Dwelling and Skill*, ed. Tim Ingold (London: Routledge, 2000), 132–51, especially 132.

47. Alan Goodman, "Towards Genetics in an Era of Anthropology," *American Ethnologist* 34, no. 2 (2007): 225–22.

48. Marks, *What It Means to Be*, 169–71; see also S. O. Y. Keita and Rick A. Kittles, "The Persistence of Racial Thinking," 543–44, especially 539; Margaret Lock, "The Alienation of Body Tissue and the Biopolitics of Immortalized Cell Lines," *Body and Society* 7, no. 2–3 (2001): 63–91, especially 80.

49. Marks, "We're Going to Tell These People," 370.

50. This text appeared on the original home page of the Genographic Project website in 2005. The site has been redeveloped since. See https://genographic.nationalgeographic.com.

51. Wells, *Deep Ancestry*, 4.

52. Hayden, "A Biodiversity Sampler."

53. Wells, *The Journey of Man*, 194.

54. This is the text from the Frequently Asked Questions section of the Genographic Project website in its 2005 iteration. The answer to the question "What will the end result be?" ended by stating, "Among other things, we hope that the findings from the project will underscore how closely related we are to one another as part of the extended human family." Accessed February 8, 2005.

55. Kimberly TallBear, *Native American DNA: Narratives of Origin and Race* (PhD diss., University of California, Santa Cruz, 2005), 241; see also Kimberly TallBear, "Narratives of Race and Indigeneity in the Genographic Project," *Journal of Law, Medicine & Ethics* 35, no. 3 (Fall 2007): 412–24.

56. James Clifford, "Varieties of Indigenous Experience: Diasporas, Homelands, Sovereignties," in *Indigenous Experience Today*, ed. Marisol de la Cadena

and Orin Starn (Oxford: Berg, 2007), 197–224; Robin Maria DeLugan, "Indigeneity across Borders: Hemispherical Migrations and Cosmopolitan Encounters," *American Ethnologist* 37, no. 1 (2010): 83–97.

57. Wells, *The Journey of Man*, 193–94.

58. Wells, *Deep Ancestry*, 5.

59. "Collective Statement of Indigenous Organizations Opposing 'The Genographic Project,' Agenda Item 4," presented on behalf of Global Indigenous Caucus, Buffalo River Dine Nation, International Indian Treaty Council (IITC), Indigenous Peoples Council on Biocolonialism (IPCB), and the Knowledgeable Aboriginal Youth Association, Fifth Session, UN Permanent Forum on Indigenous Issues, New York, May 15–26, 2006, http://www.ipcb.org/issues/human_genetics/htmls/unpf5_collstate.html; "Indigenous Peoples Oppose National Geographic & IBM Genetic Research Project That Seeks Indigenous Peoples' DNA," Indigenous Peoples Council on Biocolonialism press release, April 13, 2005, http://www.ipcb.org/issues/human_genetics/htmls/geno_pr.html; "IPCB Action Alert to Oppose the Genographic Project," April 13, 2005, http://www.ipcb.org/issues/human_genetics/htmls/action_geno.html; "United Nations Recommends Halt to Genographic Project," May 2006, http://www.ipcb.org/issues/human_genetics/htmls/unpfii_rec.html.

60. Wells, *The Journey of Man*, 195.

61. National Geographic, "Genographic Legacy Fund Charter Document," May 2006; Ellen L. Lutz, "Cultural Survival Calls for Genographics Moratorium," *Cultural Survival Quarterly* 30, no. 3 (2006): 99.

62. Ellen L. Lutz, "Genetic Research on Human Migration," *Cultural Survival Quarterly* 29, no. 4 (2005): 34; Lutz, "Cultural Survival," 99; Debra Harry and Le 'a Malia Kanehe, "Collecting Blood to Preserve Culture?," *Cultural Survival Quarterly* 29, no. 4 (2005): 34; Stella Tamang and Richard Grounds, "Genographic Project Discussion at Cultural Survival," *Cultural Survival Quarterly* 29, no. 4 (2005): 37.

63. Criticisms from indigenous organizations led by the Indigenous Peoples Council on Biocolonialism (IPCB) immediately followed the project launch in March 2005. The IPCB submitted a petition against the project to the National Geographic Society in May 2005 and were active in raising concerns about the project in the UN Permanent Forum on Indigenous Issues in 2006. This has led to the forum's request that the Genographic Project be immediately suspended and recommendation that the Human Rights Commission and the World Health Organization investigate the objectives of the project. In August 2005, the International Indian Treaty Council called for a halt of the project. In July 2006, after discussions with the project's representatives that failed to satisfy their concerns, Cultural Survival, an organization promoting indigenous rights, asked the National Geographic to suspend the project and called for a moratorium on the project (See Lutz, "Cultural Survival," 99).

64. Jenny Reardon has tracked the Genographic Project organizers' resistance to take on board the project's relation to asymmetries of economic and cultural power and argues for a much deeper recognition of the power differentials that crosscut a genuinely shared goal of "conducting genomic research in a manner that respects Indigenous People and their rights." See Jenny Reardon, "'Anti-colonial Genomic Practice?': Learning from the Genographic Project and the Chacmool Conference," *International Journal of Cultural Property* 16 (2009): 205–13, especially 208. Michael Kent's account of the use of Genographic Project research by the Uros—an indigenous group living on floating islands on Lake Titicaca in Peru—to assert their ethnic distinctiveness to support their territorial claims in conflict with the state suggests the complex and diverse ways genetic research is incorporated into political debates over indigenous identity and its relation to preexisting practices of ethnic definition. He argues that this case suggests that genetic research may be most problematic for indigenous groups whose rights and claims are already recognized but can be used as a resource for indigenous groups whose rights and claims are contested. In this case, genetic accounts of ancestry are flexibly used alongside sociocultural discourses, sometimes conflated and sometimes kept apart, and this strategic use "has so far not been matched by similar transformations in the ways they speak about identity and belonging among themselves." Michael Kent, "The Importance of Being Uros: Indigenous Identity Politics in the Genomic Age," *Social Studies of Science* 43, no. 4 (August 2013): 534–56, especially 552.

65. An earlier iteration of the Genographic Project website contained the subpages "Indigenous Representatives Profiles" and "Indigenous Representatives Tell Their Stories." They no longer appear there. Instead, a much more fully elaborated section on the ethics of gathering indigenous material has been developed. See https://genographic.nationalgeographic.com/faq/indigenous-and-traditional-communities/. Kimberly TallBear's analysis of the launch event demonstrates the ways in which the three men served the Genographic Project's attempt to portray the project as a "multiculturalist coming together of scientific and indigenous knowledge" even while indigenous knowledge is ultimately secondary to the project's search for scientific truth (TallBear, *Native American DNA*, 262).

66. Wells, *The Journey of Man*, xvi.

67. Ibid., 80.

68. Wells, "How Much We Have to Learn," 34.

69. Reardon and TallBear, "'Your DNA Is *Our* History,'" 233–45, especially 234.

70. This focus on autosomal markers rather than just Y-chromosome or mtDNA markers is one of the two strands of the second phase of the project announced in December 2012. The second strand is offering customers the chance to see whether there is evidence of "non-modern-human ancestors"—that is, Neanderthal and Denisovan ancestry—in their genome. There is no discussion of what

this incorporation of evidence of the genetic legacy of nonmodern humans, who also originated in Africa but migrated to Eurasia before the emergence of modern humans, implies for accounts of the shared human origins and the global family tree. See http://genographic.nationalgeographic.com/about.

71. Shnayerson, "The Map of Us All."

72. See, for example, Robert Kellygoss, "Black, White, Brown . . . What's the Difference?" *Daily Advance*, April 24, 2006.

73. See Spencer Wells in "A Family Story," a section of a short video titled *Written in the Blood*, available online as a supplement to the online version of *National Geographic* magazine, March 2006, http://www7.nationalgeographic.com/ngm/0603/feature2/multimedia.html.

74. McClintock, "Family Feuds," 61–80.

75. Edwards, *Born and Bred*; Janet Carsten, *After Kinship* (Cambridge: Cambridge University Press, 2003).

76. Melissa Bamford and James Leach, eds., *Kinship and Beyond: The Genealogical Model Reconsidered* (Oxford: Berghahn Books, 2009).

77. Wald, "Future Perfect," 681–708, especially 704.

78. Gillian Rose, "Family Photographs and Domestic Spacings: A Case Study," *Transactions of the Institute of British Geographers* 28, no. 1 (2003): 5–18.

79. The National Geographic Channel website included this text and individual participant biographies and "deep ancestry" results when the documentary was launched in 2009. More limited information is now available at http://channel.nationalgeographic.com/channel/a-night-of-exploration/episodes/the-human-family-tree/.

80. Strathern, "Cutting the Network," 517–35.

81. J. Philippe Rushton, "Ethnic Nationalism, Evolutionary Psychology and Genetic Similarity Theory," *Nations and Nationalism* 11, no. 4 (2005): 489–507, especially 490. Rushton's earlier work informed the notoriously racist account of intelligence in Richard J. Hernstein's *The Bell Curve: Intelligence and Class Structure in American Life* (New York: Free Press, 1994).

82. Rushton, "Ethnic Nationalism," 500. Like other evolutionary psychologists such as Frank Salter, Rushton does not argue that these drives for collective reproductive success are uncomplicated by modern political or ethical norms, but like Salter, he asserts that they are fundamental aspects of human social organization. Salter's book *On Genetic Interests: Family, Ethnicity and Humanity in the Age of Mass Migration* (Frankfurt: Peter Lang, 2003) is an account of the persistence of genetically grounded ethnic bonds despite the complexity of modern, mobile, and multicultural societies. Salter leads a recent strand of research that seeks to apply sociobiological concepts, such as the idea of the evolutionary origins of trust and risk taking as based in the drive to further the genetic survival of closest kin, to explanations of social behavior within and across ethnic groups. See Frank K. Salter,

ed., *Risky Transactions: Trust, Kinship and Ethnicity* (New York: Berghahn Books, 2002).

83. Donovan Webster, "Footsteps of My Ancestors," *National Geographic Traveller* 22, no. 7 (2005): 66–75.

84. See "Meet the Izzards," BBC Media Centre, Programme Information, http://www.bbc.co.uk/mediacentre/proginfo/2013/08/meet-the-izzards.html.

85. See IrelandsDNA home page, http://www.irelandsdna.com; BritainsDNA home page, http://www.britainsdna.com; ScotlandsDNA home page, http://www.scotlandsDNA.com; YorkshiresDNA home page, http://www.yorkshiresdna.com. There is also an IzzardsDNA site that describes the documentary and has links to the genetic ancestry tests that are also offered on the other sites. See http://www.izzardsdna.com.

86. See, for example, David Brown, "Revealed: The Indian Ancestry of William," *The Times*, June 14, 2013.

87. "Journey of Man by Private Jet," National Geographic Expeditions, Destinations, http://nationalgeographicexpeditions.com/expeditions/journey-of-man-jet-tour/detail.

3. Our Genetic Heritage

1. Wellcome Trust, "People of the British Isles," video feature, 2010, http://genome.wellcome.ac.uk/doc_WTX063757.html.

2. See the People of the British Isles website at http://www.peopleofthebritishisles.org.

3. Walter Bodmer, quoted in "Donate Your DNA to Reveal Your East Anglian Roots," University of East Anglia press release, February 21, 2006, http://www.uea.ac.uk/mac/comm/media/press/2006/feb/Donate+your+DNA+to+reveal+your+East+Anglian+roots.

4. *British, More or Less*, BBC Radio Four, broadcast July 27, 2011, http://www.bbc.co.uk/programmes/b012r6z8.

5. "Gene Geography: History's Genetic Legacy," Wellcome Trust News, 2004, http://www.wellcome.ac.uk/News/2004/Features/WTX022535.htm.

6. Joan H. Fujimura, Troy Duster, and Ramya Rajagopalan, "Race, Genetics, and Disease: Questions of Evidence, Matters of Consequence," *Social Studies of Science* 38, no. 5 (2008): 643–56; Fullwiley, "Race and Genetics," 221–37; Gannett, "Racism and Human Genome Diversity," 479–92; Koenig, Lee, and Richardson, *Revisiting Race in a Genomic Age*; Whitmarsh and Jones, *What's the Use of Race?*; Duster, *Backdoor to Eugenics*.

7. Peter Wade, "Race, Ethnicity and Nation," 1–31.

8. Steve Fenton, *Ethnicity* (Cambridge: Polity Press, 2010), 12–23.

9. M'charek, *The Human Genome Diversity Project*; Fujimura and Rajagopalan, "Different Differences," 5–30, especially 7 and 17.

10. Nikolas Rose, "The Politics of Life Itself," *Theory, Culture and Society* 18, no. 6 (2001): 1–30, especially 13; Nikolas Rose, *The Politics of Life Itself* (Princeton: Princeton University Press, 2007). See Gail Davies, "Molecular Life," in *A Companion to Social Geography*, ed. V. J. Del Casino Jr., M. E. Thomas, P. Cloke, and R. Panelli (Oxford: Wiley-Blackwell, 2011), 257–74.

11. Rose, "The Politics of Life Itself," 5.

12. Deborah Heath, Rayna Rapp, and Karen-Sue Taussig, "Genetic Citizenship," in *A Companion to the Anthropology of Politics*, ed. David Nugent and Joan Vincent (Oxford: Blackwell, 2008), 152–67; Nikolas Rose and Carlos Novas, "Biological Citizenship," in *Global Assemblages: Technology, Politics, and Ethics as Anthropological Problems*, ed. Aihwa Ong and Stephen J. Collier (Oxford: Blackwell, 2004), 439–63. Bruce Braun is critical of the lack of attentiveness to the geographical specificity of this account of the "molecularization of life." See Bruce Braun, "Biopolitics and the Molecularization of Life," *Cultural Geographies* 14, no. 1 (2007): 6–28.

13. Rose, "The Politics of Life Itself," 5.

14. Paul Rabinow, "Fragmentation and Redemption in Late Modernity," in *Essays on the Anthropology of Reason*, ed. P. Rabinow (Princeton: Princeton University Press, 1996).

15. Sujatha Raman and Richard Tutton, "Life, Science, and Biopower," *Science Technology and Human Values* 35, no. 5 (2009): 711–34; Braun, "Biopolitics and the Molecularization," 6–28.

16. Sandra Soo-Jin Lee, "Biobanks of a 'Racial Kind': Mining for Difference in the New Genetics," *Patterns of Prejudice* 40, nos. 4–5 (2006): 443–60.

17. Beth Greenhough, "Assembling an Island Laboratory," *Area* 43, no. 2 (2011): 134–38; Pálsson, *Anthropology and the New Genetics*.

18. Taussig, *Ordinary Genomes*.

19. Steve Garner, "The Entitled Nation: How People Make Themselves White in Contemporary England," *Sens Public*, 2010, http://www.sens-public.org/spip .php?article729&lang=fr; Krishan Kumar, "Negotiating English Identity: Englishness, Britishness and the Future of the United Kingdom," *Nations and Nationalism* 16, no. 3 (2010): 469–87.

20. Ben Rogaly and Becky Taylor, *Moving Histories of Class and Community: Identity, Place and Belonging in Contemporary England* (Basingstoke: Palgrave Macmillan, 2009); Chris Haylett, "Illegitimate Subjects? Abject Whites, Neo-Liberal Modernisation and Middle Class Multiculturalism," *Environment and Planning D: Society and Space* 19, no. 3 (2001): 351–70.

21. Tariq Modood, *Still Not Easy Being British: Struggles for a Multicultural Citizenship* (Stoke-on-Trent: Trentham Books, 2010).

22. Derek McGhee, *The End of Multiculturalism? Terrorism, Integration and Human Rights* (Maidenhead: Open University Press, 2008).

23. Wellcome Trust, "People of the British Isles," video feature, 2010, http://genome.wellcome.ac.uk/doc_WTX063757.html.

24. "Channel 4 and Northern Ireland Researchers Are After Your Blood!," People of the British Isles and Wag TV/Channel Four press release, December 21, 2005.

25. Fujimura and Rajagopalan, "Different Differences."

26. Wellcome Trust, "Linking Genes to Disease," 2006, http://genome.wellcome.ac.uk/doc_WTX036463.html.

27. The People of the British Isles project is not the first attempt to undertake a national genetic survey. Earlier research projects have also been couched in terms of a census of Britain or the British Isles. See Cristian Capelli, Nicola Redhead, Julia. K. Abernethy, Fiona Gratrix, James F. Wilson, Torolf Moen, Tor Hervig, Martin Richards, Michael P. H. Stumpf, Peter A. Underhill, Paul Bradshaw, Alom Shaha, Mark G. Thomas, Neal Bradman, and David B. Goldstein, "A Y Chromosome Census of the British Isles," *Current Biology* 13, no. 11 (2003): 979–84. Bryan Sykes also described his research on mtDNA and Y-chromosome research as the Oxford Genetic Atlas Project. See Bryan Sykes, *Blood of the Isles: Exploring the Genetic Roots of Our Tribal History* (London: Bantam Press, 2006). See also Martin Richards, Cristian Capelli, and James, F. Wilson, "Genetics and the Origins of the British Population," *Encyclopedia of Life Sciences* (ELS), published online July 2008, doi:10.1002/9780470015902.a0020804; K. Boyle and C. Renfrew, eds., *Archaeogenetics: DNA and the Population Prehistory of Europe* (Cambridge: McDonald Institute for Archaeological Research, 2001). I discuss the national and postcolonial politics of studies of genetic variation in Ireland in Catherine Nash, "Irish Origins, Celtic Origins: Population Genetics, Cultural Politics," *Irish Studies Review* 14, no. 1 (2006): 11–37.

28. Stephen Oppenheimer, *The Origins of the British: A Genetic Detective Story* (London: Constable, 2006); Sykes, *Blood of the Isles*; Chris Moffatt and Jim Wilson, *The Scots: A Genetic Journey* (Edinburgh: Birlinn, 2011) and the radio series of the same name, BBC Radio Scotland, February–March 2011; David Miles, *The Tribes of Britain: Who Are We? And Where Do We Come From?* (London: Phoenix, 2005).

29. Marianne Sommer explores the work of Bryan Sykes and his Oxford Ancestors genetic testing company. See Marianne Sommer, "'It's a Living History, Told by the Real Survivors of the Times—DNA': Anthropological Genetics in the Tradition of Biology as Applied History," in *Genetics and the Unsettled Past: The Collision of DNA, Race, and History*, ed. Keith Wailoo, Alondra Nelson, and Catherine Lee (New Brunswick, N.J.: Rutgers University Press, 2012), 225–46.

30. Stephen Harding, Mark Jobling, and Turi King, *Viking DNA: The Wirral and West Lancashire Project* (Birkenhead: Nottingham University Press, 2010);

Georgina R. Bowden, Patricia Balaresque, Turi E. King, Ziff Hansen, Andrew C. Lee, Giles Pergl-Wilson, Emma Hurley, Stephen J. Roberts, Patrick Waite, Judith Jesch, Abigail L. Jones, Mark G. Thomas, Stephen E. Harding, and Mark A. Jobling, "Excavating Past Population Structures by Surname-Based Sampling: The Genetic Legacy of the Vikings in Northwest England," *Molecular Biology and Evolution* 25, no. 2 (2008): 301–9.

31. John Beckett, *Writing Local History* (Manchester: Manchester University Press, 2007).

32. Turi E. King, Stéphane J. Ballereau, Kevin Schürer, and Mark A. Jobling, "Genetic Signatures of Coancestry within Surnames," *Current Biology* 16, no. 4 (2006): 384–88; Turi E. King and Mark A. Jobling, "What's in a Name? Y Chromosomes, Surnames, and the Genetic Genealogy Revolution," *Trends in Genetics* 25, no. 28 (2009): 351–60; Turi E. King and Mark A. Jobling, "Founders, Drift and Infidelity: The Relationship between Y Chromosome Diversity and Patrilineal Surnames," *Molecular Biology and Evolution* 26, no. 5 (2009): 1093–1102; Bryan Sykes and Catherine Irven, "Surnames and the Y Chromosome," *American Journal of Human Genetics* 66, no. 4 (2000): 1417–19.

33. George Redmonds, Turi King, and David Hey, *Surnames, DNA, and Family History* (Oxford: Oxford University Press, 2011); *Surnames, Genes and Genealogy*, BBC Radio Four, BBC Natural History Unit, 2001, which I discuss in more detail in Catherine Nash, "Genetic Kinship," *Cultural Studies* 18, no. 1 (2004): 1–34.

34. Bruce Winney, Abdelhamid Boumertit, Tammy Day, Dan Davison, Chikodi Echeta, Irina Evseeva, Katarzyna Hutnik, et al., "People of the British Isles: Preliminary Analysis of Genotypes and Surnames in a UK-Control Population," *European Journal of Human Genetics* 20, no. 2 (2012): 203–10.

35. Paul A. Longley, James A. Cheshire, and Pablo Mateos, "Creating a Regional Geography of Britain through the Spatial Analysis of Surnames," *Geoforum* 42, no. 4 (2011): 506–16; James A. Cheshire and Paul A. Longley, "Identifying Spatial Concentrations of Surnames," *International Journal of Geographical Information Science* 26, no. 2 (2012): 309–25.

36. "The Impact of Diasporas on the Making of Britain: Evidence, Memories, Inventions," The Impact of Diasporas, University of Leicester, http://www2.le.ac.uk/projects/impact-of-diasporas.

37. "The Roots of the British, 1000 BC–AD 1000," The Impact of Diasporas, University of Leicester, http://www2.le.ac.uk/projects/impact-of-diasporas/Roots.

38. Robert J. C. Young, *The Idea of English Ethnicity* (Oxford: Blackwell, 2008), 13.

39. Young, *The Idea of English Ethnicity*, 39.

40. James Urry, "Englishmen, Celts, and Iberians: The Ethnographic Survey of the United Kingdom, 1892–1899," in *Functionalism Historicized: Essays on British*

Social Anthropology, ed. George W. Stocking (Madison: University of Wisconsin Press, 1984), 83–105.

41. D. F. Roberts and Eric Sunderland, eds., *Genetic Variation in Britain* (London: Taylor and Francis, 1973).

42. BBC Two, *Motherland: A Genetic Journey*, television documentary, directed by Archie Baron, 2003; Channel 4, *100% English*, television documentary, directed by David Batty, 2006; BBC, *Blood of the Vikings*, television documentary series, produced by Caroline van den Brul, 2001. Richard Tutton explores the entwining of genealogy and genetics in Britain focusing in particular on Walter Bodmer's BBC television documentary *Sir Walter's Journey*, 1994, broadcast on BBC2 on March 28, 1994, in the BBC Horizon series. Richard Tutton, "'They Want to Know Where They Came From': Population Genetics, Identity, and Family Genealogy," *New Genetics and Society* 23, no. 1 (2004): 105–20.

43. Channel 4, *Face of Britain*, television documentary, directed by Martin Durkin, 2007; Robin McKie, *Face of Britain: How Our Genes Reveal the History of Britain* (London: Simon and Schuster, 2006).

44. Walter Bodmer, "Public Understanding of Science: The BA, the Royal Society and COPUS," *Notes and Records of the Royal Society* 64, no. S1 (2010): s151–61.

45. Robin McKie, "Scientists Go in Search of the True Brit," *The Observer*, August 15, 2004.

46. *People of the British Isles*, newsletter, December 1, 2006, http://www.peopleofthebritishisles.org/press.

47. McKie, *Face of Britain*, 27.

48. Young, *The Idea of English Ethnicity*, 16.

49. Ibid., 49–50.

50. Ibid., 174.

51. John Beddoe, *The Races of Great Britain: A Contribution to the Anthropology of Western Europe* (London: Trübner, 1885).

52. Oppenheimer, *The Origins of the British*; Sykes, *Blood of the Isles*.

53. Abul Taher, "British Genes Are Invasion Proof," *The Sunday Times*, June 5, 2005.

54. Gilbert Bonifas, "Reconceptualising Britishness on the Far Right: An Analysis of the British National Party's Identity Magazine," *Cycnos* 25, no. 2 (2008): http://revel.unice.fr/cycnos/index.html?id=6203.

55. Arthur Kemp, *Four Flags: The Indigenous People of Britain: DNA, History and the Right to Existence of the Native Inhabitants of the British Isles* (Deeside: Excalibur Books, 2010), 50–51.

56. Interview on December 13, 2007, Oxford.

57. Yasmin Alibhai-Brown, "Welcome to the 'Mongrel' Nation," *The Independent*, September 4, 2001; Discovery Channel, *Mongrel Nation*, television documentary, 2003.

58. Turi E. King, Emma J. Parkin, Geoff Swinfield, Fulvio Cruciani, Rosaria Scozzari, Alexandra Rosa, Si-Keun Lim, Yali Xue, Chris Tyler-Smith, and Mark A. Jobling, "Africans in Yorkshire? The Deepest-Rooting Clade of the Y Phylogeny within an English Genealogy," *European Journal of Human Genetics* 15, no. 3 (2007): 288–93. For further information about the surname project, see http://www.le.ac.uk/ge/maj4/surnames.html.

59. Roger Highfield, "An Old Yorkshire Name Reveals Roots in Africa," *The Daily Telegraph*, January 24, 2007, 15.

60. Simon Crompton, "History in Our Genes: DNA Technology Is Helping Black and White Britons to Trace Their Roots, with Surprising Results," *The Times*, March 24, 2007.

61. Jobling in Mark Henderson, "Out of Africa and All the Way to Yorkshire: Our Shared DNA," *The Times*, January 24, 2007, 9.

62. King et al., "Africans in Yorkshire," 288.

63. Interview on December 19, 2007.

64. "The Impact of Diasporas," University of Leicester, http://www2.le.ac.uk/projects/impact-of-diasporas.

65. Steven Vertovec, "Super-Diversity and Its Implications," *Ethnic and Racial Studies* 2, no. 6 (2007): 1024–54.

66. "Roots of the British Come under New Scrutiny," University of Leicester press release, September 1, 2010, http://www2.le.ac.uk/ebulletin/news/press-releases/2010-2019/2010/09/nparticle.2010-09-01.8554810763.

67. Mark A. Jobling, "The Impact of Recent Events on Human Genetic Diversity," *Philosophical Transactions of the Royal Society of Britain* 367 (2012): 793–99, especially 798.

68. Mark Gale (narrator), *100% English*, plot summary available at http://www.imdb.com/title/tt0907295/plotsummary.

69. Gale, *100% English*.

70. James F. Wilson, Deborah A. Weiss, Martin Richards, Mark G. Thomas, Neal Bradman, and David B. Goldstein, "Genetic Evidence for Different Male and Female Roles during Cultural Transitions in the British Isles," *Proceedings of the National Academy of Science* 98, no. 9 (2001): 5078–83.

71. Deborah A. Bolnick, "'Showing Who They Really Are': Commercial Ventures in Genetic Genealogy," paper presented at the American Anthropological Association Annual Meeting, Chicago, November 2003.

72. McKie, *Face of Britain*, 143.

73. Interview on December 13, 2007, Oxford.

74. Oxford Ancestors, "Tribes of Britain," http://www.oxfordancestors.com/component/page,shop.product_details/flypage,flypage/product_id,40/category_id,7/option,com_virtuemart/Itemid,67.

75. McKie, *Face of Britain*, 146.

76. Ibid., 124.

77. Interview on December 13, 2007, Oxford.

78. Anne-Marie Fortier, "Genetic Indigenisation in 'The People of the British Isles,'" *Science as Culture* 21, no. 2 (2012): 153–57.

79. *People of the British Isles*, newsletter, August 3, 2009, and no. 4, 2010, available at http://www.peopleofthebritishisles.org/press.

80. Young, *The Idea of English Ethnicity*, 130.

81. Kath Cross, "Framing Whiteness: The Human Genome Diversity Project (as seen on TV)," *Science as Culture* 20, no. 3 (2001): 411–38. See also Deborah Lynn Steinberg's critique of geneticist Steven Jones's simultaneous claims that genetics tells the truths distorted by racist ideology and the casual association of racial or nation traits and categories with genetic ancestry. Deborah Lynn Steinberg, "Reading Genes/Writing Nation: Reith, 'Race' and the Writings of Geneticist Steve Jones," in *Hybridity and Its Discontents: Politics, Science, Culture*, ed. Avtar Brah and Annie E. Coombes (London: Routledge, 2000), 137–53.

82. Shriver and Kittles, "Genetic Ancestry and the Search," 611–18.

83. Roxanne Khamsi, "Genes Reveal West African Heritage of White Brits," *New Scientist*, January 24, 2007, http://www.newscientist.com/article/dn11018-genes-reveal-west-african-heritage-of-white-brits.html.

84. Geneticists Neal Bradman and Mark Thomas, in an appreciative commentary on the paper by King et al., "Africans in Yorkshire," pick up on the issue of describing genetic lineages in relation to contemporary diversity in Britain, gently chiding the authors: "Genetic history is a discipline in which it is difficult to write both simply and with precision, and one in which offence can easily be given. We should therefore have sympathy for King et al. (2007) when they write in the first sentence of the abstract to their paper 'The presence of Africans in Britain has been recorded since Roman times, but has left no apparent genetic trace among modern inhabitants.' A 5-minute walk through the centre of any British city would suggest otherwise. We know what the writers mean but they have not written what they mean." Neal Bradman and Mark G. Thomas, "An African Y Chromosome in Yorkshiremen? Y chromosome Travelled North," *Heredity* 99 (2007): 3–4.

85. McKie, "Scientists Go in Search."

86. Fortier, "Genetic Indigenisation," 162.

87. Walter Bodmer, "Introduction," in *Face of Britain: How Our Genes Reveal the History of Britain*, ed. Robin McKie (London: Simon and Schuster, 2006), 9–11, especially 11.

88. McKie, *Face of Britain,* 21.

89. Ibid.

90. Interview on December 19, 2007, Leicester.

91. Interview on December 13, 2007, Oxford.

92. Richard Tutton, "Biobanks and the Inclusion of Racial/Ethnic Minorities," *Race/Ethnicity: Multidisciplinary Global Contexts* 3, no. 1 (2006): 75–95.

93. Helen Busby and Paul Martin, "Biobanks, National Identity and Imagined Communities: The Case of UK Biobank," *Science as Culture* 15, no. 1 (2006): 237–51.

94. Andrew Smart, Richard Tutton, Paul Martin, George T. H. Ellison, and Richard Ashcroft, "The Standardization of Race and Ethnicity in Biomedical Science Editorials and UK Biobanks," *Social Studies of Science* 38, no. 3 (2008): 407–23.

95. Richard Tutton, "Opening the White Box: Exploring the Study of Whiteness in Contemporary Genetics Research," *Ethnic and Racial Studies* 30, no. 4 (2007): 557–69, especially 563.

96. Winney et al., "People of the British Isles."

97. As Kath Cross argued in her analysis of the figuring of origins, ancestry, and belonging in the documentary *Sir Walter's Journey,* "original Britons . . . may well be simply a linguistically expedient and layperson-friendly solution to a tricky problem of nomenclature, but it is in addition an implicitly political act of demarcation, disqualifying all those Britons now living whose recent ancestors came from outside the islands." Cross, "Framing Whiteness," 423.

98. Chris Tyler-Smith and Yali Xue, "A British Approach to Sampling," *European Journal of Human Genetics* 20, no. 2 (2012): 129–30, especially 129.

99. Michaels, *The Trouble with Diversity.*

100. This debate has been intensified by Michael Gove's plans as the Conservative education secretary, in a first draft of a new national curriculum published in February 2013, to focus on a narrow, chronological, and triumphalist account of a specifically English national history designed to inspire patriotism, which was widely denounced. See Richard J. Evans, "Michael Gove's History Wars," *The Guardian,* July 13, 2013.

101. Fortier, "Genetic Indigenisation," 167.

102. Rose, *The Politics of Life Itself,* 183.

4. Finding the "Truths" of Sex in Geographies of Genetic Variation

1. Jeffrey T. Tell and Douglas C. Wallace, "The Peopling of Europe from the Maternal and Paternal Perspectives," *American Journal of Human Genetics* 67, no. 6 (2000): 1376–81; Wilson et al., "Genetic Evidence," 5078–83; Thomas D. Als, Tove H. Jorgensen, Anders D. Børglum, Peter A. Petersen, Ole Mors, and August G. Wang, "Highly Discrepant Proportions of Female and Male Scandinavian and British Isles Ancestry within the Isolated Population of the Faroe Islands," *European Journal of Human Genetics* 14, no. 4 (2006): 487–504; Agnar Helgason, Sigrún

Sigurðardóttir, Jayne Nicholson, Bryan Sykes, Emmeline W. Hill, Daniel G. Bradley, Vidar Bosnes, Jeffery R. Gulcher, Ryk Ward, and Kári Stefánsson, "Estimating Scandinavian and Gaelic Ancestry in the Male Settlers of Iceland," *American Journal of Human Genetics* 67, no. 3 (2000): 679–717; Agnar Helgason, Sigrún Sigurðardóttir, Jeffery R. Gulcher, Ryk Ward, and Kári Stefánsson, "MtDNA and the Origin of the Icelanders: Deciphering Signals of Recent Population History," *American Journal of Human Genetics* 66, no. 3 (2000): 999–1016.

2. S. Goodacre, A. Helgason, J. Nicholson, L. Southam, E. Hickey, E. Vega, K. Stefánsson, R. Ward, and B. Sykes, "Genetic Evidence for a Family-Based Scandinavian Settlement of Shetland and Orkney during the Viking Periods," *Heredity* 95, no. 2 (2005): 129–35; M. G. Thomas, H. Härke, G. German, and M. P. H. Stumpf, "Social Constraints on Interethnic Marriage/Unions, Differential Reproductive Success and the Spread of 'Continental' Y Chromosomes in Early Anglo-Saxon England," in *Simulations, Genetics and Human Prehistory*, ed. Shuichi Matsumura, Peter Forster, and A. Colin Renfrew (Cambridge: McDonald Institute for Archaeological Research, 2008), 59–68.

3. Rita Rasteiro, Pierre-Antonie Bouttier, Vítor C. Sousa, and Lounès Chikki, "Investigating Sex-Biased Migration during the Neolithic Transition in Europe, Using an Explicit Spatial Simulation Framework," *Proceedings of the Royal Society B* 279, no. 1737 (2012): 2409–16.

4. Genographic Project, Public Participation Kit leaflet, 18–19.

5. O'Rourke, "Anthropological Genetics," 101–9.

6. R. Alexander Bentley, Robert H. Layton, and Jamshid Tehrani, "Kinship, Marriage, and the Genetics of Past Human Dispersals," *Human Biology* 81, no. 2–3 (2009): 159–79.

7. See, for example, the incorporation of studies of mtDNA and Y-chromosome variation and popular accounts of the human population genetics of the British Isles into a study addressing the numbers of women and men in Norse migration to England, which adds these forms of evidence to documentary and archaeological sources: Shane McLeod, "Warriors and Women: The Sex Ratio of Norse Migrants to Eastern England Up to 900AD," *Early Medieval Europe* 19, no. 3 (2011): 332–53.

8. Eugene A. Foster, Mark A. Jobling, P. G. Taylor, P. Donnelly, P. de Knijff, Rene Mieremet, T. Zerjal, and C. Tyler-Smith, "Jefferson Fathered Slave's Last Child," *Nature* 396 (November 1998): 27–28.

9. These fears and fantasies about sex and race intersect with old and new senses of belonging and relatedness among those descendants of Sally Hemings—since some but not all were proven to have Jefferson as a paternal ancestor—whose place within the American family remains contested. Newspapers have reported on the continued controversy since the findings were published in 1998. The annual meeting of the Monticello Association is

characterized by continued resistance to the campaign for the inclusion of the Hemings-Jefferson descendants. While this genetically proven story has been made to stand as a paradigm for multicultural reconciliation ("Multicultural-ism at Monticello," *New York Times*, May 24, 2002), the genetic results have also fractured existing senses of relatedness. The Y-chromosome tests undermine the oral histories of the Jefferson lineage and the sense of relatedness for other de-scendants of Hemings since it suggests that only the last and not all her sons were the result of sex with the president (Christine Woodside, "Family Works to Prove Its Ties to Jefferson," *New York Times*, February 13, 2000, 10). The descen-dants of her other sons do not have the genetic proof of the sense of relatedness that they had had through oral genealogies. See Michael Janofsky, "Jefferson's Kin Not Ready to Accept Tie to Slave," *New York Times*, May 16, 1999, 22; Mary Dejevsky, "Jefferson Descendants Reveal Tense State of US Race Relations," *The Independent*, May 17, 1999. See Roger Williams, *Jefferson's Pillow: The Found-ing Fathers and the Dilemma of Black Patriotism* (Boston: Beacon Press, 2001); Annette Gordon-Reed, *Thomas Jefferson and Sally Hemings: An American Con-troversy* (Charlottesville: University of Virginia Press, 2000); Jan Ellen Lewis and Peter S. Onuf, eds., *Sally Hemings and Thomas Jefferson: History, Memory, and Civic Culture* (Charlottesville: University of Virginia Press, 1999).

10. See, for example, Jobling, Hurles, and Tyler-Smith, *Human Evolutionary Genetics*, 23.

11. M'charek, *The Human Genome Diversity Project*, 84–119.

12. Ibid., 99 and 101.

13. Hannah Landecker, "Immortality, In Vitro: A History of the HeLa Cell Line," in *Biotechnology and Culture: Bodies, Anxieties, Ethics*, ed. Paul E. Brodwin (Bloomington: Indiana University Press, 2000), 53–72.

14. M'charek, *The Human Genome Diversity Project*, 91.

15. Ibid., 140.

16. Nash, "Genetic Kinship," 1–34.

17. Cann, Stoneking, and Wilson, "Mitochondrial DNA and Human Evolu-tion," 31–36.

18. Lori Hager, ed., *Women in Human Evolution* (London: Routledge, 1997).

19. Rebecca Cann, "Mothers, Labels and Misogyny," in *Women in Human Evo-lution*, ed. Lori D. Hager (London: Routledge, 1997), 76–90.

20. Elizabeth Pennisi, "Tracking the Sexes by Their Genes," *Science* 291, no. 5509 (2001): 1733–34.

21. Goodacre et al., "Genetic Evidence," 129.

22. Wilkins, "Unravelling Male and Female Histories," 611–17, especially 611.

23. Tatiana Zerjal, Yali Xue, Giorgio Bertolle, R. Spencer Wells, Weidong Bao, Suling Zhu, Raheel Qamar, et al., "The Genetic Legacy of the Mongols," *American Journal of Human Genetics* 72, no. 3 (2003): 717–21.

24. Ibid., 720.

25. Nicholas Wade, "A Prolific Genghis Khan, It Seems, Helped People the World," *New York Times,* February 11, 2003; Robin McKie, "We Owe It All to Superstud Genghis: Warlord Khan Has 16m Male Relatives Alive Now, Says Study," *The Observer,* March 2, 2003; Lois Rogers, "Genghis Super-Y: The Gene for a True Alpha Male," *The Sunday Times,* June 13, 2004; Bryan Sykes, *Adam's Curse: A Future without Men* (London: Bantam Press, 2003).

26. Hillary Maynell, "Genghis Khan a Prolific Lover, DNA Data Implies," *National Geographic News,* February 14, 2003, http://news.nationalgeographic.com/news/2003/02/0214_030214_genghis.html.

27. Nicholas Wade, "Falling from Genghis's Family Tree," *New York Times,* June 21, 2006; Jerome Taylor, "Giants of the Gene Pool," *The Independent,* January 19, 2006.

28. Taylor, "Giants of the Gene Pool."

29. Laoise T. Moore, Brian McEvoy, Eleanor Cape, Katharine Simms, and Daniel G. Bradley, "A Y-Chromosome Signature of Hegemony in Gaelic Ireland," *American Journal of Human Genetics* 78, no. 2 (2006): 334–38.

30. Nicholas Wade, "Genetic Detective Work Leads to Manchu Conquerors," *International Herald Tribune,* November 3, 2005.

31. Bryan Sykes, *Adam's Curse.*

32. Venla Oikkonen, "Narrating Descent: Popular Science, Evolutionary Theory and Gender Politics," *Science as Culture* 18, no. 1 (2009): 1–12.

33. Mark Henderson, "How I Am Related to Genghis Khan," *The Times,* May 30, 2006; Nicolas Wade, "In the Body of an Accounting Professor, a Little Bit of the Mongol Hordes," *New York Times,* June 6, 2006; Nicolas Wade, "Falling from Genghis's Family Tree," *New York Times,* June 21, 2006.

34. Chirag Trivedi, "Taking the Genghis Khan Test," *BBC News Online,* July 14, 2004, http://www.news.bbc.co.uk/2/hi/uk_news/england/london/3871159.stm.

35. Pomery, *Family History in the Genes,* 22.

36. Carol Delaney, "Cutting the Ties That Bind: The Sacrifice of Abraham and Patriarchal Kinship," in *Relative Values: Reconfiguring Kinship Studies,* ed. Sarah Franklin and Susan McKinnon (Durham, N.C.: Duke University Press, 2001), 445–67.

37. Bryan Sykes, *The Seven Daughters of Eve* (London: Bantam Press, 2001). I discuss the gendering of genetic genealogy in some of the first popular accounts more fully in Nash "Genetic Kinship."

38. "Are You a Warrior?," Family Tree DNA, http://www.familytreedna.com/landing/warrior-gene.aspx.

39. Zerjal et al., "The Genetic Legacy," 719–20.

40. Quoted in Maynell, "Genghis Khan a Prolific Lover."

41. Wells, *The Journey of Man,* 174.

42. "Genetic Adam Never Met Eve," BBC News Online, October 30, 2000, http://news.bbc.co.uk/1/hi/sci/tech/999030.stm.

43. Wells, *The Journey of Man*, 177.

44. Ibid., 178.

45. Ibid.

46. Susan McKinnon, "On Kinship and Marriage: A Critique of the Genetic and Gender Calculus of Evolutionary Psychology," in *Complexities: Beyond Nature and Nurture*, ed. Susan McKinnon and Sydel Silverman (Chicago: University of Chicago Press, 2005), 106–31; Susan McKinnon, *Neo-Liberal Genetics: The Myths and Moral Tales of Evolutionary Psychology* (Chicago: Prickly Paradigm Press, 2005); Rose Hilary and Steven Rose, eds., *Alas, Poor Darwin: Arguments against Evolutionary Psychology* (New York: Harmony Books, 2000).

47. McKinnon, "On Kinship and Marriage," 106.

48. Shaoni Bhattacharya and Michael Le Page, "A Few Prehistoric Men Had All the Children," *New Scientist* 2411, September 6, 2003; "Europe's 10 Founding 'Fathers,'" BBC News Online, November 10, 2000, http://news.bbc.co.uk/1/hi/sci/tech/1015670.stm.

49. Ian Sample, "More Women Than Men Have Added Their DNA to the Human Gene Pool," *The Guardian*, September 24, 2014.

50. McKinnon, *Neo-Liberal Genetics*, 81–94.

51. Wells, *The Journey of Man*, v.

52. Wade, "A Prolific Genghis Khan."

53. Sykes, quoted in Claudia Dreifus, "A Conversation with Bryan Sykes: Is Genghis Khan an Ancestor? Mr. DNA Knows," *New York Times*, June 8, 2004.

54. Nicholas Wade, "The Ascent of Man; What's It All about, Alpha?," *New York Times*, November 7, 1999.

55. Wade, "In the Body."

56. Wade, *Before the Dawn*, 237.

57. Chris Pomery, *Family History in the Genes: Trace Your DNA and Grow Your Family Tree* (Kew, United Kingdom: National Archives, 2007).

58. McKinnon, *Neo-Liberal Genetics*, 73. The theme of "paternal uncertainly" continues to be pursued in evolutionary psychology. See, for example, T. K. Shackleford and S. M. Platek, eds., *Female Infidelity and Paternal Uncertainty: Evolutionary Perspectives on Male Anti-cuckoldry Tactics* (New York: Cambridge University Press, 2006).

59. M. H. D. Larmuseau, J. Vanoverbeke, A. Van Geystelen, G. Defraence, N. Vanderhyden, K. Matthus, and R. Decorte, "Low Historical Rates of Cuckoldry in a Western European Human Population Traced by Y-Chromosome and Genealogical Data," *Proceedings of the Royal Society B* 280, no. 1772 (2013): 1–8. This paper is indicative of a strand of work in human population genetics devoted to estimating the frequency of "nonpaternity" in different geographical contexts.

60. Mark A. Jobling, "In the Name of the Father: Surnames and Genetics," *Trends in Genetics* 17, no. 6 (2001): 353–57; Mark A. Jobling and Turi E. King, "The Distribution of Y-Chromosomal Haplotypes: Forensic Implications," *International Congress Series* 1261 (April 2004): 70–72; Sykes and Irven, "Surnames and the Y Chromosome," 1417–19.

61. Michael L. Burton, Carmella C. Moore, John W. M. Whiting, A. Kimball Romney, David F. Aberle, Juan A. Barcelo, Malcolm M. Dow, Jane I. Guyer, David B. Kronenfeld, Jerrold E. Levy, and Jocelyn Linnekin, "Regions Based on Social Structure," *Current Anthropology* 37, no. 1 (1996): 87–123.

62. Hiroki Oota, Wannaoa Settheetham-Ishida, Danai Tiwawech, Takafumi Ishida, and Mark Stoneking, "Human MtDNA and Y-Chromosome Variation Is Correlated with Matrilocal versus Patrilocal Residence," *Nature Genetics* 29, no. 1 (2001): 20–21.

63. Wells, *The Journey of Man*, 176.

64. Oota et al., "Human MtDNA and Y-chromosome Variation," 21.

65. Mark T. Seielstad, Eric Minch, and L. Luca Cavalli-Sforza, "Genetic Evidence for a Higher Female Migration Rate in Humans," *Nature Genetics* 20, no. 3 (1998): 278–80.

66. Nigel Hawkes, "Women Were the First Travellers," *The Times* (London), October 27, 1998, 6.

67. Robin McKie, "How the Women's Movement Outbred Pillaging Armies," *The Observer*, November 9, 1997.

68. Minch, quoted in McKie, "How the Women's Movement," 15.

69. Mark Stoneking, "Women on the Move," *Nature Genetics* 20, no. 3 (1998): 219–20, especially 220.

70. Ibid., 220.

71. Wells, *The Journey of Man*, 176.

72. Gayle Rubin, "The Traffic in Women: Notes on the 'Political Economy' of Sex," in *Towards an Anthropology of Women*, ed. Rayner R. Reiter (New York: Monthly Review Press, 1975), 157–210.

73. Emily Martin, "The Egg and the Sperm: How Science Has Constructed a Romance Based on Stereotypical Male-Female Roles," *Signs* 16, no. 3 (1991): 485–501.

74. Wade, *Before the Dawn*, 144.

75. Ibid., 150.

76. Jon F. Wilkins and Frank W. Marlow, "Sex-Based Migration in Humans: What Should We Expect from Genetic Data," *Bioessays* 28, no. 3 (2006): 290–300, especially 299; see also Patricia Balaresque and Mark A. Jobling, "Human Populations: Houses for Spouses," *Current Biology* 17, no. 1 (2007): 14–16.

77. Bentley, Layton, and Tehrani, "Kinship, Marriage," 159 and 175.

78. Wilkins, "Unravelling Male and Female Histories," 614.

79. Maria Cátira Bortolini, Mark G. Thomas, Lounes Chikhi, Juan A. Aguilar, Dinorah Castro-De-Guerra, Francisco M. Salzano, and Andres Ruiz-Linares, "Ribeiro's Typology, Genomes, and Spanish Colonialism, as Viewed from Gran Canaria and Colombia," *Genetics and Molecular Biology* 27, no. 1–8 (2004): 6–7.

80. Schramm, "Genomics en Route," 167–92.

81. Sykes, *The Seven Daughters of Eve.*

82. Ibid., 276.

83. McKinnon, *Neo-Liberal Genetics.*

Conclusion

1. See, for example, Phil McKenna, "Chinese Challenge 'Out of Africa' Theory," *New Scientist*, November 3, 2009, http://www.newscientist.com/article/dn18093-chinese-challenge-to-out-of-africa-theory.html; Nikhil Swaminathan, "Is the Out of Africa Theory Out?," *Scientific American*, August 8, 2007, http://www.scientificamerican.com/article.cfm?id=is-the-out-of-africa-theory-out.

2. Caspari, "'Out of Africa' Hypothesis," 391–97.

3. Kathryn Yusoff, "Geologic Life: Prehistory, Climate, Futures in the Anthropocene," *Environment and Planning D: Society and Space* 31, no. 5 (2013): 779–95.

4. See National Geographic, Genographic Project website about the project, https://genographic.nationalgeographic.com/about.

5. Hinterberger, "Categorization, Census and Multiculturalism," 204–24.

6. It informs the policies of disclosure in the regulation of adoption and, in the UK context, the removal since April 1, 2005, of the right of those donating eggs, sperm, or embryos to future anonymity. Once he or she reaches the age of eighteen, a person born as a result of donation after April 1, 2005, is entitled to request and receive his or her donor's name and last known address.

7. In the UK and U.S. contexts, new forms of relatedness are emerging as those who share a biological father, through sperm donation, seek to contact hitherto unknown half sisters or half brothers as well as donor fathers. In the United States, for example, this is being facilitated by donor family organization the Donor Sibling Registry founded in 2000. But genetic genealogy is also being used to test for suspected donor relatedness for what is dubbed "Generation Cryo" in the MTV documentary of that name, broadcast in late 2013. See http://www.donorsiblingregistry.com.

8. Sommer, "DNA and Cultures of Remembrance," 366–90.

9. For example, the Ties Program is a U.S. organization based in Wisconsin that specializes in what are described as Adoptive Family Homeland Journeys to the main source countries for children and babies in U.S. transnational adoption: Romania, Russia, Chile, Guatemala, Paraguay, Peru, Cambodia, China, India,

Korea, the Philippines, and Vietnam. Its website describes its work in providing specialized, customized international journeys to "help families reconnect with significant people and places related to their adoption." It states, "Traveling to your child's country of birth as a family will be one of the most profound, bonding, identity building opportunities in your family's life experience of adoption." See http://www.adoptivefamilytravel.com.

10. Reardon, "The Democratic, Anti-racist Genome?," 25–47.

11. Sarah Franklin, "From Blood to Genes? Rethinking Consanguinity in the Context of Geneticization," in *Blood and Kinship: Matter and Metaphor from Ancient Rome to the Present*, ed. Christopher H. Johnson, Bernhard Jussen, David Warren Sabean, and Simon Teuscher (New York: Berghahn Books, 2013), 285–306, especially 302.

Index

Abu El-Haj, Nadia, 3, 9, 13, 44, 62
admixture, genetic, 58, 127. *See also*
    mapping: admixture
adoptions, transnational, 180–81,
    218n6, 218–19n9
affinities, 17, 175–76, 177, 183. *See also*
    similarities
Africa: British connections to, 117,
    125–26, 211n84; genetic testing
    in, 45, 52, 56, 62; human origins
    from, 54–55, 69, 89, 91, 95, 132, 166;
    migrations out of, 42–43, 83, 145,
    172, 203–4n70; shared ancestry
    from, 8, 76–77, 84, 98, 121, 145–46,
    191n42. *See also* slavery and slaves
African American Lives (documen-
    tary), 50
African Americans: European ancestry
    of, 54, 141; genetic tests for, 50, 52–
    53, 55, 62; health issues of, 38–39,
    40, 194n16; sense of loss experi-
    enced by, 178–79
African Ancestry (company), 50, 55
AIMs. *See* ancestry-informative mark-
    ers (AIMs)
Alibhai-Brown, Yasmin, 116
alleles: mapping, 35, 41, 42, 78–81; risk,
    38–39. *See also* haplogroups and
    haplotypes
ancestry, 48–67; ancient, 120, 203–4n70;
    belonging based on, 64, 131, 134;

biogeographical, 39, 57–58, 65, 84,
    147; biomedical, 38–40; British, 134,
    212n97; collective, 9, 69–70, 88, 113,
    114, 182; continental models of, 39,
    46–47, 97, 133; culture of, 33, 49,
    131, 174, 187n13; deep, 13, 65, 66, 85,
    86–87, 93–94, 204n79; differentiated,
    99, 113, 144, 179, 185n2; European, 45,
    53–54, 97, 152, 157; facial types linked
    to, 122–23; Genographic Project's
    mapping of, 90, 94–95; geographies
    of, 5–6, 11, 27, 124–25, 130, 134;
    global, 31, 80–81; immigrant, 50,
    51–59, 94, 129; knowledge produc-
    tion through, 13, 179–80; male, 150,
    154–55; migration patterns of, 3, 8,
    52, 83–84, 98, 178, 180; narratives
    of, 88, 114; politics of, 4, 54, 182; race
    and, 7–8, 16–17, 44–48, 103; regional,
    122–23, 133; research in, 6, 8, 48, 58,
    66, 92, 177; science of, 1, 33, 125, 174,
    175, 187n13; shared, 22, 24, 40, 56, 73,
    91, 95–96, 175–76; slave-based, 50, 52,
    117, 125–26, 166; studies of, 2, 39–40,
    100, 171–72; surname-based, 61–62,
    111–12. *See also* descent; ethnicity:
    shared; family tree, global; genealogy,
    conventional; genealogy, genetic;
    genetic ancestry; identity: ancestral;
    kinship; lineages; origins; relatedness,
    ancestral

CATHERINE NASH is professor of human geography at Queen Mary University of London. She is author of *Of Irish Descent: Origin Stories, Genealogy, and the Politics of Belonging*.